Text Review Guide

for

ECONOMICS U$A

Fifth Edition

EDWIN MANSFIELD
DIRECTOR, CENTER FOR ECONOMICS AND TECHNOLOGY
UNIVERSITY OF PENNSYLVANIA

W. W. NORTON & COMPANY • NEW YORK • LONDON

ISBN 0-393-97206-2

W. W. Norton & Company, Inc., 500 Fifth Avenue, New York, N.Y. 10110
W. W. Norton & Company Ltd., 10 Coptic Street, London WC1A 1PU
http://www.wwnorton.com

1 2 3 4 5 6 7 8 9 0

Contents

CONTENTS

PART FIVE: THE DISTRIBUTION OF INCOME

PART SIX: GROWTH, THE GOVERNMENT, AND INTERNATIONAL ECONOMICS

Preface

This *Text Review Guide* for *Economics U$A*, Fifth Edition, has been prepared with one overriding objective—to facilitate self-paced study of introductory economics. Five cases (the first of which is new) have been included, one at the end of each part of the book (other than the introduction):

    1. Council of Economic Advisers (1997), "Does the Consumer Price Index Overstate Increases in the Cost of Living?"

    2. Council of Economic Advisers (1994) "Promoting Technology and Economic Growth"

    3. Robert Crandall and Edward Markey (1994) "Cable Television and Government Regulation"

    4. Roland Cousins (1992) "The Well-Paid Receptionist"

    5. Council of Economic Advisers (1993) "Ownership and Pricing of Natural Resources"

Each chapter parallels closely the content of the corresponding chapter in the text. In order to give comprehensive and varied coverage, a five-pronged approach has been developed:

    1. *Chapter Profiles* that highlight principal points and that are followed by a set of *Concepts for Review* that indicate the main concepts students should understand once they have completed the chapter.

    2. Limbering-up exercises in the form of *Completion Questions* that open the way to systematic review of each chapter.

    3. Self-tests in the form of numerous *True-False* and *Multiple-Choice* questions.

    4. A number of *Discussion and Extension Questions*, many rather open-ended, to stimulate classroom discussion (or for further homework assignment).

    5. Short cases in the form of *Problems* that simulate real-world situations and require the student to work with actual data in tabular and diagrammatic form.

Answers to all the objective questions and problems are contained at the end of each chapter. No answers are given for the Discussion and Extension Questions, since they are essay questions that can be answered in a variety of ways.

Since a study guide should be a flexible learning tool, I have sought to provide not only a large number of questions but also a wide range in terms of difficulty. Each chapter begins at a relatively easy level, increasing gradually in rigor as students build confidence along with competence. The more demanding an economic concept, the more extensive the amount of review material given to it. Some of the problems at the ends of chapters are hard enough so that the typical student should not expect to answer them all. Even the best students should be challenged by some of them.

    Thanks go to my wife, Lucile, for helping me with the preparation of this study guide.

E.M.

Philadelphia
1998

CHAPTER 1*

What Is Economics?

Chapter Profile

According to one standard definition, economics is concerned with the way resources are allocated among alternative uses to satisfy human wants. A resource is a thing or service used to produce goods (or services) that can satisfy wants. Not all resources are scarce. Free resources, such as air, are so abundant that they can be obtained without charge.

Those resources that are scarce are called economic resources. The test of whether a resource is an economic resource or a free resource is price: economic resources command a nonzero price but free resources do not. Economists often classify economic resources into three categories: land, labor, and capital.

Since economic resources are scarce, only a limited amount of goods and services can be produced from them, and there arises the necessity for choice. For example, if an isolated town has a certain amount of resources, it must choose how much of each good it will produce from these resources. If it increases the amount produced of one good, it must reduce the amount produced of another good. The opportunity cost (or alternative cost) of using a resource to increase the production of one good is the value of what the resource could have produced had it been used in the best alternative way.

Economists are particularly concerned with four basic questions regarding the working of an economic system, ours or any other. These questions are (1) What determines what (and how much) is produced? (2) What determines how it is produced? (3) What determines how the society's output is distributed among its members? (4) What determines the rate at which the society's per capita income will grow?

Economists often distinguish between positive economics and normative economics. Positive economics contains descriptive statements, propositions, and predictions about the world; normative economics contains statements about what ought to be, or about what a person, organization, or nation ought to do. In normative economics, the results you get depend on your basic values and preferences; in positive economics, the results are testable, at least in principle, by an appeal to the facts.

The methodology used by economists is much the same as that used in any other kind of scientific analysis. The basic procedure is the formulation and testing of models. A model must in general simplify and abstract from the real world. Its purpose is to make predictions concerning phenomena in the real world, and in many respects the most important test of a model is how well it predicts these phenomena. To test and quantify their models, economists gather data and use various statistical techniques.

---

*Some questions pertain to the Prologue as well as to Chapter 1 of the text.

Concepts for Review

Economics	Free resources	Human wants
Model	Economic resources	Choice
*Production possibilities curve	Land	Opportunity cost
*Capital goods	Labor	Alternative cost
*Consumer goods	Capital	Positive economics
Resources	Technology	Normative economics

*The starred items refer to material covered in the section "Exploring Further."

Completion Questions

1. The true cost of going to college is considerably (higher, lower)

   _____ than the out-of-pocket expenses because one

   can obtain _____ by working rather than attending
   school.

2. The growth of output has not been steady or uninterrupted; instead, output has

   tended to fluctuate and so has _____.

3. The level of _____ may tend to rise when we reduce the

   level of unemployment. In other words, _____ may occur.

4. Although relatively few people in the United States lack food desperately, about

   _____ American people, about _____
   of the population of the United States, live in what is officially designated as
   poverty.

5. Economic problems generally involve _____. There are
   often a number of alternative ways to handle a problem, and the question is

   which is _____.

6. A characteristic of many economic problems is that, to choose among a number

   of feasible solutions, one must _____ what will
   occur if each solution is adopted. This emphasis on the future necessarily

   entails some _____.

7. Economic resources are sometimes classified into the three categories of

   _____, _____, and _____.

8. _____ is society's pool of knowledge regarding the industrial arts.

9. An economic system must determine the level and composition of society's

   _____.

10. Adam Smith was among the first to describe how a free, competitive economy can function—without central planning or government interference—to allocate _____ efficiently. He emphasized the virtues of the _____ that leads the private interests of firms and individuals toward socially desirable ends, and he was suspicious of firms that are sheltered from _____, since he believed there would be _____ effects on resource allocation.

11. Smith's optimism was in keeping with the intellectual climate of his time, the Age of Enlightenment, when people believed in rationality. Leave markets _____, said Smith, and beware of firms with too much _____ and of unnecessary government _____.

12. Value judgments are in the realm of _____ economics. They (can, cannot) _____ be tested by an appeal to facts. They (can, cannot) _____ be proved in the way that the laws of physics can be.

13. The forests of the United States are an important national resource. If these forests are used for lumber, they (can, cannot) _____ be used for recreation. There (is, is not) _____ enough forest lands for both recreation and lumber. If we use a certain portion of the nation's forests for recreation, the _____ is the forgone lumber that could have been derived.

True-False

_____ 1. Somalia has been the scene of internal warfare and (sometimes) starvation; it has been operating at a point inside its production possibilities curve.

_____ 2. Adam Smith emphasized the importance of increased specialization and division of labor.

_____ 3. When economists refer to goods as being scarce, they mean that these items are monopolized by a few people. If goods were distributed equitably, there would be no problem of scarcity.

_____ 4. If every resource is so specialized that it can produce only one good or service, and if all resources are fully employed, society has no choice concerning how much of each good or service will be produced.

_____ 5. The problem of choosing what goods to produce is not likely to confront a firm, once it is established, but it does confront society.

_____ 6. Since it passes the tax laws, Congress is the only branch of the government concerned with economics.

_____ 7. Economics now plays a considerable role in the decision making of the Department of Defense.

_____ 8. Measures designed to reduce the rate of inflation may increase unemployment, unless the government is very careful.

_____ 9. Avoiding excessive unemployment is not a task that can be assigned to a particular individual, family, or firm.

Multiple Choice

1. Adam Smith emphasized how the fundamental economic problems could be solved efficiently by:

   a. command.
   b. tradition.
   c. the price system.
   d. monopoly.
   e. government agencies.

2. Economics can best be defined as:

   a. the study of financial activities.
   b. the study of interpersonal relationships.
   c. the study of making a living.
   d. the study of the allocation of scarce resources.
   e. the study of a human being's reaction to his or her environment.

3. When we reduce the level of unemployment, the effect may be:

   a. depression.
   b. inflation.
   c. decreased output.
   d. deflation.
   e. increased purchasing power of the dollar.

4. The problem of distributing society's output among its members must be resolved by:

   a. planned economies.
   b. any society that survives.
   c. any society based largely on the price system.
   d. any society based largely on tradition.
   e. any society.

5. Which of the following is *not* included as capital?

   a. a new taxicab
   b. an old taxicab
   c. a school building
   d. a pencil used by an author
   e. a hot dog eaten by an author while writing a book

6. Susan Smith's father asks her to help her younger brother with his homework. She refuses until her father promises to pay her $5. She could obtain $6 by babysitting for the equivalent length of time. The opportunity cost of having Ms. Smith help her brother in this way is:

   a. $5.
   b. $6.
   c. less than $5.
   d. more than $6.
   e. at least $8.

7. Holding constant the amount of capital and natural resources, the greater a country's labor force:

   a. the greater the amount of equipment that each worker will have to use.
   b. the greater its rate of investment.
   c. the greater its inefficiency.
   d. the greater its output of capital goods.
   e. none of the above.

Discussion and Extension Questions

1. Robinson Crusoe apparently spent a lot of his waking hours in what we would usually deem "leisure activities." Does this not imply he had a severe unemployment problem? Why would you not be worried about his unemployment but yet you would be concerned about the unemployed in the United States?

2. "The best things in life *are* free, and hence outside the realm of economics: the air we breathe, a view of a sunset, libraries, and free speech. Many other things ought to be free as well, like medical care." Discuss.

3. How do families, as opposed to an entire economy like the United States or China, solve the four basic economic problems?

4. Someone has said that economists study how people make choices and that sociologists study why people don't have any choices to make. What does that statement mean?

5. A lawyer charges what some would regard as an exorbitant sum for a simple matter like drawing up a will. How do economic principles in this chapter help you understand this?

6. What is the opportunity cost of (a) spending an evening at a movie (b) a college education?

7. What characteristics do economic problems tend to have in common?

8. Is economics concerned solely with solving practical problems?

9. If resources are not fully employed, is it true that an economy must give up some of one good in order to get more of another good?

10. Adam Smith was suspicious of firms that are sheltered from competition. Can you think of some reasons for this suspicion? Is American Telephone and Telegraph Company sheltered from competition? If so, how? Is the typical American wheat farmer sheltered from competition? Is so, how?

Problems

1. Suppose that the costs due to crime and the opportunity costs of resources used in law enforcement are as follows:

Proportion of criminals that are caught and convicted	Costs due to crime	Opportunity costs of resources used in law enforcement	Total costs
		(billions of dollars)	
0.4	60	10	70
0.5	50	—	68
0.6	40	30	—
0.7	30	50	80
0.8	—	80	100

a. Fill in the three blanks above.
b. What proportion of criminals should society try to catch and convict? Why?
c. Suppose the costs due to crime were to increase by $5 billion at each possible level of law enforcement. In other words, suppose that each of the figures in the second column of the table (headed *Costs due to crime*) were to increase by $5 billion. Would this affect the optimal proportion of criminals that society should try to catch and convict? Why or why not?

2. Suppose that the average cost per mile of operating your car (including insurance and taxes) is 18 cents. If you are contemplating taking a 200-mile trip, are you correct in assuming that your out-of-pocket costs for the trip will be 18 cents per mile? Why or why not?

3. If the opportunity cost of producing an extra million tons of steel exceeds the value of the extra million tons of steel, should society produce the extra million tons of steel? Why or why not?

4. What do you regard as the answer to the inflation problem that has plagued the United States? Since you are just beginning the study of economics, we do not expect you to have a well-thought-out answer, but you probably have some opinions on this subject. When you have formulated your answer to this question, ask yourself the following questions:

a. What theories (if any) am I employing? (And what is a theory?)

b. On what facts does my answer rest? Where did these facts come from, and how do I know they are correct?

c. What value judgments am I making? To what extent would other interested parties share these value judgments?

d. Is my answer politically feasible? Would Congress and other parts of the political system approve it?

5. Indicate whether each of the following resources is land, capital, or labor: oil deposits in Saudi Arabia _____; Thomas Edison's work on the lightbulb _____; the Empire State Building in New York City _____; the copies of this textbook on the shelves of your college bookstore _____; Big Sur _____.

6. Peter Jones stumbles accidentally on to a large cache of rifles buried in his backyard. He donates them to the local police department. The police commissioner, in a speech lauding Jones for his altruism, says that Jones has given an important resource (namely, the guns) to the city government, thus making them a free resource. From the point of view of economics, is this use of terms correct? Why or why not?

7. During the past fifty years, the U.S. economy has increased its automobile production by an enormous amount. At the same time it has increased its production of most other types of goods and services. Does this mean that the opportunity cost of the increased automobile production was negative? Why or why not?

8. In late 1993, about 6 percent of the labor force was unemployed; how can anyone say that labor is scarce?

9. Mary Mineo, a graduate student, has one 8-hour day per week that she can devote to earning extra money. She can write stories for the local newspaper, or she can babysit, or she can divide her time between the two jobs. (For example, she can spend 3 hours writing stories and 5 hours babysitting.) If she babysits, she gets $4 per hour. If she spends her day writing stories, it takes her 1 hour to write the first story, 2 hours to write the second story, and 5 hours to write the third story because she runs out of ideas and becomes less productive as time goes on. Assume that she must write an integer number of stories a day.

a. If she receives $15 per story, should she do any babysitting if she wants to maximize her income during the day?

b. If she receives $25 per story, should she do any babysitting, if she wants to maximize her income during the day?

c. What is the lowest price per story that will result in her doing no babysitting, if she maximizes her income?

    d.   If she spends the first 5 hours of the day babysitting, what is the opportunity cost to her of spending the remaining 3 hours babysitting?

    e.   If she spends the first 7 hours of the day babysitting, what is the opportunity cost to her of spending the remaining hour babysitting?

*10. Suppose that a society's production possibilities curve is as follows:

| | *Output (per year)* | |
| | *Food* | *Tractors* |
Possibility	*(millions of tons)*	*(millions)*
A	0	30
B	4	28
C	8	24
D	12	20
E	16	14
F	20	8
G	24	0

    a.   Is it possible for this society to produce 30 million tons of food per year?

    b.   Can it produce 30 million tractors per year?

    c.   Suppose this society produces 20 million tons of food and 6 million tractors per year. Is it operating on the production possibilities curve? If not, what factors might account for this?

    d.   Plot the production possibilities curve in the graph.

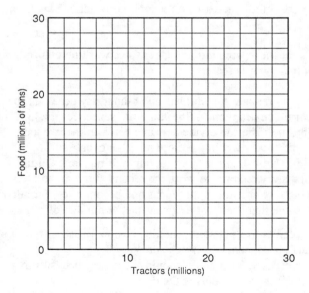

---

*The starred items pertain to material covered in the section "Exploring Further."

8

e. What is the cost to society if food output is increased from 12 to 16 million tons per year? If this increase occurs, what effect do you think it will have on this society's production possibilities curve next year?

f. Suppose that this society is governed by a dictator who feels that a tractor is worth infinitely more than a ton of food. What point on the production possibilities curve (of those presented in the table above) would the dictator choose? What problems would arise if he chooses this point?

*11. Suppose that a government faces a choice among various levels of defense, represented by the production of missiles, and of food represented by the production of corn. The following figures indicate the various combinations of missiles and corn that the country can produce:

Possibility	Missiles (number per year)	Corn (millions of bushels per year)
A	0	11
B	2	10
C	4	8
D	6	6
E	8	3
F	10	0

a. Plot the relevant production possibilities curve below.

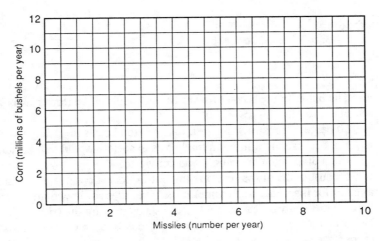

b. Can this country produce more than 12 million bushels of corn per year? Can it produce more than 10 million bushels per year? Can it produce more than 11 missiles per year? Can it produce more than 9 missiles per year?

c. Suppose that the government of this country decides that, in the interests of national security, it must produce 4 missiles per year. What is the maximum number of bushels of corn it can produce?

*The starred items pertain to material covered in the section "Exploring Further."

d.   Measured in terms of corn, what is the cost of producing 4 missiles per year rather than 2 missiles per year?
e.   Suppose that this country develops and obtains new technology that enables it to produce 50 percent more corn at each level of missile production shown in the table above. Will the new production possibilities curve be closer to, or farther from, the origin than the one graphed in part a?
f.   Under the conditions described in part e, what is the cost of producing 4 missiles per year rather than 2 missiles per year?

ANSWERS

Completion Questions

1. higher, wages   2. unemployment   3. prices, inflation   4. 37 million, 14 percent   5. choice, best   6. forecast, uncertainty   7. land, labor, capital
8. Technology   9. output   10. resources, invisible hand, competition, undesirable   11. alone, economic power, intervention   12. normative, cannot, cannot   13. cannot, is not, opportunity cost

True-False

1. True   2. True   3. False   4. True   5. False   6. False   7. True   8. True
9. True

Multiple Choice

1. c   2. d   3. b   4. e   5. e   6. b   7. e

Problems

1. a.   The blank in the second row is 18, the blank in the third row is 70, the blank in the fifth row is 20.
    b.   50 percent, because this minimizes the total costs to society.
    c.   No, because the minimum total costs to society would still be achieved when 50 percent are caught and convicted.
2. No, because some of the costs are not out-of-pocket costs. You pay a fixed amount for insurance and (some) taxes, regardless of how many miles you drive. Thus you won't increase these costs by making the trip.
3. No, because the forgone output of other goods is more valuable than the extra steel.
5. land, labor, capital, capital, land
6. No, because rifles are not free. They have a positive price in the market place, even though Jones happened to donate them.
7. No. During the past fifty years, the amount of resources and the available technology in the American economy have changed greatly, thus allowing increased production of automobiles and other goods. But if we had chosen to produce fewer automobiles, we surely could have produced more of other things. Thus the opportunity cost was positive.

8. It is not possible to get all of the labor one wants for the asking. The price of labor is positive.

9. a. She has three alternatives. (1) She can devote 1 hour to writing and 7 hours to babysitting, which will bring in $43. (2) She can devote 3 hours to writing and 5 hours to babysitting, which will bring in $50. (3) She can devote 8 hours to writing which will bring in $45. Thus, she should do some babysitting.

   b. The opportunity cost of writing the third story is $20, since this is what she could earn in 5 hours of babysitting. Since she gets $25 for this story, she is better off writing the story than devoting 5 hours to babysitting.

   c. $20.

   d. The amount that she could earn by writing two stories.

   e. The amount that she could earn by writing one story.

10. a. No.

    b. Yes.

    c. No. Inefficiency or unemployment of resources might account for this.

    d.

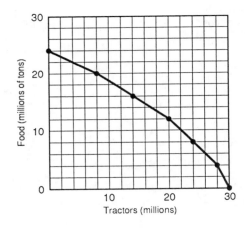

    e. Tractor output must be reduced from 20 million to 14 million. The production possibilities curve will not shift as far outward next year if this increase in food output occurs, because less tractors will be available then.

    f. 30 million tractors and no food. Mass starvation would be likely to result if such a (foolish) policy were adopted.

11. a.

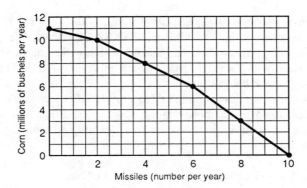

b. No. Yes. No. Yes.
c. 8 million bushels.
d. 2 million bushels of corn.
e. Farther from the origin.
f. 3 million bushels of corn.

CHAPTER 2

Markets and Prices

Chapter Profile

Consumers and firms are the basic units composing the private sector of the economy. A market is a group of firms and individuals that are in touch with each other to buy some commodity or service. When a market for a homogeneous product contains so many buyers and sellers that none of them can influence the price, economists call it a perfectly competitive market.

There are two sides to every market: the demand side and the supply side. The demand side can be represented by the market demand curve, which almost always slopes downward to the right and whose location depends on consumer tastes, the number and income of consumers, and the prices of other commodities.

The supply side of the market can be represented by the market supply curve, which generally slopes upward to the right and whose location depends on technology and resource prices.

The equilibrium price and equilibrium quantity of a commodity are given by the intersection of the market demand and market supply curves. If conditions remain reasonably stable for a time, the actual price and quantity should move close to the equilibrium price and quantity.

To determine what goods and services society will produce, the price system sets up incentives for firms to produce what consumers want. To the extent that they produce what consumers want and are willing to pay for, firms reap profits; to the extent that they don't, they experience losses.

The price system sets up strong incentives for firms to produce goods at minimum cost. These incentives take the form of profits for firms that minimize costs and losses for firms that operate with relatively high costs. To determine who gets what, the price system results in people's receiving an income that depends on the quantity of resources they own and the prices that these resources command.

The price system establishes incentives for activities that result in increases in a society's per capita income. For example, it influences the amount of new capital goods produced, as well as the amount society spends on educating its labor force and improving its technology.

There are circular flows of money and products in a capitalist economy. In product markets, firms provide products to consumers and receive money in return. In resource markets, consumers provide resources to firms, and receive money in return.

The price system, despite its many virtues, suffers from serious limitations. There is no reason to believe that the distribution of income generated by the price system is equitable or optimal. Also, there is no way for the price system to handle public goods properly, and because of external economies or diseconomies, the price system may result in too little or too much of certain goods being produced.

Concepts for Review

Consumer	Market supply curve	Public goods
Firm	Market	External economy
Market demand curve	Public sector	External diseconomy
Product market	Resource market	Circular flow
Equilibrium	Equilibrium price	Perfectly competitive market

Completion Questions

1. Since wheat can be substituted to some extent for corn as livestock feed, the quantity of wheat demanded depends on the price of corn as well as on the price of wheat. If the price of corn is high, (more, less) _____ wheat will be demanded since it will be profitable to substitute

    _____ for _____. If the price of corn is low, (more, less) _____ wheat will be demanded since it will be profitable to substitute _____ for _____.

2. Belgium is a small country; the United States is a huge country. Clearly, at a given price of wheat, the quantity demanded by American consumers will

    (exceed, be less than) _____ the quantity demanded by Belgian consumers. Even if consumer tastes, income, and other factors were held constant, this would still be true simply because the United States has so many more _____ in the relevant market.

3. As technology progresses, it becomes possible to produce commodities more

    _____, so that firms often are willing to supply a given amount of a product at a (lower, higher) _____ price than formerly. Thus technological change often causes the supply curve to shift to the (left, right) _____.

4. The supply curve for a commodity is affected by the prices of the

    _____ (labor, capital, and land) used to produce it. Decreases in the price of these inputs make it possible to produce commodities more _____. Firms may then be willing to supply a given amount of a product at a(n) _____ price, thus causing the supply curve to shift to the (left, right) _____. On the other hand, increases in the price of inputs may cause it to shift to the (left, right) _____.

5. An equilibrium is a situation where there is no tendency for

   _____. In other words, it is a situation that can

   _____. Thus an equilibrium price is a price that can be

   _____.

6. When the actual price exceeds the equilibrium price, there will be (downward,

   upward) _____ pressure on price. Similarly,
   when the actual price is less than the equilibrium price, there will be

   (downward, upward) _____ pressure on price. There is
   always a tendency for the actual price to move (toward, away from)

   _____ the equilibrium price, but it should not be assumed

   that this movement is always _____. Sometimes it takes a(n)

   _____ time for the actual price to get close to the

   equilibrium price. Sometimes the actual price _____ gets to
   the equilibrium price because by the time it gets close, the equilibrium price
   changes.

7. In general, a shift to the right in the demand curve results in a(n) (decrease,

   increase) _____ in the equilibrium price, and a shift to the

   left in the demand curve results in a(n) (decrease, increase) _____
   in the equilibrium price. This conclusion depends on the assumption that the

   supply curve slopes upward to the (left, right) _____, but this
   assumption is generally true.

8. In general, a shift to the right in the supply curve results in a(n) (decrease,

   increase) _____ in the equilibrium price, and a shift to the

   left in the supply curve results in a(n) (decrease, increase) _____
   in the equilibrium price. Of course, this conclusion depends on the assumption
   that the demand curve slopes downward to the (left, right)

   _____, but this assumption is generally true.

9. The demand curve for a product shows how much of that product consumers

   want at various _____. If consumers don't want much of a
   product at a certain price, its demand curve will indicate that fact by being

   positioned close to the _____ axis at that price. In other
   words, the demand curve will show that, at this price for the product, the

   amount consumers will buy is _____.

True-False

_____ 1. The demand curve for a free good (a good with a zero price) must be a horizontal line.

_____ 2. The demand curve for a free good (a good with a zero price) must be a vertical line.

_____ 3. No equilibrium price or equilibrium quantity exists if a good's demand curve is a horizontal line and its supply curve is a vertical line.

_____ 4. As long as the actual price exceeds the equilibrium price, there ordinarily will be a downward pressure on price.

_____ 5. A shift to the left in the demand curve results in an increase in the equilibrium price.

_____ 6. The flow of money income from firms to consumers is exactly equal to the flow of expenditure from consumers to firms, so long as consumers spend all their income.

_____ 7. The price system results in each person receiving an income that depends on the quantity of resources he or she owns and the prices they command.

_____ 8. The market supply curve depends on technology and the income of consumers.

_____ 9. One prerequisite for a perfectly competitive market is that the product sold by various producers be homogeneous.

_____ 10. A product's demand curve is an important determinant of how much firms will produce of the product, since it indicates the amount of the product that will be demanded at each price.

_____ 11. For the individual product, the question of who gets what is solved by the equality of the quantity demanded and quantity supplied.

_____ 12. The amount society invests in educating, training, and upgrading its labor resources is determined entirely outside the price system.

_____ 13. Since a shift in demand for apples leads to a change in their supply, it is impossible to say anything about what happens to either equilibrium price or quantity sold.

_____ 14. Markets for individual commodities must always be in equilibrium since the amount actually sold is always equal to the amount actually bought.

_____ 15. The demand curve for coal in a 5-year period can be derived from the demand curve for coal in a 1-year period. At each price of coal, the quantity demanded in the 5-year period is 5 times the quantity demanded in the 1-year period.

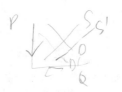

Multiple Choice

1. A decrease in the price of a good together with an increase in the quantity sold would result from:

   a. an increase in supply.
   b. a decrease in supply.
   c. an increase in demand.

   d. a decrease in demand.
   e. both a decrease in demand and a decrease in supply.

2. If the supply of fishing licenses increases:

   a. the quantity of fishing poles demanded will probably decrease.
   b. the supply of fishing poles will probably decrease.
   c. the price of fishing licenses will probably increase.
   d. the demand for fishing poles will probably increase.
   e. none of the above.

3. Between 1974 and 1979 per capita coffee consumption fell in the United States while the price per pound of coffee more than doubled. One possible explanation is that:

   a. the supply of coffee decreased during this period.
   b. the demand for coffee increased during this period.
   c. both the demand and supply of coffee increased.
   d. coffee's supply curve is a vertical line.
   e. none of the above.

4. If the government were to announce that it would no longer allow private parties to buy uranium oxide (so the government would be the sole buyer) and if it were to announce that it would buy any and all uranium oxide at $20 per pound, which of the following diagrams would represent the demand curve for uranium oxide in the United States:

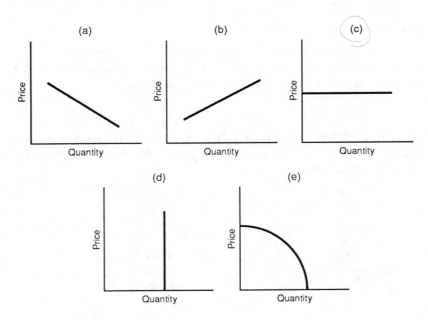

5. If people addicted to drug X must buy some given quantity of it (but not more than that quantity) and will pay whatever price is necessary (and if non-addicts do not buy drug X), which of the diagrams in the previous question represents the demand curve for drug X?

6. Which of the following will *not* affect the demand curve for fishing poles?

   a. pollution of local streams and rivers
   b. an increase in the price of fishing licenses
   c. an increase in the population
   d. an increase in the price of fish
   e. an increase in the price of a fishing pole

7. If the quantity supplied of gasoline exceeds the quantity demanded when gasoline is $1.10 a gallon, and the quantity demanded exceeds the quantity supplied at $1.00 a gallon, the equilibrium price of gasoline is:

   a. $1.00.
   b. $1.10.
   c. below $1.00.
   d. above $1.10.
   e. between $1.00 and $1.10.

8. The equilibrium price of a commodity is given by:

   a. the actual price minus the input costs.
   b. the intersection of market demand and supply curves.
   c. the first point at which market demand exceeds market supply.
   d. the actual price.
   e. none of the above.

9. The position of the supply curve is *not* directly affected by the:

   a. state of technology.
   b. prices of resources used.
   c. income level of consumers.
   d. all of the above.
   e. none of the above.

10. The price system:

   a. sets up incentives for firms to produce what consumers want.
   b. determines each person's income through the price of his or her resources.
   c. may result in unequal distribution of society's output.
   d. all of the above.
   e. none of the above.

11. The amount of new capital goods produced, the amount that society invests in education and training, and the rate of technological change are all influenced in the United States by:

   a. the price system.
   b. government action.
   c. neither a nor b.
   d. both a and b.

12. A perfectly competitive market does *not* require:

   a. a homogeneous product.
   b. so many buyers and sellers that none can influence price.
   c. a constant price.
   d. both a and b.
   e. none of the above.

Discussion and Extension Questions

1. *Business Week* has reported that, after the New York Knicks recruited star center Patrick Ewing, the team expected to sell 66 percent more tickets than in the previous year. Did Ewing's recruitment shift the demand curve for tickets to Knick games? If so, why?

2. "The supply curve influences the demand curve, since the more that is produced of a commodity, the more people want of it (or the more producers convince them they want)." Discuss and evaluate.

3. According to *Business Week*, consumers have turned to meat that is low in calories and cholesterol, like chicken and turkey. What is the effect of such a trend on the beef market? The lamb market? The pork market?

4. When we placed controls on gasoline prices in 1973–74 there still remained the problem of rationing a scarce good. How did we do it? Would you regard the mechanism we used as better or worse than alternative methods of rationing? Why?

5. The discussion about an equilibrium point in the text focused on the equilibrium price and situations where the actual price was either above or below that equilibrium price. To see if you understand the argument, explain the adjustment mechanism in terms of equilibrium quantity. Begin with a quantity which is less than the equilibrium quantity; what pressures exist to move toward an equilibrium? When the price is too low for equilibrium we say that, at the prevailing price, the quantity people want to buy exceeds the amount suppliers want to sell. What is the counterpart if the quantity is too low for equilibrium?

6. What factors influence the position of the market demand curve for corn? What factors influence the position of the market supply curve for corn? What will happen to the equilibrium price of corn if the market demand curve shifts to the right? What will happen if it shifts to the left?

7. What will happen to the equilibrium price of corn if the market supply curve shifts to the right? What will happen if it shifts to the left?

Problems

1. Suppose that the market demand curve for corn is as follows:

Price of corn (dollars per bushel)	Quantity of corn demanded (millions of bushels per year)
0.50	100
1	80
2	60
3	40
4	30
5	20

   a.   How much corn would be demanded if the price were 50 cents? Plot the demand curve below:

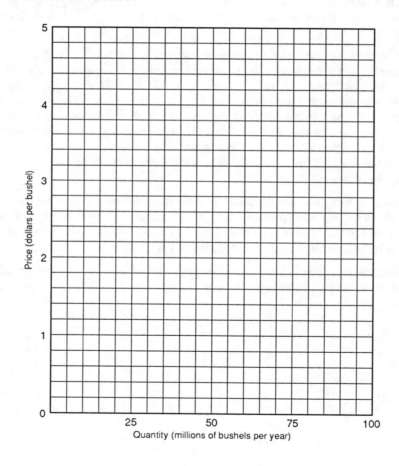

b. Suppose that the market supply curve for corn is as follows:

Price of corn (dollars per bushel)	Quantity of corn supplied (millions of bushels per year)
0.50	10
1	30
2	60
3	70
4	80
5	90

How much corn would be supplied if the price were 50 cents? $2? Plot the supply curve below:

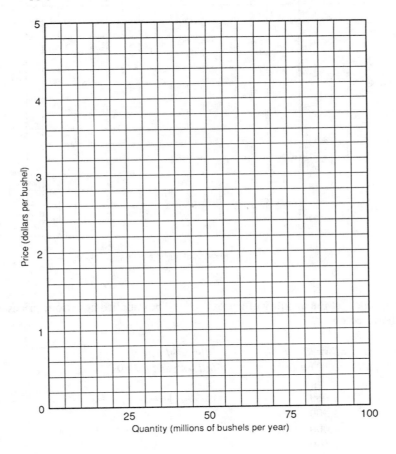

c. Using the data above, what is the equilibrium price for corn? Plot the demand and supply curves, and relate these curves to the equilibrium price.

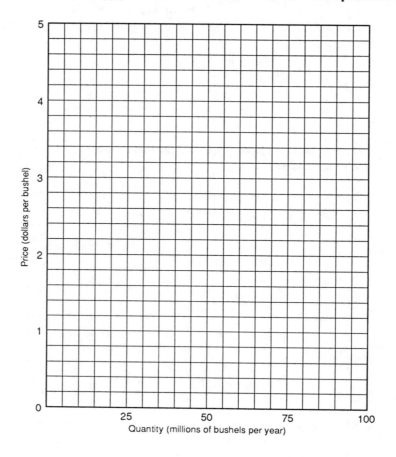

2. Suppose that the quantity of wheat that will be supplied at various prices is as shown below:

Quantity of wheat supplied (millions of bushels)	Price of wheat (dollars per bushel)
1,000	1
1,500	2
2,000	3
2,500	4

a. Plot the supply curve for wheat in the following graph. How much will be produced if the price is $3.50 per bushel (and if the supply curve is linear)?

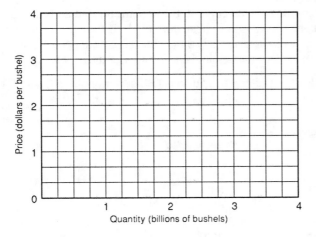

b. Suppose that because of a technological change—a new, drought-resistant type of grain—farmers are willing to supply 20 percent more wheat at each price. Plot the new supply curve below:

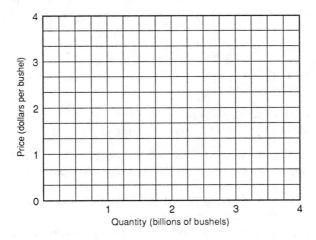

c. Suppose that the demand curve for wheat is as follows:

Quantity of wheat demanded (millions of bushels)	Price of wheat (dollars per bushel)
3,000	1
2,500	2
2,000	3
1,500	4

Plot this demand curve in the graphs in parts a and b above.

   d. Under these new circumstances, will the equilibrium price be higher or lower than under the old circumstances, assuming that the demand curve remains constant?

   e. Suppose that the demand curve in the new circumstances is unknown, but that the supply curve is as indicated in part b. If the equilibrium price under the new circumstances is $3 per bushel, at what point along the horizontal axis does the demand curve intersect the supply curve?

3. Suppose that the demand curve for tickets to the Metropolitan Opera for a performance of *Carmen* is as follows:

Price of a ticket (dollars)	Quantity demanded
56	3,000
60	2,800
64	2,600
68	2,400
72	2,200
76	2,000
80	1,800

   a. If the Metropolitan Opera House has 2,400 seats, and if it sets a price of $72 per ticket, will the house be full? If not, how many seats will be vacant?

   b. What is the equilibrium price of a ticket for this performance?

   c. What is the shape of the supply curve for tickets?

   d. Is there a "shortage" or "surplus" of tickets? In a free market, would the price of a ticket rise or fall?

4. The demand curve for fishing poles is $P = 50 - 10Q$, where P is the price of a fishing pole (in dollars) and Q is the quantity demanded per year (in millions).

   a. If the government orders the producers of fishing poles to produce 1 million fishing poles per year, what will be the equilibrium price of a fishing pole?

   b. If the current price of a fishing pole is $60, would you expect the price to rise or fall, once the government order occurs?

   c. Suppose that after it issues the above order, the government sets a ceiling of $30 on the price of a fishing pole. Will a surplus or shortage result? How big will it be?

*5. If supply and demand in a competitive market both increase, one can predict the direction of change of output but not of price. If supply increases but demand decreases, one cannot, without further knowledge, be certain about the direction of either the price or the quantity change. Do you agree with this statement? Explain.

---

*The starred items pertain to material covered in the section "Exploring Further."

*6. Use a diagram to show that a rise in the price of margarine could be a response to a rise in the price of butter.

*7. According to *Business Week*, all major chocolate makers shared a basic problem some time ago. Production costs were going up, sales were going down, and the price of a standard candy bar rose from 30¢ to 40¢. Depict this situation graphically and explain why a successful attempt to make candy appealing to more customers would only cause a further rise in price.

8. How do you reconcile the hypothesis that "the quantity demanded varies inversely with price" (law of demand), with the statement that "a rise in demand will lead to a rise in price, other things equal?"

*9. It is impossible for the price of a commodity to fall at the same time the demand for the commodity is rising. Comment, using supply and demand curves.

10. Distinguish between a "change in demand" and a "change in quantity demanded."

*11. "When it is said that there are shortages in some market, we know that that market is out of equilibrium. Take natural gas for instance. In the late 1970s there were shortages. Some people argued that they were due to the government price controls while others claimed that they were due to cold winters combined with the stockpiling of natural gas because firms and individuals feared a shortage might develop. The first group of people worried that releasing the controls would lead to very high prices, while the second group concluded that the shortage would disappear as soon as it warmed up and people became less worried." Explain each side's argument using diagrammatic analysis.

ANSWERS

Completion Questions

1. more, wheat, corn, less, corn, wheat   2. exceed, consumers   3. cheaply, lower, right   4. resources, cheaply, lower, right, left   5. change, persist, maintained   6. downward, upward, toward, rapid, long, never   7. increase, decrease, right   8. decrease, increase, right   9. prices, vertical, small

---

*The starred items pertain to material covered in the section "Exploring Further."

True-False

1. False   2. False   3. False   4. True   5. False   6. True   7. True   8. False
9. True   10. True   11. True   12. False   13. False   14. False   15. False

Multiple Choice

1. a   2. d   3. a   4. c   5. d   6. e   7. e   8. b   9. c   10. d   11. d
12. c

Problems

1. a.   100 million bushels.

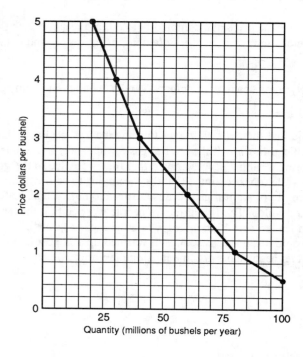

b. 10 million bushels, 60 million bushels.

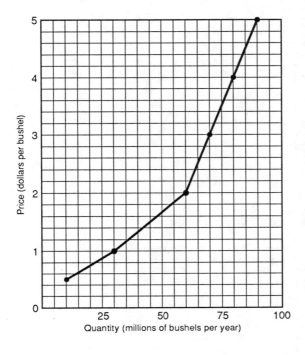

c. $2 a bushel.

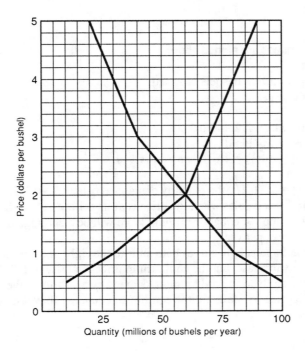

2. a. 2,250 million bushels.

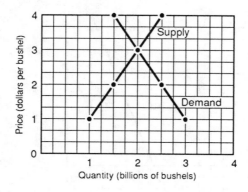

b. The new supply curve is below.

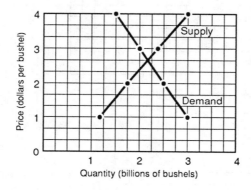

    c. The demands are plotted above.
    d. Lower.
    e. At 2,400 million bushels of wheat.

3. a. No. 200 seats.
    b. $68.
    c. A vertical line at 2,400 tickets.
    d. Surplus. It would fall.

4. a. Since $50 - 10(1) = 40$, the answer is $40.
    b. Fall.
    c. Since $Q = 5 - 0.1P$, the quantity demanded equals $5 - 0.1(30) = 2$ million fishing poles when the price is at its ceiling of $30. Since the quantity supplied equals 1 million, there will be a shortage of 1 million fishing poles per year.

5. If the demand and supply curves both shift to the right, the equilibrium quantity must increase, but the equilibrium price may rise or fall. If the supply curve shifts to the right but the demand curve shifts to the left, the equilibrium price will fall, but the equilibrium quantity may rise or fall.

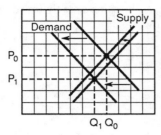 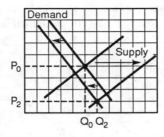

The left-hand panel above shows a case where it falls (from Q_0 to Q_1); the right-hand panel above shows a case where it rises (from Q_0 to Q_2).

6. Butter and margarine are substitutes. An increase in the price of butter might shift the demand curve for margarine to the right, as shown below, the result being an increase (from P to P') in the price of margarine.

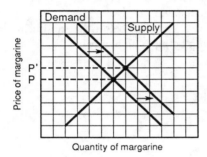

7. These facts seem to suggest that the supply curve for candy bars shifted to the left, as shown below.

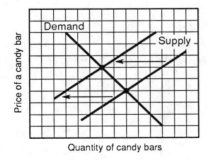

If candy is made appealing to more customers, this means that the demand curve shifts to the right, which causes a further rise in price.

8. The first hypothesis states that the demand curve slopes downward and to the right. The second hypothesis states that a shift of the demand curve to the right results in an increase in the equilibrium price. There is no contradiction between them.

9. If the supply of the commodity is rising at the same time that its demand is rising, the price may fall, as shown below:

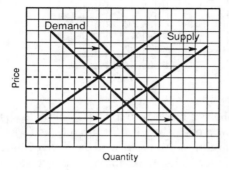

10. A change in demand is a shift in the demand curve, which is quite different from a change in the quantity demanded.
11. The first group felt that the price, P_c, was set below the equilibrium price by government controls, the situation being as shown below:

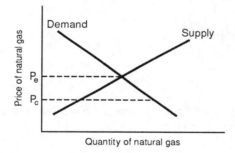

If the controls are released, the price will rise to P_e.

The second group felt that the demand curve had shifted to the right and that the price had not increased, so there was a shortage of $Q_D - Q_S$, as shown below:

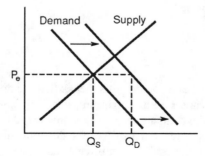

If the demand curve shifts back to its original position when the weather warms up and people become less worried, the shortage will disappear.

CHAPTER 3

National Income and Product

Chapter Profile

One of the key indicators of the health of any nation's economy is the gross domestic product, which measures the total value of the final goods and services the nation produces in a particular period. Since gross domestic product is affected by the price level it must be deflated by a price index to correct for price-level changes. When deflated in this way, GDP is called real GDP, or GDP in constant dollars.

There are many pitfalls in calculating the gross domestic product. One must avoid counting the same output more than once. Purely financial transactions that do not reflect current production must be excluded. Also, some final goods and services that must be included in GDP are not bought and sold in the marketplace, so they are valued at what they cost.

GDP is not an ideal measure of total economic output, let alone a satisfactory measure of economic well-being. It takes no account of a nation's population, the amount of leisure time, or the distribution of income. It does not reflect many changes in the quality of goods and many social costs like pollution.

One approach to GDP is the expenditures approach, which regards GDP as the sum of all expenditures that are involved in taking the total output of final goods and services off the market. To determine GDP in this way, one must add up all the spending on final goods and services. Economists distinguish among four broad categories of spending: personal consumption expenditures, gross private domestic investment, government purchases, and net exports. GDP equals the sum of these four items.

Another approach to GDP is the income approach, which regards GDP as the sum of incomes derived from the production of this year's output (plus depreciation and indirect business taxes). To determine GDP in this way, one must add up all the income stemming from the production of this year's total output (plus depreciation and indirect business taxes). Economists identify five broad categories of income: compensation of employees, rents, interest, proprietors' income, and corporate profits. GDP equals the sum of these five items (plus depreciation and indirect business taxes).

Concepts for Review

Gross domestic product
National income accounts
Final goods and services
Intermediate good
Transfer payments
Base year
Current dollars
Constant dollars
Real gross domestic
  product
Price index

Deflating
Value-added
Expenditure approach
  to GDP
Personal consumption
  expenditure
Gross private domestic
  investment
Government purchases
Net exports

Income approach to
  GDP
Compensation of
  employees
Rents
Interest
Proprietors' income
Corporate profits
Depreciation
Indirect business
  taxes

Completion Questions

1. The four parts of the total amount spent on final goods and services are

    _____, _____, _____,

    and _____.

2. The value in money terms of the total output of final goods and services in the economy during a certain period of time is called the _____.

3. Bread purchased by a consumer is a(n) (final, intermediate) _____ good, but flour to be used in manufacturing bread is a(n) (final, intermediate)

    _____ good. Clearly, we would be double counting if we counted both the bread and the flour used to make the bread as

    _____. To avoid this, we include only the value of (final, intermediate) _____ goods and services in gross domestic product.

4. Government transfer payments are payments made by the government to individuals who (do, do not) _____ contribute to production in exchange for them. Since these payments are not for _____, it would be (correct, incorrect) _____ to include them in GDP.

5. Private transfer payments are gifts or other transfers of wealth from one

_____ or _____ to another. These are not

payments for _____, so they are not included in GDP.

6. Expressed in (current, constant) _____ dollars, gross
domestic product is affected by changes in the price level. Expressed in

(current, constant) _____ dollars, gross domestic product is
not affected by the price level because the prices of all goods are maintained

at their _____ level. In recent years, inflation has caused

gross domestic product expressed in (current, constant) _____
dollars to increase more rapidly than gross domestic product in (current,

constant) _____ dollars.

7. An important function of a price index is to convert values expressed in

(current, constant) _____ dollars into values expressed in

(current, constant) _____ dollars. This conversion, known as

_____, can be achieved simply by dividing values expressed

in (current, constant) _____ dollars by the price
index.

8. The contribution of a firm or industry to the final output is measured by the

concept of _____. Wheat and the _____ of
flour mills and bakers are part of the value-added in the process of making
bread. GDP figures indicate that the American economy is turning more

toward producing _____, rather than _____.

9. Gross domestic product equals the income paid out (or owed) as

_____, _____, _____,

and _____, plus two other items; indirect business taxes and

depreciation. Indirect business taxes are _____ taxes,

_____ taxes, and other taxes that firms consider as part of
their costs. In other words, gross domestic product exactly equals the total

_____ on output.

10. If consumers regard a pound of butter as 10 times as valuable as a pencil, and if an economy's 1994 and 1995 outputs were as shown below, the economy's total output (as measured by its value to consumers) was (greater, less)

    _____ in 1995 than in 1994. Specifically, it (increased,

    decreased) _____ by _____ percent. In

    national income accounting, a good's _____ is used to
    measure the value consumers attach to it.

	Output	
	1994	*1995*
Pencils (millions)	200	220
Butter (millions of pounds)	30	29

11. Suppose that $100 worth of apples are used (together with $100 worth of labor by cider producers) to make $200 worth of apple cider, and that $200 worth of apple cider (together with $100 worth of labor by drink producers) are used to make $300 worth of a potent apple drink that is marketed at New England colleges on football weekends. If we consider $600 worth of this

    apple drink, the value added by the apple producers equals _____,

    the value added by the cider producers equals _____, and the

    value added by the apple drink producers equals _____. The
    total value added by these three groups of firms is (greater than, equal to, less

    than) _____ the value of the apple drink sold to consumers.

12. If gross domestic product expressed in constant dollars is 50 percent greater than in 1980 and if the price index is 50 percent higher than in 1980, then

    gross domestic product in current dollars is _____ percent
    greater than in 1980. If the price index does not take proper account of quality improvements in goods during this period, the rise in the price level

    since 1980 is probably (greater, less) _____ than 50 percent

    and the rise in real GDP since 1980 is probably (greater, less) _____
    than 50 percent.

13. An economy consists of only two firms, Macy's and Bloomingdale's. During 1995, Macy's reduces its inventories by $2 million, while Bloomingdale's increases its inventories by $3 million. At the beginning of 1995, each firm had inventories of $10 million. If there were no other gross private domestic investment in 1995, domestic gross private investment during that year equaled

    _____.

True-False

_____ 1. Corporate profits, as defined in the national income accounts, do not include retained earnings.

_____ 2. Part of the annual production of a commodity can be counted as an intermediate good while the rest can be counted as a final good. It frequently is incorrect to categorize a commodity as totally a final good or totally an intermediate good.

_____ 3. During 1995, the Acme Washing Machine Company produces $10 million worth of washing machines but sells only $9 million of them. The remaining $1 million worth of washing machines will be included in GDP in 1996 when they are sold.

_____ 4. Gross domestic product does not include intermediate goods.

_____ 5. When expressed in current dollars, the gross domestic product is not affected by changes in the price level.

_____ 6. Expenditures by General Motors on paper, typewriters, and fuel oil are all included in consumption expenditure.

_____ 7. The smallest part of the total amount spent on final goods and services in the United States is net exports of goods and services.

_____ 8. Gross domestic product has one drawback as a measure that must be faced; it does not take into account the fact that plant and equipment wear out with use.

_____ 9. If a new type of drug is put on the market at the same price as an old drug, and if the output and cost of the new drug are the same as the old drug, GDP will not increase, even though the new drug is twice as effective as the old one.

_____ 10. Consumption includes your expenditures on meals and clothing, and your parents' expenditures on the family car or on an electric washer and dryer.

_____ 11. The capital consumption allowance in the national income accounts includes the wear and tear on an automobile owned by a college professor who drives it to and from work.

_____ 12. If the Lehman Real Estate Company buys 20 acres of land in Palo Alto, California, with an eye toward the possible construction of houses on this land in future years, this purchase would be included in gross private domestic investment.

_____ 13. If the Malone family buys a 15-year-old house from Mr. D. Teece, a (hypothetical) real estate speculator, this purchase would be included in gross private domestic investment.

_____ 14. Net exports include goods but not services.

_____ 15. If a retired naval officer builds himself a bookshelf, this is included in the gross domestic product.

_____ 16. If the president of General Motors drives his car to his office, this is included in the gross domestic product.

Multiple Choice

1. Which of the following would *not* be included in gross private domestic investment?

   a. an increase in McDonald's inventory of hamburger rolls
   b. expenditures on a new Broadway theater
   c. the purchase of a new taxi by Yellow Cab Company
   d. the purchase of a new washing machine by the Jones family
   e. the purchase of a new washing machine by the Acme Laundry

2. Which of the following would *not* be included in government purchases of goods and services?

   a. the Defense Department's expenditure of $1 billion on a new missile
   b. the National Science Foundation's expenditure of $1 billion for basic research
   c. the Department of Health, Education, and Welfare's expenditure of $1 billion on welfare
   d. Iowa's expenditure of $1 billion on the construction of schools
   e. none of the above

3. Which of the following is *not* an indirect business tax?

   a. Pennsylvania's general sales tax
   b. New York's cigarette tax
   c. U.S. corporate income tax
   d. Pennsylvania corporation income tax
   e. both c and d

4. Which of the following transactions would be included in the gross domestic product?

   a. Bill White buys a secondhand bicycle for $70.
   b. Bill Green gives his bicycle to his cousin.
   c. John Black buys a new bicycle for $150.
   d. Jerry Brown buys 2 shares of stock in a bicycle firm.
   e. Mort Gray steals John Black's new bicycle.

5. In the national income accounts, indirect business taxes include:

   a. government transfer payments.
   b. private transfer payments.
   c. all personal taxes.
   d. excise taxes.
   e. personal income taxes.

6. If a set of goods and services costs $5,000 in constant dollars (1960 prices) and $7,000 in current dollars, by about how much has their price changed between 1960 and now?

   a. 20%   d. 70%
   b. 40%   e. 80%
   c. 50%

7. GDP takes no account of:

   a. exports.   d. all of the above.
   b. services produced.   e. a and b above.
   c. the social costs of environmental pollution.

8. It is customary for gross domestic product to be expressed in terms of:

   a. current dollars.   d. a or b above.
   b. constant dollars.   e. all of the above.
   c. price index.

9. Marantz produces a hi-fi receiver in 1994 which is sold to a retailer in December 1994. It is sold to a consumer in 1995. This receiver is included in:

   a. consumption expenditure in 1995.
   b. investment in 1994.
   c. disinvestment in 1995.
   d. all of the above.
   e. none of the above.

10. Mrs. Harris spends the morning cleaning her house and cooking lunch. This is not included in the GDP because it is:

   a. already included in the value of her husband's output.
   b. a nonmarket transaction.
   c. valued at cost.
   d. unproductive of any economic output.
   e. none of the above.

Discussion and Extension Questions

1. "Value added is a poor measure of an industry's contribution to GDP because it does not take any account of the environmental pollution caused by the industry. Also, it is based entirely on market prices." Discuss and evaluate.

2. What difficulties would you encounter in trying to compare levels of economic welfare across countries (say, for example, the United States versus Great Britain, India, Sweden, Mexico, and China) using gross domestic product as your yardstick?

3. "Gross domestic product is a sexist measure because it discriminates against women, many of whom work in the home." Comment and evaluate.

4. Does the gross domestic product include the value of all goods and services produced? If not, which ones does it include?

5. How are government services valued in computing GDP? Why is the sale of secondhand goods excluded from GDP?

6. "If you don't subtract depreciation in the calculation of total national output, you are making a mistake similar to double counting intermediate goods." In what ways are the two mistakes similar? In what ways are they different?

7. If each taxpayer hired his or her neighbor to fill out his or her tax return, would this affect the gross domestic output? If so, how? Would you favor including in GDP the value of time spent by citizens filling out tax returns? Why or why not?

8. "Aid to the poor is not included in government purchases of goods and services; consequently, it is not included in GDP. Yet such aid is of enormous benefit to the population and the improvement in the income distribution should be regarded as an output of the economic system." Comment in detail.

Problems

1. a. Gopherland is a country where the price level has been rising at a rate of 5 percent per year. Gross domestic product in current dollars was 10 percent higher in 1994 than in 1993, and 3 percent higher in 1993 than in 1992. In terms of constant dollars, how much greater was Gopherland's GDP in 1994 than in 1992?
   b. Gopherland's largest firm, the Gopherland Iron Company, sold $3 million worth of iron in 1994. It purchased $1.2 million worth of goods and services from other firms, paid $0.5 million in interest, and paid $0.3 million in excise and property taxes. Since its depreciation allowance was $0.3 million, its profit was $0.7 million. How much was its value-added in 1994?
   c. In 1990, Gopherland's exports equaled its imports, and its gross private domestic investment equaled its government expenditures. Its personal consumption expenditure was double its government expenditure, and equaled $400 million. What was its GDP in 1990?

2. Suppose that we could add up all of the money transactions in the United States during this year. Would this total amount equal, exceed, or be less than this year's GDP? Why?

3. The nation of Erewhon reports that its capital consumption allowance in 1994 is negative. What would this mean? Is it possible or not?

ANSWERS

Completion Questions

1. consumption expenditure, investment, government purchases of goods and services, net exports   2. gross domestic product   3. final, intermediate, output, final   4. do not, production, incorrect   5. person, private organization, production   6. current, constant, base-year, current, constant   7. current, constant, deflating, current   8. value-added, services, services, goods   9. wages, rent, interest, profits, sales, excise, claims   10. greater, increased, 2, price   11. $200, $200, $200, equal to   12. 125, less, greater   13. $1 million

True-False

1. False   2. True   3. False   4. True   5. False   6. False   7. True   8. True   9. True   10. True   11. False   12. False   13. False   14. False   15. False   16. False

Multiple-Choice

1. d   2. c   3. e   4. c   5. d   6. b   7. c   8. d   9. d   10. b

Problems

1. a. Gross domestic product in current dollars in 1994 equals $1.10 \times 1.03 \times$ gross domestic product in current dollars in 1992. The price level in 1994 is 10 percent higher than in 1992. Thus, in terms of 1992 dollars, GDP in 1994 is $\dfrac{1.10}{1.10} \times 1.03 \times$ GDP in 1992. In other words, it is 3 percent higher than in 1992.
   b. $1.8 million.
   c. $800 million.
2. It would exceed GDP because transactions involving intermediate goods and secondhand goods, as well as purely financial transactions, would be included in this total, but they are excluded from GDP.
3. This would mean that a negative amount of plant and equipment wore out, which clearly is unrealistic.

CHAPTER 4

Business Fluctuations and

Unemployment

Chapter Profile

National output tends to rise and approach its potential (that is, its full-employment) level for a while, then falter and fall below this level, then rise to approach it once more, and so on. These ups and downs are called business fluctuations, or business cycles. Each cycle can be divided into four phases: trough, expansion, peak, recession. These cycles are very irregular and highly variable in length and amplitude. Unemployment tends to be higher at the trough than at the peak; inflation tends to be higher at the peak than at the trough.

Until the 1930s, most economists were convinced that the price system, left to its own devices, would ensure the maintenance of full employment. They thought it unlikely that total spending would be too small to purchase the full-employment level of output, and argued that prices would be cut if any problem of this sort developed. A notable exception was Karl Marx, who felt that the capitalistic system would suffer from worse and worse unemployment, leading to the system's eventual collapse.

John Maynard Keynes, in the 1930s, developed a theory to explain how the capitalist economic system remained mired in the Great Depression, with its tragically high levels of unemployment. Contrary to the classical economists, he concluded that there was no automatic mechanism in a capitalistic system to generate and maintain full employment—or, at least, to generate it quickly enough to be relied on in practice.

The aggregate demand curve shows the level of real national output that will be demanded at each price level. One reason why it slopes downward and to the right is that (a) increases in the price level push up interest rates, and (b) increases in interest rates reduce real national output.

The short-run aggregate supply curve shows the level of real national output that will be supplied at each price level if the prices of all inputs are fixed. Since increases in the price level tend to raise the profitability of firms' increasing output, the short-run aggregate supply curve tends to slope upward to the right.

The equilibrium level of real national output and the equilibrium price level are given by the intersection of the aggregate demand and supply curves.

Unemployment is of various types: frictional, structural, and cyclical. The overall unemployment rate conceals considerable differences among types of people. The Bureau of Labor Statistics publishes monthly data concerning unemployment rates for various segments of the population. High levels of unemployment impose great costs on society.

*In the long run, when input prices can adjust fully to eliminate the unemployment or shortage of inputs (like labor), the aggregate supply curve is vertical. Real national output is at its potential level.

Concepts for Review

Business cycle
Trough
Expansion
Peak
Recession
Depression
Prosperity
Aggregate demand curve

Frictional unemployment
Structural unemployment
Cyclical unemployment
Potential GDP
Full employment
Short-run aggregate supply curve
Say's Law
*Long-run aggregate supply curve

Completion Questions

1. When there is substantial unemployment, the short-run aggregate supply curve may be (vertical, downward sloping, close to horizontal) _____.

   There (is, is not) _____ so much upward pressure on prices as output increases because there are plenty of unemployed workers and other resources.

2. An increase in the price level (increases, decreases) _____ interest rates, which (reduces, increases) _____ total output. Thus, the aggregate demand curve slopes _____.

3. When an economy's resources are fully employed, its short-run aggregate supply curve tends to be (horizontal, upward-sloping, vertical) _____. This is because further increases in the price level will result in (considerable, no) _____ extra output.

4. A rightward shift of the aggregate demand curve will increase total output but not the price level if the economy is situated at the (horizontal, positively sloped, vertical) _____ range of the short-run aggregate supply curve. It will increase the price level but not total output if the economy is situated at the (horizontal, positively sloped, vertical) _____ range of the short-run aggregate supply curve. It will increase both the price level and total output if the economy is situated at the (horizontal, positively sloped, vertical) _____ range of the short-run aggregate supply curve.

---

*The starred items pertain to material covered in the section "Exploring Further."

5. When the unemployment rate has been very high and the government has wanted to reduce unemployment, it frequently has used its fiscal and monetary policies to shift the aggregate demand curve to the (right, left)

   _____. If inflation is a serious problem and the government wants to keep a tight lid on the price level, it often uses its fiscal and monetary policies to shift the aggregate demand curve to the (right, left)

   _____.

6. If the short-run aggregate supply curve shifts to the right, the result is likely to

   be (increased, decreased) _____ total output and a (higher,

   lower) _____ price level. If the short-run aggregate supply

   curve shifts to the left, the result is likely to be (increased, decreased)

   _____ total output and a (higher, lower) _____

   price level.

7. A decrease in the price level (reduces, increases) _____ the real value of the currency and government bonds held by the public. This

   results in a(n) (increase, decrease) _____ in consumption expenditures. A decrease in the price level (increases, decreases)

   _____ the average money cost of a transaction, thus

   (increasing, decreasing) _____ the demand for money, which

   will (increase, decrease) _____ the interest rate. Thus the

   aggregate demand curve slopes _____ and to the

   _____.

8. The _____ is the point where national output is lowest

   relative to its potential level. The _____ is the point where national output is highest relative to its potential level.

9. During the Great Depression, the aggregate demand curve shifted to the (left,

   right) _____. During World War II, the aggregate demand

   curve shifted to the (left, right) _____.

10. During the 1970s, the short-run aggregate supply curve shifted to the (left,

    right) _____ because of the actions of Arab and other oil-

    producing countries which (increased, decreased) _____ the price of oil substantially.

11. If a peak occurs in March 1997, we can be sure that an expansion (will, will

    not) _____ begin in March 1997. If a recession ends in

    January 1996, we can be sure that a trough (will, will not) _____ occur in January 1996. If a peak occurs in April 1998, we (can, cannot)

_____ be sure that April 1998 is a time of prosperity.

12. Between 1929 and 1933, real GDP fell by almost _____.
Two factors that contributed to this debacle was the contraction of

_____ and the reduction in the _____

supply. Unemployment rates were excessive until _____.

True-False

_____ 1. The aggregate demand curve assumes that the money supply is fixed.

_____ 2. In a typical year the production of soft drinks tends to be over 20 percent higher in July or August than in January or February. This is an example of the business cycle.

_____ 3. Regardless of the shape of the short-run aggregate supply curve, a shift of the aggregate demand curve upward and to the right will result in inflation.

_____ 4. If the short-run aggregate supply curve is very steep, expansionary policies will result in considerable inflation but a relatively small increase in real output.

_____ 5. Inflation generally is eliminated by a rightward shift of the aggregate demand curve.

_____ 6. The aggregate demand curve slopes downward and to the right for the same reasons that a demand curve for an individual commodity slopes downward and to the right.

_____ 7. If the money supply is fixed, increases in the price level will reduce interest rates.

_____ 8. Increases in interest rates reduce total output because banks become more important in the economy.

_____ 9. In the horizontal range of the short-run aggregate supply curve, it is assumed that there is little or no downward pressure on prices as output decreases because of the rigidity of wages and of prices.

_____ 10. The vertical range of the short-run aggregate supply curve is a simplification because it is always possible to get a bit more output from any economic system.

_____ 11. In the horizontal range of the short-run aggregate supply curve, a rightward shift of the aggregate demand curve has no effect on output.

_____ 12. In the vertical range of the short-run aggregate supply curve, a leftward shift of the aggregate demand curve has no effect on the price level.

_____ 13. To reduce unemployment, governments often try to shift the aggregate demand curve to the right.

_____ 14. During any decade, the number of troughs must equal the number of peaks.

Multiple Choice

1. During the typical business cycle, there is more variation in:
   a. the output of consumer goods than in the output of capital goods.
   b. the output of agriculture than in nonfarm output.
   c. the output of breakfast cereals than in the output of machine tools.
   d. none of the above.
   e. all of the above.

2. An upward shift of the aggregate demand curve will *not* result in:
   a. an increase in both the price level and real output.
   b. an increase in the price level but no increase in real output.
   c. no increase in the price level but an increase in real output.
   d. an increase in the price level and a decrease in real output.
   e. none of the above.

3. Suppose that the aggregate demand curve is $P = 120 - Q$, where P is the price level and Q is real output (in billions of dollars). If the short-run aggregate supply curve (which is a horizontal line) shifts upward from $P = 105$ to $P = 110$, real output will:
   a. fall from $10 billion to $5 billion.
   b. increase from $5 billion to $10 billion.
   c. fall from $15 billion to $10 billion.
   d. increase from $10 billion to $15 billion.
   e. none of the above.

4. Suppose that the short-run aggregate supply curve is $P = 20Q$, where P is the price level and Q is real output (in billions of dollars). If the aggregate demand curve shifts from $P = 105 - Q$ to $P = 115.5 - Q$, the price level will:
   a. increase from 100 to 105.   d. increase from 100 to 115.5.
   b. increase from 105 to 115.5.   e. none of the above.
   c. increase from 100 to 110.

5. A leftward shift of the aggregate demand curve will have the same effect as a rightward shift of the aggregate demand curve if:
   a. the economy is in the horizontal range of the short-run aggregate supply curve.
   b. the economy is in the vertical range of the short-run aggregate supply curve.
   c. the economy is in the positively sloped range of the short-run aggregate supply curve.

    d.   the economy is in a depression.

    e.   none of the above.

6. If the price level rises and output falls, this could be due to:

    a.   a rightward shift of the aggregate demand curve.

    b.   a leftward shift of the aggregate demand curve.

    c.   a rightward shift of the short-run aggregate supply curve.

    d.   a leftward shift of the short-run aggregate supply curve.

    e.   none of the above.

7. If the price level rises and output rises, this could be due to:

    a.   a rightward shift of the aggregate demand curve.

    b.   a leftward shift of the aggregate demand curve.

    c.   a rightward shift of the short-run aggregate supply curve.

    d.   a leftward shift of the short-run aggregate supply curve.

    e.   none of the above.

Discussion and Extension Questions

1. In the summer of 1988, many economists said that they did not believe that the expansion would end soon. What measures would you look at to see whether an expansion is ending? Explain in detail why you think that each would be a good indicator. Also comment on the limitations of each one.

2. What measures would you look at to see whether a recession is beginning? Explain in detail why you think that each would be a good indicator. Also comment on the limitations of each one.

3. During the business cycle, would you expect that ice cream purchases would vary as much as expenditures on machine tools? Would you expect that shoe sales would vary as much as the sales of bulldozers? Would you expect that cosmetics purchases would vary as much as expenditures on computers?

4. In nation X, output and employment rise, but the price level remains unchanged. Using aggregate demand and supply curves, explain how this combination of events could have occurred. Can you be sure that it was due solely to a shift in one of these curves? If so, can you tell whether the aggregate demand or the aggregate supply curve shifted?

5. Booms in the nineteenth century were associated with events like railroad building and the California gold rush. Why do you think that these events were associated with boom periods? Suppose that a vast new space program was begun. Do you think that it would promote a boom? Why or why not?

6. President Reagan, in his 1982 Economic Report, said that, "To spur further business investment and productivity growth, the new [1981] tax law provides faster write-offs for capital investment [that is, depreciation of equipment over

shorter periods of time]. . . . Research and development expenditures are encouraged with a new tax credit. Small business tax rates have been reduced." Explain in detail how each of these tax changes affects the aggregate supply curve. Based on what you have learned thus far, can you say anything about the magnitude of their effects?

Problems

1. The aggregate demand curve for economy A is shown below:

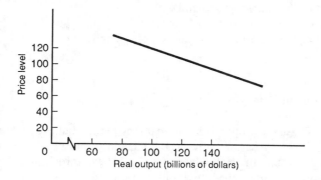

a.   If the short-run aggregate supply curve is a vertical line at real output = $140 billion, what is the price level?
b.   If the short-run aggregate supply curve is a horizontal line at price level = 120, what is real output?
c.   If the equation for the short-run aggregate supply curve is $P = -40 + Q$, where P is the price level and Q is real output (in billions of dollars), what is the price level and real output?

2. The aggregate demand curve and the short-run aggregate supply curve for economy B are shown below. As you can see, the aggregate demand curve shifts downward and to the left.

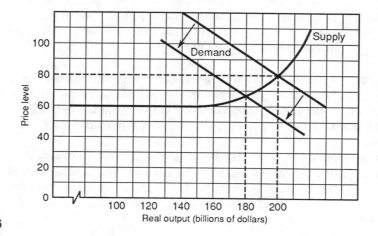

a. What is the effect of the shift of the aggregate demand curve on the price level? Specifically, what is the price level before and after the shift?

b. What is the effect of the shift of the aggregate demand curve on real output? Specifically, what is real output before and after the shift?

c. If economy B is devastated by an earthquake that reduces its productive capacity by 50 percent, how will the aggregate supply curve be affected?

3. Nation C's aggregate demand curve is $P = 1,000 - 2Q$, where P is the price level and Q is total real output in billions of dollars. Nation C is operating on the positively sloped range of its short-run aggregate supply curve: When P increases by 1, Q increases by $1 billion. Suppose that the aggregate demand curve shifts to $P = 990 - 2Q$.

a. Is this a shift of the aggregate demand curve to the left or to the right?

b. What is the effect of this shift on the price level?

c. What is the effect of this shift on total real output?

4. In nation D, the aggregate demand curve is $P = 5,000 - 5Q$, where P is the price level and Q is total real output (in billions of dollars). The short-run aggregate supply curve (in the relevant range) is $P = 0.5Q$.

a. What is the equilibrium value of the total real output?

b. What is the equilibrium value of the price level?

ANSWERS

Completion Questions

1. close to horizontal, is not   2. increases, reduces, downward and to the right
3. vertical, no   4. horizontal, vertical, positively sloped   5. right, left
6. increased, lower, decreased, higher   7. increases, increase, decreases, decreasing, decrease, downward, right   8. trough, peak   9. left, right
10. left, increased   11. will not, will, cannot   12. one-third, investment, money, World War II

True-False

1. True   2. False   3. False   4. True   5. False   6. False   7. False   8. False
9. True   10. True   11. False   12. False   13. True   14. False

Multiple Choice

1. d   2. d   3. c   4. c   5. e   6. d   7. a

Problems

1. a. 100.
   b. 100.
   c. The price level is 100 and real output is 140.
2. a. The price level falls from 80 to about 68.
   b. Real output falls from 200 to 180 billions of dollars.
   c. It will shift upward and to the left.
3. a. To the left.
   b. The equation for the short-run aggregate supply curve is $P = C + Q$, where C is an unknown constant. Thus, before the shift of the aggregate demand curve, the equilibrium price level is

$$P = C + Q = 1,000 - 2Q.$$

Thus, $3Q = 1,000 - C$, or $Q = \dfrac{1,000 - C}{3}$, which means that

$$P = \frac{3C + 1,000 - C}{3} = \frac{1,000 + 2C}{3}.$$

After the shift of the aggregate demand curve, the equilibrium price level is

$$P = C + Q = 990 - 2Q.$$

Thus, $3Q = 990 - C$, or $Q = \dfrac{990 - C}{3}$, which means that

$$P = \frac{3C + 990 - C}{3} = \frac{990 + 2C}{3}.$$

Consequently, the effect of this shift in the aggregate demand curve is to reduce the price level by $\dfrac{1,000 + 2C}{3} - \dfrac{990 + 2C}{3} = 10/3.$

   c. Q decreases from $\dfrac{1,000 - C}{3}$ to $\dfrac{990 - C}{3}$. In other words, Q decreases by 10/3 billions of dollars.
4. a. $P = 5,000 - 5Q = 0.5Q.$
   Thus, $Q = 5,000 \div 5.5 = 909.$
   b. $P = 0.5Q = 5,000 \div 11 = 454.5.$

CHAPTER 5

The Determination of National

Output and the Keynesian

Multiplier

Chapter Profile

The consumption function—the relation between personal consumption expenditure and disposable income—is at the heart of the Keynesian theory of the determination of national output. There have been many studies of the consumption function, some based on cross-section data, some based on time-series data. From the consumption function, one can determine the marginal propensity to consume, which is the proportion of an extra dollar of income that is spent on consumption, as well as the saving function (the relationship between total saving and disposable income) and the marginal propensity to save (the proportion of an extra dollar of income that is saved).

The level of gross private domestic investment is determined by the expected rate of return from capital and the interest rate. The expected rate of return from capital is the perceived rate of return that businesses expect to obtain if new buildings are put up, new equipment is added, or inventories are increased. The interest rate is the cost of borrowing money.The level of investment is directly related to the expected rate of return from capital, and inversely related to the interest rate.

The equilibrium level of gross domestic product will be at the point where intended spending on final goods and services equals GDP. If intended spending exceeds GDP, GDP will tend to increase. If intended spending falls short of GDP, GDP will tend to fall.

If GDP is below its equilibrium level, the total amount spent on goods and services will exceed the total amount produced, so that firms' inventories will be reduced. Firms will step up their output rates, thus increasing GDP. If GDP is above its equilibrium value, the total amount spent on goods and services will fall short of the total amount produced, so that firms' inventories will rise. Firms will cut their output rates, thus reducing GDP.

Investment expenditure tends to vary from year to year by greater percentages than does consumption expenditure. This is due in part to the irregularity of innovation, the durability of capital goods, and the differences from year to year in the extent to which existing productive capacity is utilized.

A $1 billion change in intended investment will result in a change in equilibrium GDP of (1/MPS) billions of dollars, where MPS is the marginal propensity to save. In other words, the multiplier equals (1/MPS). The multiplier can be interpreted in terms of—and derived from—the successive stages of the spending process.

*Holding disposable income constant, personal consumption expenditure is likely to depend on the amount of wealth in the hands of the public, the ease and cheapness with which consumers can borrow money, the expectations of the public, the amount of durable goods on hand, the income distribution, and the size of the population. Changes in these factors are likely to cause shifts in the consumption function. A shift in the consumption function will also have an amplified effect on GDP, a $1 billion shift in the consumption function resulting in a change of (1/MPS) billions of dollars in GDP.

Concepts for Review

Consumption function
Marginal propensity to consume
Average propensity to consume
*Shifts in the consumption function
Expected rate of return
Interest rate

45-degree line
Saving function
Income-expenditure analysis
Multiplier
Marginal propensity to save

Completion Questions

1. The level of investment is influenced heavily by the _____ of business executives. If business executives believe that their _____ are about to drop, they will be unlikely to invest much in additional capital goods. On the other hand, if they believe that their _____ are about to increase greatly, they may be led to invest heavily in

   _____.

2. The relation between consumption expenditure and disposable income is called the _____.

3. If the consumption function is:

$$C = 400 + 0.7D,$$

   where D is disposable income, the average propensity to consume (increases, decreases) _____ as income rises. When $D = 1,000$, the average propensity to save is (positive, negative) _____. The marginal propensity to consume equals _____.

---

*The starred items pertain to material covered in the section "Exploring Further."

4. In general, a (more, less) _____ rapid rate of technological change is likely to result in more investment. Also, as a firm's sales go (up, down) _____, its need for plant, equipment, and inventories goes up. And the more (optimistic, pessimistic) _____ business expectations are, the greater the amount of investment.

5. If consumption expenditure is proportional to disposable income, the average propensity to consume is (greater than, less than, equal to) _____ the marginal propensity to consume, and the average propensity to save is (greater than, less than, equal to) _____ the marginal propensity to save.

6. If the consumption function is:

$$C = .8D^2,$$

the marginal propensity to consume (increases, decreases, does not change) _____ as disposable income increases. This (is, is not) _____ a typical situation.

7. The equilibrium value of GDP will be at the point on the horizontal axis where the _____ line intersects the _____ line. If GDP is below this point, intended spending (exceeds, is less than) _____ GDP. If GDP is above this point, intended spending (exceeds, is less than) _____ GDP.

True-False

_____ 1. If the marginal propensity to consume is 0.8, and disposable income is $200 billion, personal consumption expenditure equals $160 billion.

_____ 2. If the average propensity to consume is 0.9, and disposable income is $100 billion, personal consumption expenditure equals $90 billion.

_____ 3. The marginal propensity to save plus the marginal propensity to consume equals the average propensity to save plus the average propensity to consume.

_____ 4. The proportion of total income consumed must always equal the marginal propensity to consume.

_____ 5. The marginal propensity to save is equal to the slope of the consumption function.

_____ 6. The marginal propensity to consume will not in general equal the average propensity to consume.

_____ 7. The level of investment is influenced by the level of sales and the stock of capital goods needed to produce the output to be sold.

_____ 8. Since the cost of an investment is bound to increase, all other things equal, with the increase in the rate of interest, a given investment will be less profitable when the interest rate is high than when it is low.

_____ 9. Investment expenditures are not influenced by the cost of capital goods.

Multiple Choice

1. The marginal propensity to save increases as disposable income rises. Consequently, the difference between the marginal propensity to consume and the marginal propensity to save:

   a. decreases as disposable income rises.
   b. increases as disposable income rises.
   c. increases and then decreases as disposable income rises.
   d. decreases and then increases as disposable income rises.
   e. remains constant as disposable income rises.

2. Which of the following relationships is a direct one?

   a. The relationship between consumption expenditure and disposable income.
   b. The relationship between saving and disposable income.
   c. The relationship between saving and the rate of interest.
   d. The relationship between consumption expenditure and population.
   e. All of the above.

3. Which of the following relationships is *not* an inverse one?

   a. The relationship between the rate of interest and investment.
   b. The relationship between the average propensity to consume and disposable income.
   c. The relationship between the average propensity to save and disposable income.
   d. The relationship between the percent of the existing capital stock that is utilized and investment.
   e. both c and d.

4. The level of investment is influenced by:

   a. the interest rate.
   b. the optimism or pessimism of expectations.
   c. the rate of technological change.
   d. the level of output relative to the capacity of existing plant and equipment.
   e. all of the above.

5. At any particular level of disposable income, the marginal propensity to save plus the marginal propensity to consume must equal:

a. 0.
b. 1.
c. 100.

d. 1,000.
e. 10,000.

6. Intended investment increases by $1,000 in an economy where the marginal propensity to save is .2. The amount of extra spending in the *first* stage of the spending and respending process is:

a. $200.
b. $400.
c. $600.

d. $800.
e. $1,000.

7. Continuing question 6, the amount of extra spending in the *second* stage of the spending and respending process is:

a. $200.
b. $400.
c. $600.

d. $800.
e. $1,000.

8. Continuing question 6, the amount of extra spending in *all* stages of the spending and respending process is:

a. $1,000.
b. $2,000.
c. $3,000.

d. $4,000.
e. $5,000.

Discussion and Extension Questions

1. "The consumption function is a deficient concept because many of the items people consume are provided by the government—for example, police protection and public education—and the amount people spend on these items is not included in the economist's concept of consumption expenditure." Discuss and evaluate.

2. John Roberts is a wealthy dentist whose income in 1995 is $25,000 because he took most of the year off to vacation in Florida. His younger brother, Bill, is a high-school teacher who made $25,000 in 1995 as a result of full-time employment. Do you think that the consumption expenditures of these two brothers will be the same in 1995? Why or why not?

3. Discuss the importance of nonincome factors on consumption expenditure. Include in your discussion facts concerning postwar American experience.

4. As it stands, can the simple model described in this chapter be used to forecast GDP? Why or why not?

5. "Because of habit and inertia, the level of personal consumption expenditure in one year depends on its level in the previous year, as well as on disposable income." Do you agree? Why or why not?

Problems

1. In the nation of Chaos-on-the-Styx, there is the following relationship between consumption expenditure and disposable income:

Consumption expenditure (billions of dollars)	Disposable income (billions of dollars)
120	100
200	200
270	300
330	400
380	500
420	600

a. Plot the consumption function for this nation below:

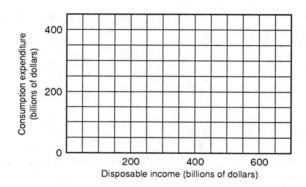

b. What is the marginal propensity to consume when disposable income is between $100 and $200 billion? When disposable income is between $300 and $400 billion? When disposable income is between $500 and $600 billion?

c. If the nation of Chaos-on-the-Styx consumes $5 billion more at each level of disposable income than shown above is this a shift in the consumption function or a movement along the consumption function?

d. Based on the data shown above, plot the saving function for Chaos-on-the-Styx below:

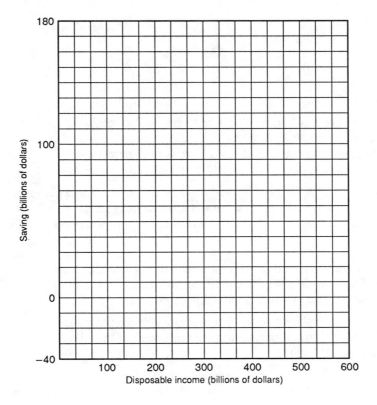

e. What is the marginal propensity to save when disposable income is between $100 billion and $200 billion? When disposable income is between $300 billion and $400 billion? When disposable income is between $500 billion and $600 billion?

f. Combining your answers to parts b and e, what is the sum of the marginal propensity to consume and the marginal propensity to save under the three situations covered there?

g. If, as described in part c, the nation consumes $5 billion more at each level of disposable income than shown above, draw the new consumption function (in the graph provided in part a) and the new saving function (in the graph provided in part d). If no change occurs in either function, write "no change" as your answer.

2. Suppose that the Bugsbane Music Box Company is considering investing in 7 projects, identified as A to G. The expected rate of return from each project is given on the next page.

Project	Expected rate of return (percent)
A	12
B	8
C	7
D	15
E	25
F	11
G	9

a. If the firm can borrow money at 10 percent interest, which projects are clearly unprofitable?

b. Suppose that the interest rate increases to 13 percent. Which projects are unprofitable now?

3. Suppose that $1 of income is transferred from a person whose marginal propensity to consume is 0.9 to someone whose marginal propensity to consume is 0.8. What is the effect on total consumption expenditure? On saving?

4. Country X's consumption function is such that personal consumption expenditure equals $90 billion if disposable income equals $100 billion. The marginal propensity to save equals 1/3.

a. Fill in the value of personal consumption expenditure and the average propensity to consume corresponding to each of the following values of disposable income:

Disposable income (billions of dollars)	Personal consumption expenditure (billions of dollars)	Average propensity to consume
150	_____	_____
200	_____	_____
250	_____	_____
300	_____	_____

b. In 1995 Country X's economists believe that the consumption function described above is no longer valid. In that year disposable income is $200 billion and personal consumption expenditure is $175 billion. Is there evidence of a shift in the consumption function?

c. Can we tell what the new marginal propensity to consume is? If so, how? If not, why not?

5. Suppose that each of the following events occurred in 1995. Taken by itself, would it increase the amount that firms want to invest?

   a. A major invention occurs which makes it possible to convert coal into gasoline cheaply.
   b. A major recession occurs.
   c. One-fifth of California's capital stock is obliterated because of an earthquake.
   d. Interest rates fall by about 2 percentage points.
   e. Because of decreases in productivity, costs rise rapidly in the construction industry.

6. Suppose that each of the following events occurred in 1995. Taken by itself, would it shift the consumption function upward, downward, or have no effect?

   a. The liquid assets held by consumers increase by $50 billion.
   b. The *Wall Street Journal* and other leading newspapers print stories indicating that there may be severe shortages of many goods.
   c. Disposable income goes up by $30 billion.
   d. A substantial increase in population occurs.
   e. Convincing evidence is found that the world will soon come to an end.

7. Assume that there are no government expenditures in Muppetland, that the economy is closed (that is, no exports or imports), and that there are no taxes or government transfer payments or undistributed corporate profits. In 1995, suppose that firms want to invest $200 billion and that the consumption function is as follows:

Disposable income (billions of dollars)	Consumption expenditure (billions of dollars)
900	750
1,000	800
1,100	850
1,200	900
1,300	950
1,400	1,000

a. Plot the consumption function below:

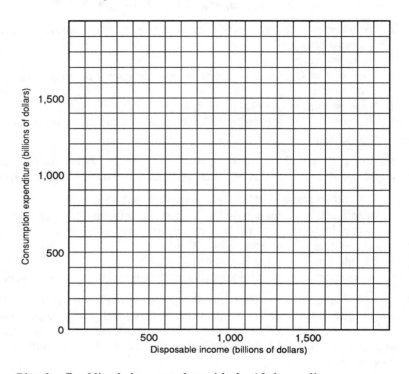

b. Plot the $C + I$ line below, together with the 45-degree line:

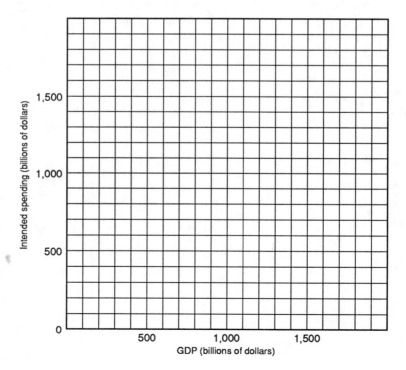

c. Will GDP be at its equilibrium level if it equals $900 billion? Why or why not?

d. Will GDP be at its equilibrium level if it equals $1,100 billion? Why or why not?

e. Will GDP be at its equilibrium level if it equals $1,000 billion? Why or why not?

f. If GDP is $1,000 billion, what is the value of the multiplier?

g. If intended investment increases by $1 billion, by how much will equilibrium GDP increase?

h. If the consumption function shifts upward by $1 billion, by how much will equilibrium GDP increase?

ANSWERS

Completion Questions
1. expectations, sales, sales, capital goods   2. consumption function
3. decreases, negative , 0.7   4. more, up, optimistic   5. equal to, equal to
6. increases, is not   7. C + I, 45-degree, exceeds, is less than

True-False
1. False   2. True   3. True   4. False   5. False   6. True   7. True   8. True
9. False

Multiple Choice
1. a   2. e   3. e   4. e   5. b   6. e   7. d   8. e

Problems
1. a.

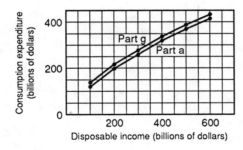

b. 0.8, 0.6, 0.4

c. A shift in the consumption function, because consumption expenditure is higher at each level of disposable income.

d.

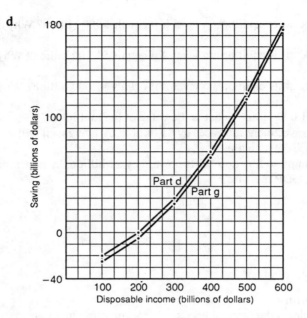

e. 0.2, 0.4, 0.6
f. 1 in each case.
g. See answers to parts a and d.
2. a. Projects *B, C,* and *G.*
   b. Projects *A, B, C, F,* and *G.*
3. Consumption expenditure falls by 10 cents and saving increases by 10 cents.
4. a. $123 1/3 billion   0.82
      $156 2/3 billion   0.78
      $190 billion   0.76
      $223 1/3 billion   0.74
   b. Yes.
   c. No, because we know only one point on the new consumption function.
5. a. Yes.
   b. No.
   c. Yes.
   d. Yes.
   e. No.
6. a. Upward.
   b. Upward.
   c. No effect.
   d. Upward.
   e. Upward.

7. a.

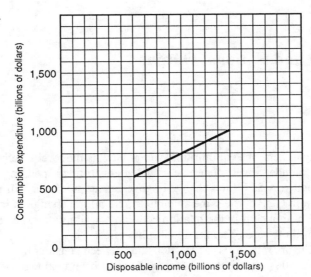

b.

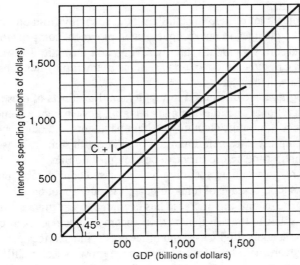

   c. No. Intended spending will exceed GDP, and there will be an unintentional decline in inventories.

   d. No. GDP will exceed intended spending, and there will be an unintentional increase in inventories.

   e. Yes. GDP will equal intended spending.

   f. 2.

   g. $2 billion.

   h. $2 billion.

CHAPTER 6

Fiscal Policy and National Output

Chapter Profile

If net exports equal zero, the equilibrium level of GDP is the level where intended consumption plus intended investment plus intended government spending equal gross domestic product. A $1 billion change in government purchases will result in a change in equilibrium GDP of the same amount as a $1 billion change in intended investment or a $1 billion shift in the relation between consumption expenditures and GDP. In any of these cases, there is a multiplier effect.

An increase in the tax rate shifts the relationship between consumption expenditure and GDP downward, thus reducing the equilibrium value of GDP. A decrease in the tax rate shifts the relationship upward, thus increasing the equilibrium value of GDP.

Policymakers receive a lot of help in stabilizing the economy from our automatic stabilizers—automatic changes in tax revenues, unemployment compensation and welfare payments, corporate dividends, family saving, and farm aid. However, the automatic stabilizers can only cut down on variations in unemployment and inflation, not eliminate them.

Discretionary programs are often used to supplement the effects of these automatic stabilizers. Such discretionary actions include changing government expenditure on public works and other programs, changing welfare payments and other such transfers, and changing tax rates. An important problem with some of these tools of fiscal policy is the lag in time before they can be brought into play.

In the past 60 years, government spending has increased considerably both in absolute terms and as a percentage of total output. (It is now about one-third of our total output.) To a large extent, this increase has been due to our greater military responsibilities, as well as to the fact that as their incomes have risen, our citizens have demanded more schools, highways, and other goods and services provided by government. Also, government transfer payments have grown substantially.

To get the money to cover most of these expenditures, governments collect taxes from individuals and firms. At the federal level, the most important form of taxation is the personal income tax; at the local level, the property tax is very important; and at the state level, sales (and excise) taxes are the biggest money raisers.

If a recession is imminent, or if a considerable amount of resources is unemployed, governments frequently try to push the aggregate demand curve to the right. Fiscal policy is often used for this purpose. If it appears likely that there will be a substantial increase in the price level, the government is likely to try to use fiscal policy to induce a leftward shift of the aggregate demand curve, thus causing the price level to be lower than it otherwise would be.

*If net exports are not zero, the equilibrium level of GDP is where intended

---

*The starred items refer to material covered in the section "Exploring Further."

spending on GDP—which equals intended consumption expenditure plus intended investment plus government spending plus intended net exports—equals GDP.

Concepts for Review

$C + I + G$ line

Council of Economic Advisers

Automatic stabilizers

Discretionary fiscal policy

Government transfer payments

$C + I + G + (X - M_i)$ line

Completion Questions

1. If the marginal propensity to consume is 0.75, an extra $1 billion in government expenditure will increase equilibrium GDP by _____ billion. A reduction of $5 billion in government expenditure will reduce equilibrium GDP by _____ billion.

2. Two major economic targets the government should aim at are _____ and _____. If there is full employment but unacceptable inflation, the government might (increase, reduce) _____ spending. Structural features of our economy which tend to iron out business fluctuations and push in the direction of full employment at stable prices are called _____.

3. The slope of the relationship between consumption and GDP (increases, decreases) _____ as the tax rate decreases. This means that the "marginal propensity to consume out of GDP" (increases, decreases) _____ as the tax rate decreases. Consequently, the multiplier—the amount by which GDP changes if intended investment changes (or the consumption function shifts, or government expenditures change)—(increase, decreases) _____ as the tax rate goes down, and (increases, decreases) _____ as the tax rate goes up. In other words, as the tax rate increases, GDP becomes (more, less) _____ sensitive to changes in investment, government spending, and the consumption function.

4. The amount of income tax collected by the federal government goes (down, up) _____ with increases in GDP and goes (down, up) _____ with decreases in GDP. Moreover, because the income tax is progressive, the average tax rate goes (down, up) _____ with increases in GDP, and goes (down, up) _____ with decreases in GDP.

5. When GDP falls off and unemployment increases, tax collections (fall, rise)

_____, so _____ falls less than GDP, thus

_____ falls less, which tends to (cut, increase)

_____ the fall in GDP. When GDP rises too quickly and
the economy begins to suffer from serious inflation, tax collections (fall, rise)

_____, which tends to (cut, increase) _____
the increase in GDP.

6. When GDP falls off and unemployment increases, the tax collections which

finance unemployment compensation go (down, up) _____

because of (increased, lower) _____ employment. At the
same time, the amount paid out to unemployed workers goes (down, up)

_____. But, when GDP rises too quickly and inflation besets
the economy, the tax collections to finance unemployment compensation go

(up, down) _____, while the amount paid out goes (up, down)

_____ because there is much (less, more)

_____ unemployment.

7. Because corporations generally maintain their dividends even though their
sales fall off and also limit the increase in dividend payments even when their
sales rise, their dividend policies tend to (stabilize, destabilize)

_____ the economy. To the extent that consumers tend to

be (fast, slow) _____ to raise or lower their spending in
response to increases or decreases in their income, this too tends to

(stabilize, destabilize) _____ the economy.

8. When there is high unemployment, the government may (cut, increase)

_____ tax rates (as it did in 1981). If inflation is the

problem, the government may (cut, increase) _____ taxes (as
it did in 1968).

True-False

_____ 1. Walter Heller played an important role in getting the tax cut of 1964
enacted.

_____ 2. Public works are an automatic stabilizer.

_____ 3. If the marginal propensity to save is 0.2 and taxes are imposed so
consumers must pay $1 billion to the government at each level of

GDP, consumption expenditure at each level of GDP will be $200 million less than before the imposition of the taxes.

_____ 4. If the marginal propensity to save is 0.2, and if both taxes and government expenditures on goods and services are increased by $1 billion, the equilibrium level of GDP will increase by $5 billion.

_____ 5. Government discretionary programs like varying tax rates and welfare payments are not the same as the automatic stabilizers.

_____ 6. The sum total of government expenditures—federal, state, and local— was about $2.3 trillion in 1993.

Multiple Choice

1. Suppose that the amount of consumption expenditure at each level of disposable income is as follows:

Consumption expenditure (billions of dollars)	Disposable income (billions of dollars)
300	500
315	520
330	540
345	560

If taxes are zero, investment equals $60 billion, and government expenditures on goods and services equal $150 billion, the equilibrium value of GDP is:

a. $500 billion.   d. $560 billion.
b. $520 billion.   e. none of the above.
c. $540 billion.

2. Suppose that the amount of consumption expenditure at each level of disposable income is as shown in the previous question. If taxes equal $100 billion at each level of GDP, if investment equals $100 billion, and if government expenditure on goods and services equals $200 billion, the equilibrium value of GDP is:

a. between $520 billion   c. $540 billion.
    and $540 billion.   d. $560 billion.
b. $520 billion.   e. none of the above.

3. If there is high unemployment, Keynes would say that the government should *not*:

a. reduce taxes.
b. decrease government expenditures.
c. enact tax credits.
d. change depreciation.
e. do any of the above.

4. Which of the following is not considered an automatic stabilizer?

   a. automatic changes in tax revenues
   b. unemployment compensation
   c. farm aid programs
   d. government expenditure for public works
   e. corporate dividend policies

5. To supplement the effects of automatic stabilizers, discretionary programs are used, such as:

   a. redistricting.
   b. changing of tax rates.
   c. increasing congressional vacations.
   d. family saving.
   e. all of the above.

Discussion and Extension Questions

1. "The whole purpose of automatic stabilizers is to reduce the value of the multiplier." Discuss.

2. One member of the Federal Reserve Board once said: "If we attempted a more stimulative program, business would spend less." Explain what he meant and indicate its significance for public policy. Do you agree or not? Why?

3. "Fiscal policy is a political subterfuge whereby the government spends and taxes more and more until the economy is socialized." Comment and evaluate.

4. "If defense spending were cut, we would have mass unemployment. Regardless of the worthiness of defense spending, it is required to prevent a massive, longterm depression." Comment and evaluate, using a production possibilities curve.

5. "Fiscal policy is of no importance because temporary changes in income due to government spending and tax changes do not alter people's spending much. For example, the tax increase of 1968 did not curb inflationary pressures because it was viewed as temporary." Comment and evaluate.

6. If the economy is suffering from an undesirably high rate of unemployment, what measures can the government take to improve the situation? How quickly can these measures be adopted? If the economy is suffering from an undesirably high rate of inflation, what measures can the government take to improve the situation? How quickly can these measures be adopted?

7. What are the automatic stabilizers for the U.S. economy? What are the major tools of discretionary fiscal policy? How do they differ? Why are both considered important?

Problems

1. Suppose that the consumption function in Gopherland is as follows:

Disposable income (billions of dollars)	Consumption expenditure (billions of dollars)
900	750
1,000	800
1,100	850
1,200	900
1,300	950
1,400	1,000

a. Suppose that intended investment is $200 billion and that government expenditure is $100 billion. Plot the $C + I + G$ curve and the 45-degree line in the graph below. (Full-employment GDP equals $1,400 billion.)

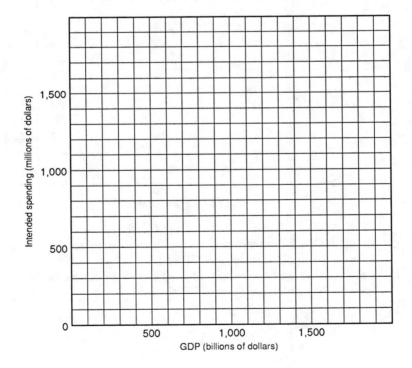

b. What is the equilibrium value of GDP?
c. What sorts of measures can be taken by the government to promote non-inflationary full employment?
d. What would be the effect on the equilibrium level of GDP of a $1 billion increase in government expenditure?

e. What would be the effect on the equilibrium level of GDP of a $1 billion decrease in government expenditure?

f. Plot the relationship between consumption expenditure and GDP if taxes equal 10 percent of GDP. Suppose that intended investment is $200 billion and that government expenditure is $100 billion. Plot the $C + I + G$ line and the 45-degree line in the graph below. What is the equilibrium level of GDP?

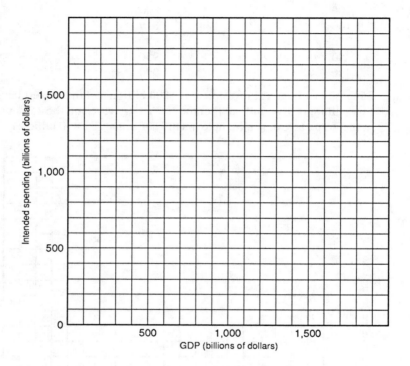

g. Holding other factors constant, what effect will an increase in the tax rate have on the equilibrium level of GDP?

h. Holding other factors constant, what effect will a decrease in the tax rate have on the equilibrium level of GDP?

2. a. In the country of Badger, the consumption function is as follows:

Disposable income (millions of dollars)	Consumption expenditure (millions of dollars)
900	700
1,000	750
1,100	800
1,200	850
1,300	900

Suppose that intended investment is $100 million. What is the equilibrium level of GDP if government expenditures are $200 million (and taxes are zero)?

b. Suppose that Badger increases its government expenditures by $10 million. What will be the effect on its equilibrium GDP? Will GDP increase or decrease? By how much?

c. Suppose that the government of Badger imposes a personal income tax which takes 16 2/3 percent of everyone's pretax income. What now will be the relationship between GDP and consumption expenditure? Specifically, fill in the blanks below:

GDP (millions of dollars)	Consumption expenditure (millions of dollars)
_____	700
_____	750
_____	800
_____	850
_____	900

d. What is the equilibrium value of Badger's GDP if intended investment is $100 million and government expenditure is $350 million?

e. Plot the consumption function in Badger in the graph below.

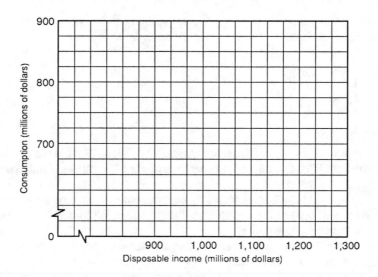

f. Plot below the relationship between consumption expenditure and GDP after Badger imposes the personal income tax.

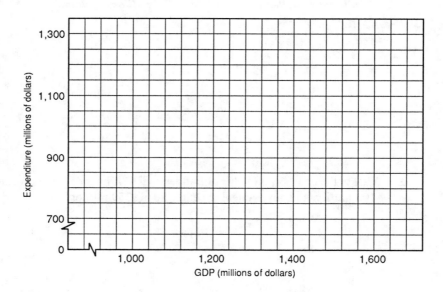

g. In the above graph, plot the $C + I + G$ line for Badger under the conditions described in part d. Where does this line intersect the 45-degree line? What is the significance of this intersection point?

h. Suppose that $1,100 billion is the full-employment GDP. What sorts of measures can the government of Badger take to produce noninflationary full employment?

3. Suppose that the following set of equations defines a model of our Basic Economy:

(1) $C_d = 200 + .8Y_d$
(2) $GDP = Y_d$
(3) $I_d = 160$

where C_d equals intended consumption expenditure, I_d equals intended investment, and Y_d equals disposable income. We now add a government sector to this model. In particular, let both government spending (on goods and services) and taxes equal 500. (All figures are in millions of dollars.)

a. Represent this economy in the grid below:

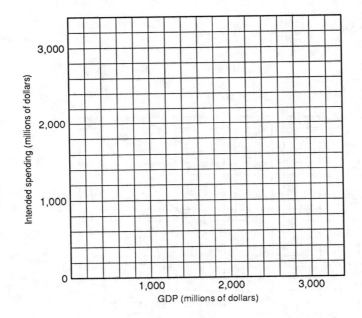

b. Determine equilibrium GDP and show it in your diagram.
c. What is the multiplier for this economy? Demonstrate that your result is correct.
d. Government spending increases to 700, while everything else remains constant. What happens to equilibrium GDP?

ANSWERS

Completion Questions

1. $4, $20   2. full employment, a stable price level, reduce, automatic stabilizers
3. increases, increases, increases, decreases, less   4. up, down, up, down   5.
fall, disposable income, consumption, cut, rise, cut   6. down, lower, up, up,
down, less   7. stabilize, slow, stabilize   8. cut, increase

True-False

1. True   2. False   3. False   4. False   5. True   6. True

Multiple Choice

1. c   2. e   3. b   4. d   5. b

Problems

1. a.

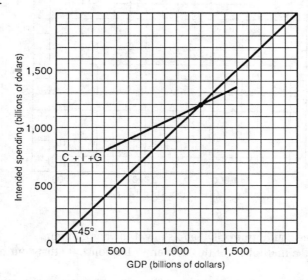

b. $1,200 billion.
c. The government could increase its expenditures by $100 billion, or it
    could encourage private investment.
d. It would increase equilibrium GDP by $2 billion.
e. It would reduce equilibrium GDP by $2 billion.

f.

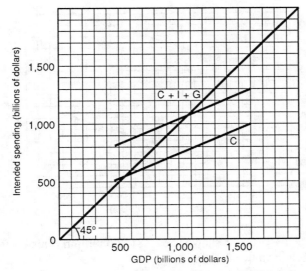

$1,091 billion.

g. It will reduce the equilibrium value of GDP.

h. It will increase the equilibrium value of GDP.

2. a. $1,100 million.

b. Equilibrium GDP will increase by $20 million.

c.
> *GDP*
> *(millions of dollars)*
> 1,080
> 1,200
> 1,320
> 1,440
> 1,560

d. $1,200 million.

e.

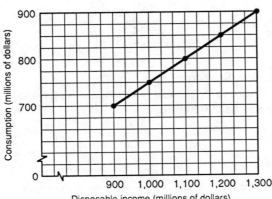

f.

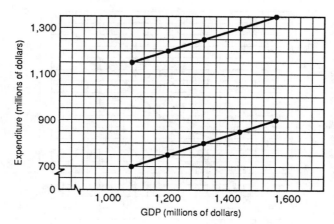

g. The $C + I + G$ line is shown above. $1,200 million. This is the equilibrium value of GDP.

h. The government can increase taxes, decrease its spending, and/or discourage private spending on investment.

3. a.

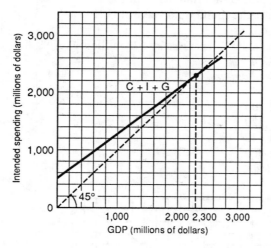

b. $2,300 million. See part a.

c. 5. A $1 increase in investment will increase GDP by $5.

d. It increases by $1,000 million.

CHAPTER 7

Inflation

Chapter Profile

Inflation is a general upward movement of prices. Runaway inflation occurs when the price level increases very rapidly, as in Germany after World War I. Creeping inflation occurs when the price level rises a few percent per year, as in the United States during the 1950s and 1960s. The Consumer Price Index, published monthly by the Bureau of Labor Statistics, is a key measure of the rate of inflation.

High rates of inflation produce considerable redistribution of income and wealth. People with relatively fixed incomes, such as the elderly, tend to take a beating from inflation. Inflation hurts lenders and benefits borrowers, since it results in the depreciation of money. Inflation can also have a devastating effect on savers. The penalties (and rewards) resulting from inflation are meted out arbitrarily, with no regard for society's values or goals. Substantial rates of inflation may also reduce efficiency and total output.

Demand-side inflation can be viewed, in the extreme, as a case where the aggregate demand curve is shifting up along the vertical portion of the short-run aggregate supply curve.

The Phillips curve shows the relationship between the rate of increase of the price level and the level of unemployment. If the Phillips curve remains fixed, it poses an awkward dilemma for policymakers. If they reduce unemployment, inflation increases; if they reduce inflation, unemployment increases. During 1955–69, there was a fairly close relationship between the inflation rate and the unemployment rate.

During the 1970s and early 1980s, the Phillips curve shifted upward and to the right. High unemployment and high inflation occurred simultaneously. During the late 1980s and early 1990s, inflation was lower.

Concepts for Review

Inflation

Runaway inflation

Demand-side inflation

Phillips curve

Supply-side inflation

Creeping inflation

Consumer Price Index

Money income

Real income

Completion Questions

1. Inflation hurts _____ and benefits _____, since it results in the depreciation of money.

2. The most widely quoted measure of inflation in the United States is the

    _____.

3. Runaway inflation is likely to result in (increased, reduced) _____ national output.

4. The Consumer Price Index equaled 186.1 in December 1977 (where 1967 = 100). If the Consumer Price Index equals 200 this month, the price level has

    risen by about _____ percent between December 1977 and this month. One limitation of the Consumer Price Index is that it does not

    include the prices of _____ or _____. A more

    inclusive index is the _____ deflator.

5. If the Murphy family's money income is increasing at 10 percent per year, and its real income is increasing at 8 percent per year, the price level must be

    rising at _____ percent per year. If the price level continues to rise at this rate and if you invest in a bond yielding 6 percent

    interest per year, you will receive _____ percent interest in real terms.

6. If lenders foresee an inflation rate of 10 percent per year, they are unlikely to lend money at 10 percent or less because it would mean they would receive

    an interest rate of _____ percent or less in real terms. If lenders anticipate increased inflation, they will tend to (increase, decrease)

    _____ interest rates.

True-False

_____ 1. If deflation occurs at 5 percent per year, a family living on a fixed dollar income would experience an increase in its real income of about 5 percent per year.

_____ 2. Deflation is a general *downward* movement of the price level. An unanticipated deflation would tend to redistribute income from borrowers to lenders.

_____ 3. Inflation tends to cut everyone's income.

_____ 4. All changes in output, employment, and the price level are due to the business cycle.

_____ 5. When actual GDP equals potential GDP, a large increase in total spending will result in inflation since little or no increase in real output can occur.

_____ 6. Land, gold, diamonds, and works of art are traditional investments made by people who want to hedge against inflation.

_____ 7. In the economy as a whole wages always rise much more slowly than prices, so inflation hurts the wage-earner more than owners of property.

_____ 8. During periods of rapid inflation, firms find it difficult to plan ahead and invest efficiently, because they are very uncertain about what future prices will be. The result is inefficiency and waste. Thus both inflation and unemployment result in social waste.

Multiple Choice

1. Inflation tends to benefit:

   a. the older generation.
   b. lenders who anticipate the rate of inflation correctly.
   c. lenders who underestimate the rate of inflation.
   d. borrowers who obtain money from lenders who anticipate the rate of inflation correctly.
   e. none of the above.

2. Increases in spending tend to be inflationary when:

   a. there is full employment.
   b. actual GDP equals potential GDP.
   c. the labor force is not increasing.
   d. a and b.
   e. all of the above.

3. During a period of sustained and accelerating inflation, interest rates tend to:

   a. fall because the value of money falls.
   b. fall because the unemployment rate tends to fall.
   c. rise because the value of money falls.
   d. rise because the unemployment rate tends to fall.
   e. be unaffected.

4. During a deflation, you would be wise to invest in:

   a. land.   d. gold.
   b. diamonds.   e. government bonds.
   c. a or b.

5. During inflation, government receipts tend to:

   a. rise because the nation's taxpayers move into higher tax brackets where the average tax rate is higher.
   b. fall because Congress reduces tax rates to offset inflation.
   c. rise because more receipts are needed to pay the higher interest costs on the national debt due to inflation.
   d. remain constant.
   e. none of the above.

6. In the short run, creeping inflation is likely to:

   a. reduce national output sharply.
   b. be directly related to the level of unemployment.
   c. wipe out the savings of people on fixed incomes.
   d. hurt lenders and benefit borrowers.
   e. all of the above.

7. There are only two goods, X and Y. Consumers spend half of their income on X and half on Y. Between 1994 and 1995, the price of X rose by 5 percent, and the price of Y rose by 15 percent. If the Consumer Price Index equals 100 in 1994, what does it equal in 1995?

   a. 100   d. 115
   b. 105   e. none of the above
   c. 110

8. In the previous question, suppose that consumers spend more than half of their income on X. Under these circumstances, what would the Consumer Price Index be in 1995?

   a. 105   d. between 110 and 115
   b. 110   e. 115
   c. between 105 and 110

Discussion and Extension Questions

1. Prior to his election in 1976, President Carter was quoted by the *New York Times* as saying, "I'd put my emphasis on employment and take my chances on inflation." Using the concepts developed in this chapter, explain in your own words what he meant. Do you think that President Reagan's attitude was the same as Carter's?

2. Suppose that the unemployed refuse to work unless they receive unrealistically high wages. For example, a high school dropout worth no more than $2 per hour may insist on receiving $6 per hour. If so, isn't it inflationary and foolish to try to achieve full employment?

3. "High unemployment rates are due to high inflation rates. Wives have to enter the labor force to supplement their husbands' incomes to balance their family budgets. The wives have difficulties getting jobs so the unemployment rate goes up." Do you agree? Why or why not?

4. "Unless some people benefited from inflation, the nation would not tolerate it." Do you agree? Why or why not?

5. In his 1979 *Economic Report*, President Carter said, "A large part of the worsening of inflation last year . . . stemmed from poor productivity." By poor productivity he meant that output per hour of labor did not increase as fast as in previous years. Why would this affect the rate of inflation?

Problems

1. In Israel the annual inflation rate was about 50 percent in 1978, and nearly 100 percent during the summer of 1979, according to William C. Freund of the New York Stock Exchange. In the *New York Times* on June 24, 1979, Freund concluded that: "The solution lies in marshalling the necessary political courage and consensus. . . . It is political fortitude, above all else, which is needed now—to cut back on excess claims against resources, to promote production and productivity, and to relieve intense demand pressures." Indicate how this advice is related to the discussion presented in this chapter. What specific measures would you suggest to accomplish these results?

2. Commenting on the above-cited inflation in Israel, the *Jerusalem Post* observed that "75 percent of Israeli families live in flats they own. Most of these were bought with government assistance and low interest mortgages. The payments on these mortgages are peanuts in light of our current inflation spiral. Someone who received a loan of 200,000 Israeli pounds at the beginning of the year—even at 32 percent interest—will have earned about 65,000 Israeli pounds by the end of it, clear and nontaxable. This sum is possibly more than his annual wages, so why complain?" Does this prove that inflation is of no consequence? Why or why not? Explain in detail.

3. Mr. Rich has $1 million in cash, bank accounts, and savings and loan accounts. They are his only assets.

    a.   If the inflation rate is 8 percent, how much must Mr. Rich save per year in order to maintain the real value of his assets?

    b.   If all Mr. Rich's income is taxable, what is the minimum amount that Mr. Rich must make per year if he wants to maintain the real value of his assets? (He must pay 70 percent of his income in taxes.)

4. Suppose that there are only three commodities, X, Y, and Z. The price per pound of each commodity in 1994 is shown below, together with the number of pounds of each commodity consumed in 1994.

1994

Commodity	Price per pound (dollars)	Number of pounds consumed (millions)
X	1	5
Y	2	8
Z	3	12

    a.   What is the total amount spent on these commodities in 1994?

    b.   The price per pound of each commodity in 1995, together with the number of pounds of each commodity consumed in 1995, is shown below:

1995

Commodity	Price per pound (dollars)	Number of pounds consumed (millions)
X	$1.08	6
Y	$2.15	8
Z	$3.30	13

What is the total amount spent on these commodities in 1995?

    c.   If we divide the answer to part b by the answer to part a, do we get a proper price index? Why or why not?

    d.   If we average the 1995 prices of the three commodities, we get

$$\frac{\$1.08+\$2.15+\$3.30}{3} = \frac{\$6.53}{3} = \$2.177$$

If we average the 1994 prices of the three commodities, we get

$$\frac{\$1+\$2+\$3}{3}=\frac{\$6}{3}=\$2.$$

One way to obtain a price index is to divide $2.177 by $2.00 and multiply the result by 100. If we do this, we get 108.8. Why do statisticians regard an index number of this sort as being too crude for most purposes?

    e.   Another way to calculate a price index is by calculating how much the amounts of these commodities consumed in 1994 would have cost in 1995 and by dividing this cost by how much they actually cost in 1994. (The result should be multiplied by 100.) Compute this price index, using the above data. What advantages do you think this price index has over the one computed in part d?

5.   a.   Suppose that the Phillips curve in France in 1993 was as shown on the following graph. What rate of increase of the price level would be associated with a 5 percent unemployment rate? What unemployment would be associated with a 6 percent rate of increase of the price level?

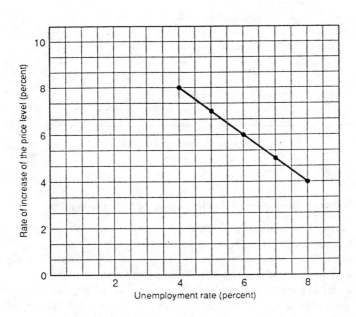

b. The Phillips curve in part a pertained to 1993. Suppose that the Phillips curve in France in 1995 is as follows:

Unemployment rate (percent)	Rate of increase of the price level (percent)
2	6
4	5
6	4
8	3

Plot the 1995 Phillips curve in the graph provided below:

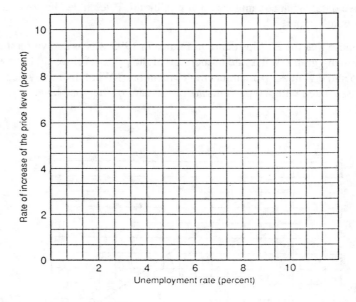

6. The Phillips curve in economy D shifts upward and to the right.

a. Economy D's leading liberal legislator says that this shift means an increase in unemployment. Is he right?
b. Economy D's leading conservative legislator says that this shift means an increase in inflation. Is she right? Why or why not?
c. Economy D's prime minister says that, despite this shift, his administration will reduce both unemployment and inflation. Is he right? Why or why not?

ANSWERS

Completion Questions
1. lenders, borrowers   2. Consumer Price Index   3. reduced   4. 7.5, industrial machinery, raw materials, GDP   5. 2, 4   6. zero, increase

True-False
1. True   2. True   3. False   4. False   5. True   6. True   7. False   8. True

Multiple Choice
1. e   2. d   3. c   4. e   5. a   6. d   7. c   8. c

Problems
1. Total spending is so great that the price level is being pushed up at a very rapid rate. The government might reduce its own expenditures and/or increase taxes.
2. No, even though some people may have protected themselves, many others are hurt by the resulting redistribution of income. Also, an inflation of this sort is likely to affect the efficiency of the economy.
3. a. About $80,000.
    b. $266,667, since he must make at least $80,000 after taxes. If all of his income is subject to a tax of 70 percent, he must make $80,000 ÷ .3, or $266,667 before taxes.
4. a. $57 million.
    b. $66.58 million.
    c. No, because the amount consumed of each commodity is not held constant.
    d. Because the price of each commodity is not weighted by the amount of the commodity that is consumed. Also, the result will depend on the units to which the prices pertain. For example, if the price of commodity Y pertains to an ounce, not a pound, the result will differ.
    e. [$62.20 million ÷ $57 million] × 100 = 109.1. This index does not have the limitations cited in part d.

5. a. 7 percent, 6 percent.
   b.

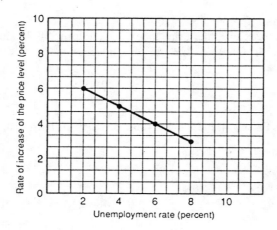

6. a. Not necessarily. If the country is willing to tolerate more inflation, it may
       be able to avoid an increase in unemployment.
   b. Not necessarily. If the country is willing to tolerate more unemployment,
       it may be able to avoid an increase in inflation.
   c. No, not unless the curve can be shifted downward and to the left.

CASE 1

Does the Consumer Price Index Overstate Increases

in the Cost of Living?

COUNCIL OF ECONOMIC ADVISERS

Many researchers have argued that the Consumer Price Index (CPI) overstates increases in the cost of living. Much of this research comes from the Bureau of Labor Statistics (BLS), which produces the CPI. This research has identified several possible sources of bias; the degree of consensus on the importance of each varies.

Substitution Bias

The CPI prices a fixed market basket of commodities. Shares of these commodities in the basket are based on spending patterns observed in a base period. But consumers do not buy the same basket of goods from year to year. When the prices of some goods rise more quickly than those of other goods, consumers often substitute away from those that have become relatively expensive and toward others that have become relatively cheap. Increases in the CPI measure how much additional income a typical consumer would need to buy the base-period market basket at the new prices. In contrast, a true cost-of-living index would measure how much more income a consumer needs to maintain the same level of economic well-being, taking into account the ability to substitute among goods. By ignoring substitution, the CPI overstates increases in the cost of living.

Substitution bias takes place at two levels, given the way the CPI is constructed. At the "upper" level, substitution occurs among the basic categories that make up the CPI's market basket—for example, when consumers switch from apples to oranges (2 of the 207 categories). But these 207 categories are themselves made up of numerous individual items. For example, the apples category consists of a sample of Delicious, Granny Smith, Macintosh, and other varieties. Thus a second, "lower" level of substitution takes place within categories when the price of, say, Delicious apples rises and consumers shift to other varieties. . . .

This article comes from *The Economic Report of the President* (Washington, D.C.: U.S. Government Printing Office, 1997), pp. 67–72.

Quality Adjustment

Measuring inflation properly requires distinguishing between changes in the underlying price and changes in quality. The BLS measures quality changes when it can. Some are easy to measure, for example when bakers double the size of their chocolate chip cookies. Others are more difficult but straightforward: for example, optional automobile equipment that later becomes standard, such as air bags or antilock brakes, can be quality-adjusted by its price when it was sold as an option. Quality adjustments generally have a significant effect on price increases as measured by the CPI. For example, the BLS estimates that in 1995 quality adjustment reduced the increase in the CPI by 2 percentage points compared with what it would have been based on listed prices.

The BLS does not adjust for other, more difficult problems because the agency cannot make direct quality adjustments in the absence of quantifiable data. For example, televisions are less likely to need repair than they were a decade ago, and some surgical procedures are more likely to be successful today than in the past. But repair rates for televisions and success rates for surgery cannot be computed until years after the purchase. Several studies on quality adjustment are available; most suggest that BLS methods fail to capture a wide range of quality changes. However, these studies focus on a relatively few categories of the CPI—possibly those where the quality bias is presumed largest—making it difficult to assess the magnitude of the overall quality bias in the CPI.

New Products

New products, such as air conditioners in the 1950s or videocassette recorders in the 1980s, usually decline sharply in price during the first years they are available for sale. But these products are not usually included in the CPI basket until years after their introduction, and so the CPI never records their initial price declines.

Outlet Substitution

Over time, consumers may change their shopping patterns, shifting from high-priced to low-priced outlets, where the quality of service is often lower. Current methods assume that all of the difference in price between high- and low-priced outlets reflects differences in the quality of service. To the extent this assumption is not appropriate, current methods overlook one source of price decline.

To sum up, recent research has identified several possible sources of bias in the CPI. A commission appointed by the Senate Finance Committee recently reported on these sources of bias. The magnitudes of some of these biases are based on hard estimates around which there is broad agreement. On the magnitudes of other biases however, consensus has yet to emerge.

Implications of CPI Bias for Other
Economic Statistics

The CPI is used as an input for calculating many other economic statistics, and therefore the potential biases in its measurement have consequences beyond our view of inflation. The accuracy of many economic measures is critically dependent on how well we measure price changes. . . . Most of the biases in the CPI result in an overdeflation, of GDP, biasing real output growth downward. . . . Productivity is also calculated from real GDP, so overestimates of CPI inflation would lead us to underestimate productivity growth. The accuracy of many other statistics, such as real median household income and real earnings, that are directly converted from nominal values by the CPI would also be affected.

Although removing CPI bias would change some of the details of our views of productivity and income trends, it would not radically alter our views on such fundamental issues as the productivity slowdown that began around 1973 or the increase in income inequality over the past two decades. Although bias in the CPI would mean that real growth and productivity have been higher recently than official measures indicate, that bias would also apply to longer term measures of growth and productivity. To explain away the decrease in productivity growth, the CPI would have to be not merely biased but *increasingly* biased over time. It is certainly plausible that the increased share of the service sector in the economy has made it harder to measure quality, with the consequence that the approximately 2-percentage-point estimate of the slowdown in productivity overestimates the true reduction. Yet it would require an implausibly large increase in CPI bias to explain away the entire slowdown as an artifact of mismeasurement.

Similarly, CPI bias might be depressing measures of real wages, but that does not change the fact that real wages today are growing more slowly than in the 1950s and 1960s. Also, the increase in income inequality . . . is one widely discussed phenomenon that is completely unaffected by CPI measurement. . . .

Discussion Questions

1. Explain how the Consumer Price Index ignores the ability of consumers to substitute among goods.

2. Why does the proper measurement of inflation require distinguishing between changes in the underlying price of a good and changes in quality?

3. Would the removal of errors in the Consumer Price Index show that there was no productivity slowdown after 1973?

4. Would the removal of these errors show that there has been no increase in income inequality in the past twenty years?

CHAPTER 8

Money and the Banking System

Chapter Profile

Money performs several basic functions. It serves as a medium of exchange, a standard of value, and a store of value. The money supply, narrowly defined, is composed of coins, currency, demand deposits, and other checkable deposits. Economists include demand (and other checkable) deposits as part of the money supply because you can pay for goods and services about as easily by check as with cash. Besides this narrow definition of money, broader definitions include savings and time deposits (and money market mutual fund balances and money market deposit accounts). It is not easy to draw a line between money and nonmoney, since many assets have some of the characteristics of money.

Commercial banks have two primary functions. First, they hold demand (and other checkable) deposits and permit checks to be drawn on them. Second, they lend money to firms and individuals. Most of our money supply is not coin and paper currency, but demand (and other checkable) deposits. This money is created by banks.

Whereas the earliest banks held reserves equal to deposits, modern banks practice fractional-reserve banking. That is, their reserves equal only a fraction of their deposits. The Federal Reserve System requires every commercial bank (and other thrift institutions with checkable deposits) to hold a certain percentage of its deposits as reserves. The major purpose of these legal reserve requirements is to control the money supply.

Banks have become much safer than 60 or 100 years ago, in part because of better management and regulation as well as the government's stated willingness to insure and stand behind their deposits. However, bank failures still occur, and bank regulation is not as stringent as it might be.

*The banking system as a whole can increase its demand deposits by an amount equal to its excess reserves divided by the legally required ratio of reserves to deposits. Thus, if excess reserves in the banking system equal a certain amount, the banking system as a whole can increase demand deposits by the amount of the excess reserves divided by the legally required ratio of reserves to deposits.

*If there is a deficiency in reserves in the banking system, the system as a whole must decrease demand deposits by the amount of this deficiency divided by the

---

*The starred items pertain to material covered in the section "Exploring Further."

legally required ratio of reserves to deposits. Demand deposits are decreased by banks' selling securities or refusing to renew loans, just as demand deposits are increased by banks' making loans and investments.

Concepts for Review

Coins	*M*-1
Currency	*M*-2
Demand deposits	Legal reserve requirements
Fractional-reserve banking	Excess reserves

Completion Questions

1. Bank A has no excess reserves. Its balance sheet is below. (All figures are in millions of dollars.)

Assets		*Liabilities and assets*	
Reserves	20	Demand deposits	100
Loans and securities	_____	Net worth	30

Its loans and securities equal _____. The reserve requirement is

_____ percent.

2. Bank B has excess reserves of $3 million. Its balance sheet is below. (All figures are in millions of dollars.)

Assets		*Liabilities and assets*	
Reserves	_____	Demand deposits	_____
Loans and securities	_____	Net worth	10

If Bank B maintains demand deposits equal to 90 percent of its assets and if the reserve requirement is 20 percent, Bank B's demand deposits equal

_____, its reserves equal _____, and its

loans and securities equal _____.

3. _____ is when banks hold reserves that are much less than the amount they owe their depositors.

4. In the text, we assume that the Federal Reserve requires about $1 dollar in reserves for every _____ of demand deposits.

5. A commercial bank can lend the amount by which its reserves are in excess of the _____.

6. The higher is the required ratio of reserves to deposits, the (larger, smaller) _____ is the amount by which the banking system can increase the money supply on the basis of a given amount of excess reserves.

*7. If there is a $10,000 decrease in reserves (and the required ratio of reserves to deposits is 1/6), the entire banking system will reduce demand deposits by _____ if there are no excess reserves.

8. The _____ can influence the money supply by influencing the amount of reserves and the legal reserve requirements.

9. Banks tend to hold large excess reserves when _____ or _____.

10. The _____ insures the accounts of depositors in practically all banks so that, even if a bank fails, the depositor will get his money back—up to _____, as of 1996.

*11. When excess _____ are made available to the banking system, the system as a whole can increase _____ by an amount equal to the amount of excess reserves multiplied by the _____ of the required ratio of reserves to deposits. For instance, if the banking system has excess reserves of $10,000 and the required ratio of reserves to deposits is 1/6, to determine how much the banking system can increase demand deposits, we must divide _____ by _____. The increase in demand deposits is _____.

*12. If the banking system has a deficiency of reserves, the system as a whole will reduce _____ by an amount equal to the deficiency in reserves multiplied by the _____ of the required ratio of reserves to deposits.

*13. To obtain the total decrease in demand deposits resulting from a deficiency in reserves, divide the deficiency by the _____.

14. A bank creates money by lending or investing its _____ reserves. If banks had to keep reserves equal to their deposits, they (could, could not) _____ create money.

---

*The starred items pertain to material covered in the section "Exploring Further."

True-False

_____ 1. If Bank X's loans and securities are higher than Bank Y's, Bank X's legally required reserves are higher than Bank Y's.

_____ 2. If the reserve requirement is 20 percent, this means that a bank belonging to the Federal Reserve System must maintain legal reserves equal to 20 percent of its assets.

_____ 3. If Marcia Jones pays back a $1,000 loan from her cousin, this results in a $1,000 decline in the money supply.

_____ 4. If Marcia Jones pays back a $1,000 loan from the First National Bank, the supply of money is reduced by $1,000, when she pays by check or cash.

_____ 5. If the Third National Bank buys a $1,000 municipal bond from Merrill Lynch, this has a different effect on the money supply than if the Third National Bank lends $1,000 to Marcia Jones.

_____ 6. A bank may have less than 20 percent of its total demand deposits in cash reserves.

_____ 7. The most important reason for legal reserve requirements is to keep banks from failing.

_____ *8. To obtain the total increase in demand deposits that can result from a certain amount of excess reserves, divide the amount of excess reserves by the legally required ratio of reserves to deposits.

_____ 9. Commercial banks invest in local, state, and federal government bonds.

_____ 10. Many banks experience an increase in reserves at about the same time.

_____ 11. The safety of a bank depends entirely on the level of its legal reserves.

_____ 12. One noteworthy characteristic of any bank's balance sheet is the fact that a very large percentage of its liabilities must be paid on demand.

_____ 13. The earliest banks held reserves equal to the amount they owed depositors, and were simply places where people stored their gold.

_____ *14. The banking system as a whole can increase the money supply by r dollars—where r is the required ratio of reserves to deposits—for every $1 in excess reserves.

---

*The starred items pertain to material covered in the section "Exploring Further."

Multiple Choice

1. The Third National Bank has demand deposits of $1 million, and the legal reserve requirement is 15 percent. If its excess reserves are equal to its legal reserves, its total reserves are:

   a. $100,000.
   b. $150,000.
   c. $300,000.
   d. not obtainable from the information given.
   e. none of the above.

2. The Fourth National Bank has demand deposits of $20 million and excess reserves of $1 million. Then the legal reserve requirement is raised by 5 percentage points, after which the bank no longer has any excess reserves. The new legal reserve requirement is:

   a. 10 percent.
   b. 15 percent.
   c. 20 percent.
   d. not obtainable from the information given.
   e. none of the above.

3. Bank X has excess reserves of $2,000. Then Shirley Morrison deposits $1,000 in cash in Bank X, which sends this amount to the Federal Reserve bank. If the legal reserve requirement is 20 percent, Bank X's excess reserves now are:

   a. $2,000.
   b. $2,200.
   c. $2,800.
   d. $3,000.
   e. none of the above.

4. In the previous question, Bank X's total reserves increase by the following amount because of Ms. Morrison's deposit and Bank X's deposit at the Fed:

   a. $200.
   b. $800.
   c. $1,000.
   d. not obtainable from the information given.
   e. none of the above.

5. Jimmy Brown deposits $500 in currency in Bank Y. Then Bank Y lends $1,000 to Bill Barry. Because of these transactions, the money supply:

   a. falls by $1,000.
   b. falls by $500.
   c. is unaffected.
   d. increases by $500.
   e. none of the above.

6. If Mr. Duke withdraws $5,000 from the Broken Wheel National Bank, and if the legal reserve requirement is 15 percent, the bank, if it has no excess reserves, must:

   a. reduce demand deposits by $4,000.
   b. reduce demand deposits by $750.
   c. increase reserves by $750.
   d. increase reserves by $4,250.
   e. increase reserves by $1,500.

7. An increase in legal reserve requirements is likely to have the least effect on the quantity of demand deposits if:

    a. banks have no excess reserves.
    b. banks have excess reserves of $1,000.
    c. banks have excess reserves of $10,000.
    d. banks have excess reserves of $10 million.
    e. banks have excess reserves of $1 billion.

8. If a commercial bank receives a deposit of $15,000 and it maintains the legally required reserves (which are 20 percent of deposits), it can lend against this deposit:

    a. $2,500.
    b. $5,000.
    c. $12,000.
    d. $15,000.
    e. all of the above.

9. A bank can increase its reserves by:

    a. selling securities.
    b. creating currency.
    c. decreasing employee vacations.
    d. all of the above.
    e. none of the above.

10. The major purpose of legal reserve requirements is to:

    a. control interest rates.
    b. control the money supply.
    c. avoid simultaneous contraction.
    d. satisfy demands in case there is a "run" on the bank.
    e. none of the above.

11. The safety of a bank depends on:

    a. the level of its reserves.
    b. the wisdom of its loans and investments.
    c. the amount of its assets that can readily be turned into cash.
    d. all of the above.
    e. none of the above.

Discussion and Extension Questions

1. Stephen Neal, former chairman of the House Banking Committee, has contended ". . . that the Federal Reserve has played politics in the past. He cites the big increase in money growth during the 1972 election year, calling it 'destructive'." Why would the Fed want to increase the money supply in an election year? Does the Fed agree with this contention? What do you think?

2. Secondary reserves are securities held by banks that have a ready market and that can easily and quickly be sold. Suppose that your local banker says that the secondary reserves held by the bank consist of real estate and stock in a South African mining company. Would you be concerned? Why or why not?

3. "Commercial banks should have to pay high interest rates on money left in checking accounts. It is inefficient, unjust, and anticompetitive for them not to do so." Comment and evaluate.

4. So long as there is no panic and so long as the bank makes sound loans and investments, could most banks get along with less reserves than they hold at present? Why do commercial banks hold as much in the way of reserves as they do?

5. Why does the Federal Reserve impose legal reserve requirements? Are the banks safer than they were 50 or 100 years ago? Why or why not?

6. Suppose that someone receives $10,000 in newly printed currency and that he deposits it in his bank.

    a.   Can this bank create $50,000 of additional new money, if the legal reserve requirement is 16 2/3 percent?

    b.   Can this bank create $8,333 in new money? If so, how?

    c.   Can the banking system as a whole create $50,000 of additional new money?

*7. a.   Suppose that the legally required ratio of reserves to deposits is 20 percent. If there are no excess reserves and if the total reserves of the banking system are reduced by $5 billion, what will be the effect on demand deposits?

    b.   If the legal reserve requirement is 20 percent, what effect would currency withdrawals or excess reserves have on the amount of demand deposits that the banks can support?

Problems

1. Suppose that the balance sheet of Crooked Arrow National Bank is currently as follows:

Assets (millions of dollars)		Liabilities and net worth (millions of dollars)	
Reserves	0.5	Demand deposits	2.5
Loans and securities	3.0	Net worth	1.0

The bank is legally required to hold reserves equal to at least 20 percent of its demand deposits.

---

*The starred items pertain to material covered in the section "Exploring Further."

a. Suppose the depositors withdraw $100,000. Indicate what the individual items on the bank's balance sheet will be after this withdrawal:

Assets (millions of dollars)		Liabilities and net worth (millions of dollars)	
Reserves	_____	Demand deposits	_____
Loans and securities	_____	Net worth	_____

b. Will the bank have the required legal reserves after the withdrawal? If not, what courses of action are open to it?

2. Suppose that depositors deposited $100,000 of new money in the Crooked Arrow National Bank, rather than withdrew $100,000.

a. What effect will this have on the bank's reserves? By how much can the bank increase its loans?

b. Suppose that Crooked Arrow National Bank lends out the maximum amount that it can, under these circumstances. It lends this amount to John Brown, who uses it to buy a piece of equipment from the Ace Machine Tool Company, which deposits it in the First National Bank. Show the effect of this transaction together with the $100,000 deposit on the balance sheet of the Crooked Arrow National Bank by filling in the blanks below.

Crooked Arrow National Bank

Change in reserves _____

Change in demand deposits _____

Change in loans and securities _____

Change in net worth _____

c. Show the effect of the transaction in part b on the balance sheet of the First National Bank by filling in the blanks below.

First National Bank

Change in reserves _____

Change in demand deposits _____

Change in loans and securities _____

Change in net worth _____

d. Can the First National Bank increase its loans? If so, by how much?

e. Suppose that the First National Bank lends the maximum amount (according to part d) to William Cooper, who buys land from James Jones, who deposits the amount to his account at the Second National Bank. Show the effect of this transaction together with Brown's deposit on the balance sheet of the First National Bank by filling in the blanks below.

First National Bank

Change in reserves _____

Change in demand deposits _____

Change in loans and securities _____

Change in net worth _____

f. Show the effect of the transaction in part e on the balance sheet of the Second National Bank by filling in the blanks below.

Second National Bank

Change in reserves _____

Change in demand deposits _____

Change in loans and securities _____

Change in net worth _____

g. Can the Second National Bank increase its loans? If so, by how much?
h. How much bank money can the banking system as a whole support on the basis of $100,000 of new reserves?

3. a. Suppose that the Federal Reserve reduces the reserve requirement from 20 to 15 percent while the bank's balance sheet is as shown in problem 1. After the reduction, will the bank have excess reserves? If so, how much?
   b. Suppose that the Federal Reserve increases the reserve requirement from 20 to 25 percent while the bank's balance sheet is as shown in problem 1. After the increase, will the bank be short of the legally required reserves? If so, by how much?

4. Bank C lends $5,000 to a depositor, Mary Monroe, by crediting her checking account balance with a $5,000 deposit.

   a. What is the effect of this transaction on the bank's assets?
   b. What is the effect of this transaction on the nation's money supply (defined as *M*-1)? What is its effect on *M*-2?
   c. If Mary Monroe transfers the $5,000 from her checking account to her savings account at the bank, what is the effect on *M*-1? What is the effect on *M*-2?

*5. Suppose that commercial bank reserves are $50 billion, the legal reserve requirement is 20 percent, and currency (and coins) in the hands of the public is $10 billion.

    a.   If there are no excess reserves, what does M-1 equal?

    b.   If commercial bank reserves fall to $49 billion while currency in the hands of the public increases to $11 billion, what would be M-1, if the other assumptions remain valid?

    c.   Suppose that the reserve requirement increases to 25 percent (but that the other assumptions in part b remain valid). What is M-1?

6. What is the effect on M-1 of each of the following transactions (taken alone)?

    a.   Mary Malone deposits $2,000 in currency in First Federal Savings and Loan.

    b.   The Chase Bank sells a $5,000 U.S. government bond to Merrill Lynch, a large stock brokerage firm, which pays Chase with a check.

    c.   The Chase Bank sells a $5,000 U.S. government bond to Mary Malone, who pays for the bond in currency, which Chase adds to the cash it holds.

7. Bank E has the following balance sheet:

Assets (millions of dollars)		Liabilities and net worth (millions of dollars)	
Cash	1	Demand deposits	29
Reserves at Fed	5	Net worth	1
Loans	10		
Securities	14		

All cash is held in the bank's vault and is part of its legal reserves. The item "Reserves at Fed" is the bank's legal reserve deposit at the Federal Reserve. Indicate the effect on this balance sheet of each of the following transactions (taken alone):

    a.   Bank E increases its vault cash by $1,000 by obtaining this amount from the Fed. Then it uses this $1,000 to cash ten $100 checks of depositors.

    b.   A depositor at Bank E writes a check for $10,000 on Bank E, which is deposited in Bank F and clears.

    c.   A depositor at Bank F writes a check for $10,000 on Bank F, which is deposited in Bank E and clears.

8. Bank G has the following balance sheet:

Assets (millions of dollars)		Liabilities and net worth (millions of dollars)	
Reserves	30	Demand deposits	80
Loans and securities	70	Net worth	20

---

*The starred items pertain to material covered in the section "Exploring Further."

a. Suppose that the legal reserve requirement is 15 percent. Indicate below what Bank G's balance sheet will look like if it makes all the new loans it can (and if all the money it lends is checked out to depositors at other banks).

Assets (millions of dollars)		Liabilities and net worth (millions of dollars)	
Reserves	_____	Demand deposits	_____
Loans and securities	_____	Net worth	_____

b. Suppose that the legal reserve requirement is 20 percent. Indicate below what Bank G's balance sheet will look like if it makes all the new loans it can make (and if all the money it lends is checked out to depositors at other banks).

Assets (millions of dollars)		Liabilities and net worth (millions of dollars)	
Reserves	_____	Demand deposits	_____
Loans and securities	_____	Net worth	_____

*9. The consolidated balance sheet for all commercial banks in the economy is as follows:

Assets (billions of dollars)		Liabilities and net worth (billions of dollars)	
Reserves	23	Demand deposits	99
Loans and securities	86	Net worth	10

Suppose that the public deposits $1 billion in currency in the banks and that the banks send the $1 billion to the Federal Reserve.

a. Suppose that the legal reserve requirement is 15 percent. Indicate below what the consolidated balance sheet for all commercial banks will look like if the banking system makes all the new loans it can.

Assets (billions of dollars)		Liabilities and net worth (billions of dollars)	
Reserves	_____	Demand deposits	_____
Loans and securities	_____	Net worth	_____

---

*The starred items pertain to material covered in the section "Exploring Further."

b. Suppose that the legal reserve requirement is 20 percent. Indicate below what the consolidated balance sheet for all commercial banks will look like if the banking system makes all the new loans it can.

Assets *(billions of dollars)*		*Liabilities and net worth* *(billions of dollars)*	
Reserves	_____	Demand deposits	_____
Loans and securities	_____	Net worth	_____

ANSWERS

Completion Questions

1. $110 million, 20   2. $90 million, $21 million, $79 million
3. Fractional-reserve banking   4. $6   5. legally required reserves   6. smaller
7. $60,000   8. Federal Reserve System   9. loans seem to be very risky, interest rates are very low   10. FDIC, $100,000   11. reserves, demand deposits, reciprocal, $10,000, 1/6, $60,000   12. demand deposits, reciprocal   13. legally required ratio of reserves to deposits   14. excess, could not

True-False

1. False   2. False   3. False   4. True   5. False   6. True   7. False   8. True
9. True   10. True   11. False   12. True   13. True   14. False

Multiple Choice

1. c   2. d   3. c   4. c   5. e   6. d   7. e   8. c   9. a   10. b   11. d

Problems

1. a.

Assets *(dollars)*		*Liabilities and net worth* *(dollars)*	
Reserves	400,000	Demand deposits	2,400,000
Loans and securities	3,000,000	Net worth	1,000,000

b. No. It can refuse to renew loans or sell securities.

2. a.   Reserves will increase by $100,000. The bank can increase its loans by $80,000.

b.

Crooked Arrow National Bank

Change in reserves	+20,000
Change in demand deposits	+$100,000
Change in loans and securities	+80,000
Change in net worth	none

c.

First National Bank

Change in reserves	+80,000
Change in demand deposits	+80,000
Change in loans and securities	none
Change in net worth	none

d. Yes. $64,000.

e.

First National Bank

Change in reserves	+16,000
Change in demand deposits	+80,000
Change in loans and securities	+64,000
Change in net worth	none

f.

Second National Bank

Change in reserves	+64,000
Change in demand deposits	+64,000
Change in loans and securities	none
Change in net worth	none

g. Yes. $51,200.
h. $500,000.
3. a. Yes. $125,000.
   b. Yes. $125,000.
4. a. They increase by $5,000.
   b. Both M-1 and M-2 rise by $5,000.
   c. M-1 decreases by $5,000, but there is no effect on M-2.
5. a. $260 billion.
   b. $256 billion.
   c. $207 billion.
6. a. No effect.
   b. M-1 decreases by $5,000.
   c. M-1 decreases by $5,000.
7. a. Reserves at Fed −$1,000   Demand deposits −$1,000
   b. Reserves at Fed −$10,000   Demand deposits −$10,000
   c. Reserves at Fed +$10,000   Demand deposits +$10,000

8.	a.	Reserves	12	Demand deposits	80
		Loans and securities	88	Net worth	20
	b.	Reserves	16	Demand deposits	80
		Loans and securities	84	Net worth	20
9.	a.	Reserves	24	Demand deposits	160
		Loans and securities	146	Net worth	10
	b.	Reserves	24	Demand deposits	120
		Loans and securities	106	Net worth	10

CHAPTER 9

The Federal Reserve and

Monetary Policy

Chapter Profile

The Federal Reserve System is responsible for regulating and controlling the money supply. Established in 1913, the Federal Reserve System is composed of the commercial banks, 12 regional Federal Reserve Banks, and the Federal Reserve Board, which coordinates the activities of the system. The Federal Reserve is the central bank of the United States.

Monetary policy is concerned with the money supply and interest rates. Its purpose is to attain and maintain full employment without inflation. When a recession seems imminent, the monetary authorities are likely to increase the money supply and reduce interest rates. On the other hand, when the economy is in danger of overheating and inflation threatens, the monetary authorities are likely to rein in the money supply and push up interest rates.

Monetary policy and fiscal policy are influenced by Congress, the Treasury, and other segments of the government and the public at large. The chief responsibility for the formulation of monetary policy lies with the Federal Reserve Board and the Federal Open Market Committee. To a very large extent monetary policy operates by changing the quantity of bank reserves.

The most important tool of monetary policy is open market operations, which involve the buying and selling of government securities in the open market by the Federal Reserve. When the Fed buys government securities, this increases bank reserves. When the Fed sells government securities, this reduces bank reserves.

The Fed can also tighten or ease money by increasing or decreasing the discount rate or by increasing or decreasing legal reserve requirements.

Concepts for Review

Federal Reserve Board
Federal Open Market Committee
Discount rate
Federal Reserve Banks
Legal reserve requirements

Completion Questions

1. If the monetary authorities think that a recession is developing, they tend to (increase, decrease) _____ the reserves of the banks.

2. When a serious inflation seems imminent, the monetary authorities are most likely to (increase, decrease) _____ the rate of growth of the money supply and to (increase, decrease) _____ interest rates.

3. Increases in the legal reserve requirement are likely to (increase, reduce) _____ the amount of demand deposits the banking system can support.

4. The _____ is composed of the Federal Reserve Board plus the presidents of five Federal Reserve Banks.

5. Loans to commercial banks are _____ on the consolidated balance sheet of the Federal Reserve Banks.

6. When the economy is at appreciably less than full employment, many economists believe that increases in the money supply tend to (increase, decrease) _____ real national product, and decreases in the money supply tend to (increase, decrease) _____ real national product, with relatively little effect on the _____ level.

7. As full employment is approached, increases in the money supply tend to affect the _____ level, as well as real _____.
    And once full employment is reached, increases in the money supply result primarily in (increases, decreases) _____ in the price level, since real output cannot (increase, decrease) _____ appreciably.

8. If the banking system has $1 billion in _____, it can support $6.25 billion in demand deposits when the legal reserve requirement is 16 percent. It can only support $5 billion in demand deposits when the legal reserve requirement is 20 percent. Thus increases in the legal reserve requirements tend to (increase, decrease) _____ the amount of demand deposits the banking system can support.

9. If the banking system has $1 billion in reserves and $5 billion in demand deposits, there are no _____ when the legal reserve requirement is 20 percent. If the Federal Reserve lowers the legal reserve requirement to 16 percent, the amount of legally required reserves is

_____ million. The banks then have _____
million in excess reserves—which means that they can (increase, decrease)
_____ the amount of their demand deposits.

True-False

_____ 1. The discount rate is the rate of interest that the state governments pay member banks on their reserves kept with the Fed.

_____ 2. The excess reserves of the commercial banks are increased by $1/r$ dollars (where r is the legal reserve requirement) for every dollar of government securities that the Fed buys from the public.

_____ 3. A reduction in the discount rate has a direct effect on member bank reserves; it increases them in much the same way that open-market purchases of government securities by the Fed increases them.

_____ 4. Banks are expected to borrow from the Federal Reserve only for short periods.

_____ 5. The policies of the Federal Reserve are always dictated by the Treasury's financing needs.

_____ 6. Open market operations are the most important techniques used by the Fed to control the money supply.

_____ 7. Although the Federal Reserve is responsible to Congress, Congress has established no clear guidelines for its behavior. Thus the Federal Reserve has had wide discretionary powers over monetary policy.

_____ 8. The commercial banks that are members of the Federal Reserve System can borrow from the Federal Reserve when their reserves are low (if the Fed is willing).

_____ 9. Changes in the discount rate have an effect on people's expectations.

_____ 10. There is often a long lag between an action by the Fed and its effect on the economy.

_____ 11. When the Fed buys government securities, bank reserves are decreased.

_____ 12. Often the Fed is criticized for paying too little attention to the long lags between its actions and their effects on the economy.

Multiple Choice

1. If the Federal Reserve sells $50 million of U.S. government securities, this will result in the following change in member bank reserves:

   a. increase them by $50 million.
   b. decrease them by $50 million.
   c. increase them by more than $50 million.
   d. decrease them by more than $50 million.
   e. leave them unaffected.

2. If the Federal Reserve increases the legal reserve requirement from 15 to 20 percent, and if this reduces excess reserves by $5 billion, total demand deposits in the economy must equal:

   a. $50 billion.
   b. $75 billion.
   c. $100 billion.
   d. $150 billion.
   e. none of the above.

3. If the legal reserve requirement is 20 percent, and if commercial banks borrow $1 billion from the Federal Reserve, this has the following immediate effect on their reserves:

   a. reserves fall by $1 billion.
   b. reserves fall by $5 billion.
   c. reserves increase by $1 billion.
   d. reserves increase by $5 billion.
   e. none of the above.

4. If the public wants to hold $1 in currency for every $3 in demand deposits, and if the legal reserve requirement is 0.1, an increase of $1 million in the money supply (M-1) results in an increase in the amount of currency in the hands of the public of:

   a. $100,000.
   b. $250,000.
   c. $333,333.
   d. $400,000.
   e. none of the above.

   (Assume that demand deposits are the only checkable deposits.)

5. If total demand deposits equal $2 billion, bank reserves equal $500 million, and excess reserves equal $100 million, the legal reserve requirement is:

   a. 15 percent.
   b. 16 2/3 percent.
   c. 20 percent.
   d. 25 percent.
   e. 30 percent.

6. The most important method used by the Federal Reserve Board to influence bank reserves is:

   a. changing legal reserve requirements.
   b. issuing new government securities.
   c. open market operations.
   d. changing the discount rate.
   e. Congressional testimony.

7. The major effect of an increase in the discount rate is:

   a. on people's expectations.
   b. easier money.
   c. an increase in reserves.
   d. an increase in the prices of stocks and bonds.

8. The Federal Reserve cannot:

   a. provide facilities for check collection.
   b. lend money to banks.
   c. change the discount rate.
   d. regulate mortgage terms and installment contracts.
   e. do any of the above.

9. If banks have little or no excess reserves and the legal reserve requirement is raised, they may:

   a. sell securities.
   b. refuse to renew loans.
   c. reduce their demand deposits.
   d. all of the above.
   e. none of the above.

10. The discount rate:

    a. can be increased or decreased by the Fed.
    b. usually is changed only once or twice a decade.
    c. if it is increased, encourages borrowing.
    d. determines how much the Fed can borrow from the banks.
    e. all of the above.

Discussion and Extension Questions

1. During World War II and up until 1951, the Federal Reserve agreed with the U.S. Treasury to keep the interest rates on Treasury bonds low and stable so as to keep the Treasury's borrowing costs as low as possible.

   a. Explain how the Federal Reserve might accomplish this goal.
   b. Do you think that such an agreement might limit the Federal Reserve's ability to counteract undesirable swings in aggregate demand? Explain your response.

2. According to the *New York Times*, "Puerto Rico cannot print money like the government of the United States or any other sovereign government. It must therefore balance its budget and live within its means—old-fashioned prescriptions for sound economics that were strongly emphasized by the Tobin Committee when its members reviewed the strained financial structure of the island." Explain in your own words what this passage means, and indicate whether you agree, and why or why not.

3. According to Thomas Dernburg and Duncan McDougall, "The initiative in conducting open market operations is firmly in the hands of the Fed. In contrast, the effect of a change in the discount rate depends on the unpredictable response of commercial banks." Comment and evaluate.

4. Suppose that the Fed buys $1 million of government securities from Bethlehem Steel. What is the effect on the quantity of bank reserves? Suppose it sells $1 million of government securities to Bethlehem Steel. What is the effect on the quantity of bank reserves?

5. What is the effect on the amount of demand deposits of increases in the legal reserve requirements? Use a numerical example in your response.

6. What is the effect of changes in the discount rate? What variables has the Fed looked at to determine whether or not to change the discount rate?

Problems

1. Suppose that the Crooked Arrow National Bank has the following balance sheet:

Assets *(millions of dollars)*		*Liabilities and net worth* *(millions of dollars)*	
Reserves	0.5	Demand deposits	2.5
Loans and securities	3.0	Net worth	1.0

   a.   If the legal reserve requirement is 20 percent, does the bank have any excess reserves? If so, how much?
   b.   Suppose that the Fed lowers the reserve requirement, with the result that the bank has excess reserves of $25,000. What is the new legal reserve requirement?
   c.   Suppose that the Fed lowers the reserve requirement, with the result that the bank has excess reserves of $100,000. What is the new legal reserve requirement?

2. Suppose that on May 1, 1995, the Federal Reserve sells $100 million of U.S. government securities to the public, which pays for them by check.

   a.   Show below the effect of this sale on the balance sheets of the Federal Reserve and the commercial banks:

Federal Reserve

Assets		*Liabilities*	
Government securities	_____	Member bank reserves	_____

Commercial banks (balance sheet for all banks combined)

Assets		*Liabilities*	
Reserves	_____	Demand deposits	_____

   b.   Does this transaction have any effect on the balance sheets of the members of the public who bought the bonds? If so, what is the effect?

c. If the commercial banks had no excess reserves before the sale of these bonds, do they have any excess reserves after the sale? Do they have less than the legally required reserves after the sale?

d. Suppose that the Fed bought, rather than sold, $100 million of U.S. government securities, and that these securities were bought from the general public. Would this transaction result in an increase or decrease in member bank reserves? By how much would reserves increase or decrease? Is this the sort of result that the Fed would have desired during the period in 1981 when it was trying hard to fight inflation?

3. Suppose that the banking system has no excess reserves, that total reserves are $50 billion, and total demand deposits are $200 billion. Suppose that the graph below shows the net amount that the banking system will borrow (i.e., net of repayments) from the Federal Reserve, if the discount rate equals the levels shown there.

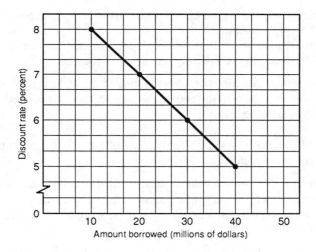

a. How much will the banking system borrow if the discount rate is 7 percent? 5 percent? What is the legal reserve requirement?

b. If the Fed wants to increase the money supply by $40 million, what discount rate should it set? (Assume that banks maintain no excess reserves.)

c. If the Fed wants to have the same effect on bank reserves as if it bought $20 million worth of government securities in the open market, what discount rate should it set?

4. From the following figures, construct the consolidated balance sheet of the twelve Federal Reserve Banks. (All figures are in billions of dollars.)

Gold certificates	10	Reserves of banks	30
Other liabilities and net worth	5	Other assets	10
Securities	100	Treasury deposits	5
Outstanding Federal Reserve Notes	90	Loans to commercial banks	10

5. Given the consolidated balance sheet which you have constructed in problem 4, what effect will each of the following transactions (taken by itself) have on this balance sheet?

   a. The Federal Reserve sells $100 million in securities to the public (which pays by check).
   b. The Federal Reserve lowers the discount rate, which results in banks borrowing $50 million from the Fed.
   c. The U.S. government buys $1 billion worth of aerospace equipment, which is paid for by checks on the Treasury's deposits at the Fed.

6. Given that each of the transactions described in problem 5 occurs (separately), what is the effect in each case on the potential money supply, if the legal reserve requirement is 20 percent?

7. Suppose that the Federal Reserve purchases $100 million of U.S. government securities from *commercial banks.*

   a. What will be the effect on the balance sheet of the Federal Reserve Banks?
   b. What will be the effect on the balance sheet of the commercial banks?
   c. What is the effect on the potential money supply, if the legal reserve requirement is 20 percent?

8. Suppose that the Federal Reserve sells $100 million of U.S. government securities to *commercial banks.*

   a. What will be the effect on the balance sheet of the Federal Reserve banks?
   b. What will be the effect on the balance sheet of the commercial banks?
   c. What is the effect on the potential money supply, if the legal reserve requirement is 25 percent?

9. The public wants to hold $1 in currency for every $3 in demand deposits. The legal reserve requirement is 20 percent, and commercial banks hold no excess reserves. There are no checkable deposits other than demand deposits.

   a. If the Federal Reserve wants to reduce the quantity of money by $2 billion, how much of a decrease must occur in demand deposits?
   b. To obtain this decrease in demand deposits, by how much must bank reserves decline?

    c.   To reduce bank reserves by this amount, how many billions of dollars worth of government securities should the Federal Reserve sell? (Be careful: note that because of the $2 billion decrease in the quantity of money, the public wants to hold $0.5 billion less in currency.)

10. The public wants to hold $1 in currency for every $3 in demand deposits. The legal reserve requirement is 25 percent, and commercial banks hold no excess reserves. There are no checkable deposits other than demand deposits.

    a.   If the Federal Reserve wants to increase the quantity of money by $6 billion, how much of an increase must occur in demand deposits?

    b.   To obtain this increase in demand deposits, by how much must bank reserves increase?

    c.   To increase bank reserves by this amount, how many billions of dollars worth of government securities should the Federal Reserve buy?

ANSWERS

Completion Questions

1. increase   2. decrease, increase   3. reduce   4. Federal Open Market Committee   5. assets   6. increase, decrease, price   7. price, output, increases, increase   8. total reserves, decrease   9. excess reserves, $800, $200, increase

True-False

1. False   2. False   3. False   4. True   5. False   6. True   7. True   8. True
9. True   10. True   11. False   12. True

Multiple Choice

1. b   2. c   3. c   4. b   5. c   6. c   7. a   8. d   9. d   10. a

Problems

1. a.   No. Its reserves are just equal to the legally required amount.
    b.   19 percent.
    c.   16 percent.

2. a.

Federal Reserve

Assets		Liabilities	
(millions of dollars)			
Government securities	−100	Member bank reserves	−100

Commercial banks

Assets		Liabilities	
(millions of dollars)			
Reserves	−100	Demand deposits	−100

    b. Yes. The public has $100 million more in U.S. government securities and $100 million less in demand deposits.

    c. No. Yes.

    d. An increase. $100 million. No.

3. a. $20 million, $40 million, 25 percent.

    b. 8 percent.

    c. 7 percent.

4.

Assets		Liabilities and net worth	
Gold certificates	10	Outstanding Federal	
Securities	100	Reserve Notes	90
Loans to commercial		Reserves of banks	30
banks	10	Treasury deposits	5
Other assets	10	Other liabilities and	
	130	net worth	5
			130

5. a. Securities − $100 million   Reserves of banks − $100 million

    b. Loans to commercial banks + $50 million   Reserves of banks + $50 million

    c. Treasury deposits − $1 billion   Reserves of banks + $1 billion

6. a. It decreases by $500 million.

    b. It increases by $250 million.

    c. It increases by $5 billion.

7. a. Securities + $100 million   Reserves of banks + $100 million

    b. Securities − $100 million   Reserves + $100 million

    c. It increases by $500 million.

8. a. Securities − $100 million   Reserves of banks − $100 million

    b. Securities + $100 million   Reserves − $100 million

    c.   It decreases by $400 million.
9. a. $1.5 billion.
    b. $300 million.
    c. $0.8 billion.
10. a. $4.5 billion.
    b. $1.125 billion.
    c. $2.625 billion.

CHAPTER 10

Stagflation and Anti-Inflationary

Measures

Chapter Profile

The Phillips curve shows the relationship between the rate of increase of the price level and the level of unemployment. If the Phillips curve remains fixed, it poses an awkward dilemma for policymakers. If they reduce unemployment, inflation increases; if they reduce inflation, unemployment increases. During 1955–69, there was a fairly close relationship between the inflation rate and the unemployment rate. But then something unforeseen by most economists occurred. The inflation and unemployment rates subsequently did not conform at all closely to the relationship that prevailed in the sixties. Both the unemployment rate and the inflation rate tended to be much higher than in the sixties.

The accelerationists, led by Milton Friedman, believe that the downward-sloping Phillips curve is only a short-run relationship. In the long run, they believe that it is vertical. In their view, expansionary policies that result in inflation will only reduce unemployment temporarily, with the result that the government, if it sets out to reduce unemployment to below its natural level, will have to permit higher and higher rates of inflation.

To reduce the inflation rate (at a given unemployment rate) governments have tried price and wage controls. Although a few economists favor such controls during peacetime, most do not agree. Such controls are likely to distort the allocation of resources, to be difficult to administer, and to run counter to our desire for economic freedom.

Many countries have experimented with various kinds of incomes policies. An incomes policy contains targets for prices and wages for the economy as a whole, more detailed guides for price and wage decisions in particular industries, and some mechanisms to get firms and unions to follow these guides. The Kennedy-Johnson guidelines were one form of incomes policy. Although guidelines of this sort have a short-term effect on the price level, how much effect they have in the long run is hard to say.

A variety of types of tax-based incomes policies have been proposed in recent years. Such policies use the tax system or subsidies to induce firms to hold down prices and workers to hold down wages.

Although it is very unlikely that a catastrophe like the Great Depression will recur, our recent experience indicates that we have a long way to go before we understand the workings of the economy well enough to achieve continuous full employment without inflation. Also, even if the advice of its economists were always correct, there is no assurance that the government would always pursue policies leading toward economic stabilization.

Concepts for Review

Supply-side inflation   Incomes policies
Wage-price spiral   Accelerationists
Wage and price controls

Completion Questions

1. One basic cause of supply-side inflation is the market power of

    _____ and _____.

2. The more inflation people expect, the further _____ and

    _____ from the origin the short-run Phillips curve is likely
    to be.

3. The ability of labor to increase its wage is likely to depend to a considerable

    extent on the _____.

4. The _____ shows the relationship between the rate of
    increase of the price level and the level of unemployment.

5. _____ have an overall target, detailed guides for wage
    and price decisions, and a mechanism to get firms and unions to observe the
    guides.

6. The wage-price spiral sometimes is at the core of _____.

7. Expectations of increased inflation tend to push the Phillips curve (upward,

    downward) _____.

8. The government would like to shift the Phillips curve (upward, downward)

    _____.

9. The tax system might be used to _____ firms that grant large

    pay increases and to _____ firms that grant small pay
    increases. It has also been suggested that, if firms and workers agreed to hold

    down price and wage increases, they would receive a _____.

    However, there are significant _____ problems in
    implementing such policies.

True-False

_____ 1. The Phillips curve is likely to be different in different countries and to shift over time in the same country.

_____ 2. The wage-price spiral is the basis for demand-side inflation.

_____ 3. In the face of supply-side inflation, most economists advocate government controls of wages and prices.

_____ 4. Both an incomes policy and price and wage controls use persuasion to induce firms and unions to follow their guides voluntarily.

_____ 5. Guidelines are not effective when there are strong inflationary pressures due to improper monetary and fiscal policies.

_____ 6. No existing economic model can provide policymakers with reliable quantitative estimates of the way the money supply, government expenditures, or tax rates should be altered to provide full employment with stable prices.

_____ 7. Judging from the experience of the past 40 years, we seem to have learned how to avoid very serious depressions, but we have not yet learned how to attain full employment with stable prices.

_____ 8. Until we can better estimate the quantitative effects of policy changes of various magnitudes, it will be unreasonable to expect that monetary and fiscal policies can be used with precision to achieve our national goals.

_____ 9. Even if economic models were completely accurate and the government knew how to achieve full employment at stable prices, it would not always choose to do so.

_____ 10. During World War II—and some other wartime emergencies—the government has imposed controls on wages and prices.

_____ 11. Some economists feel that reliance on guidelines is dangerous because it focuses attention on symptoms rather than causes of inflation.

_____ 12. If fiscal or monetary policy is generating strong inflationary pressures, such as existed in the late 1960s, it is foolish to think that guidelines can save the situation.

Multiple Choice

1. The position of the Phillips curve is likely to be influenced least by:

    a. education of workers.

    b. increased mobility of workers.

    c. reduced discrimination.

    d. intellectual property rights.

    e. people's expectations about inflation.

2. A major disadvantage of wage and price controls is:

   a. they do not stabilize basic living costs.
   b. distortion of the allocation of resources.
   c. absence of ceiling prices on basic raw materials.
   d. all of the above.
   e. none of the above.

3. The least effective approach to reducing supply-side inflation is:

   a. to reduce the market power of unions and firms.
   b. government controls of prices and wages.
   c. an incomes policy.
   d. cutting taxes.

4. With an incomes policy, the government uses:

   a. persuasion and pressure on firms.
   b. mandatory controls.
   c. a dictator.
   d. an increase in the money supply.
   e. all of the above.

5. Most economists oppose wage and price controls because they:

   a. result in a distortion of the allocation of resources.
   b. are expensive to administer.
   c. impair economic freedom.
   d. all of the above.
   e. none of the above.

6. The wage rate in industry A increases from $6.40 to $7.20 per hour, and labor productivity in industry A increases from 80 to 90. Unit labor cost:

   a. increases by 12 1/2 percent.
   b. increases by about 27 percent.
   c. decreases by about 12 1/2 percent.
   d. decreases by about 27 percent.
   e. none of the above.

7. In 1995 suppose that the relationship between the inflation rate and the unemployment rate is $i = 12 - u$, where i is the inflation rate (in percentage points) and u is the unemployment rate (in percentage points). In 1996 suppose that this relationship is $i = 13 - u$. If the unemployment rate in 1995 is 1 percentage point below that in 1996, the inflation rate in 1996 is:

   a. 1 percentage point below that in 1995.
   b. 1 percentage point above that in 1995.
   c. 2 percentage points below that in 1995.
   d. 2 percentage points above that in 1995.
   e. none of the above.

Discussion and Extension Questions

1. During 1994, many economists, including Alan Greenspan, felt that inflationary forces were building; others disagreed. Briefly try to explain why this disagreement occurred. Pretend you must give your presentation to two separate groups: (a) a meeting of economists, and (b) a local civic organization interested in contemporary problems.

2. Does it make any difference if the government, to finance a budget deficit, borrows from the Fed rather than the general public?

3. What is the nature of supply-side inflation? What factors can cause shifts in the Phillips curve? What does the Phillips curve look like in the long run?

4. What are the disadvantages of adopting price and wage controls? What are the three elements of an incomes policy? Can guidelines save the day if monetary and fiscal policies are generating strong inflationary pressures?

5. Two distinguished economists, Sidney Weintraub and Henry Wallich, proposed a measure whereby the corporate tax system would be used to help keep money wage increases within certain bounds. How might such a measure work? Do you favor its adoption?

6. Discuss the role of lags in stabilization policy. Economists often distinguish between expenditure lags (lags before money is spent) and policy lags (lags due to the policymakers). Do you think that there are differences between fiscal and monetary policy in the length of these lags? If so, what are these differences? What role do these lags play in causing our current difficulties in stabilizing the economy?

7. Some economists believe that there no longer is a trade-off between inflation and unemployment. Do you agree with them? Why or why not?

Problems

1. Labor productivity is increasing at an annual rate of 2 percent in economy C.

   a. If the wage level is increasing at an annual rate of 3 percent, are unit labor costs increasing or decreasing, and at what rate are they increasing or decreasing?

   b. Suppose that the wage level in the economy increases at a rate such that unit labor costs remain stable. At what rate is the wage level increasing?

   c. If the wage level in economy C's steel industry increases at the rate indicated in part b, at what rate will unit labor costs rise in the steel industry if labor productivity in steel is increasing at 1 percent per year?

   d. If the steel industry's price level increases at the same rate as its unit labor costs, at what rate will it rise under the circumstances in part c?

   e. Wage and price guidelines are established in economy C. Wages are allowed to increase at a rate equal to the rate of increase of labor productivity in the economy as a whole. Prices are allowed to increase at a rate equal to the rate of increase of unit labor costs. Will prices increase in all industries? If not, in which industries will prices not increase?

2. The following table applies to a firm in economy D, which has an incomes policy stating that wage rates should rise by 8 percent per year. Assume that the firm and the union adhere to this policy.

Year	Wage rate per hour	Hours of labor	Wage bill	Total output	Price of product	Profits and non-wage costs
1994	$8.00	200	_____	1,500	$2	_____
1995	_____	_____	$1,728	1,650	$2	_____
1996	_____	200	_____	1,800	$2	_____

a. Fill in the blanks in the table.
b. What is the rate of increase of labor productivity between 1994 and 1995? Between 1995 and 1996?
c. What is the rate of increase of unit wage costs between 1994 and 1995? Between 1995 and 1996?
d. What is the rate of increase of unit profits and non-wage costs between 1994 and 1995? Between 1995 and 1996?
e. What changes occur in the proportion of total revenue going to labor?

ANSWERS

Completion Questions
1. unions, firms   2. upward, out   3. unemployment rate   4. Phillips curve
5. Incomes policies   6. supply-side inflation   7. upward   8. downward
9. penalize, reward, tax rebate, administrative

True-False
1. True   2. False   3. False   4. False   5. True   6. True   7. True   8. True
9. True   10. True   11. True   12. True

Multiple Choice
1. d   2. b   3. d   4. a   5. d   6. e   7. e

Problems

1. a. They are increasing at 1 percent per year.
   b. 2 percent per year.
   c. 1 percent per year.
   d. 1 percent per year.
   e. No. They will not increase in industries where the rate of increase of labor productivity is higher than in the economy as a whole.

2. a.

1994	$8.00	200	$1,600	1,500	$2	$1,400
1995	$8.64	200	$1,728	1,650	$2	$1,572
1996	$9.33	200	$1,866	1,800	$2	$1,734

   b. 10 percent. 9 percent.
   c. 2 percent decline. 1 percent decline.
   d. 2 percent increase. 1 percent increase.
   e. It is 53 percent in 1994, 52 percent in 1995, and somewhat less than 52 percent in 1996.

CHAPTER 11

Productivity, Growth, and

Technology Policy

Chapter Profile

Compared with that of other major industrial countries, America's rate of growth of per capita output generally was quite impressive over the past century, because of rapid technological change, increases in education and training, investment in plant and equipment, plentiful natural resources, and our social and entrepreneurial climate.

However, during the latter 1960s and the 1970s, the United States experienced a notable slowdown in its rate of increase of output per hour of labor. Among the factors that were often cited as being responsible for the slowdown were (1) the increase in the proportion of youths and women in the labor force, (2) the reduction in the rate of growth of the capital-labor ratio, (3) increased government regulation, and (4) the reduction in the proportion of GDP devoted to research and development.

According to many observers, the productivity slowdown has been due in part to a decline in the rate of innovation in the United States. R and D tax credits, federal R and D grants and contracts, and expanded work by federal laboratories are among the measures that have been proposed to help deal with whatever underinvestment in R and D that exists. In 1981, an incremental R and D tax credit was enacted.

America's investment in plant and equipment (as a percentage of output) is considerably lower than that of some of its major international competitors, such as Germany and Japan. In 1981, the Congress passed a tax bill that permitted accelerated depreciation of plant and equipment. This bill was intended to encourage such investment.

One of the strongest influences on the rate of innovation is the general economic climate. Measures that encourage economic growth, saving and investment, and price stability are quite likely to enhance our technological position. Indeed, improvements in our general economic climate may have more impact on the state of U.S. technology than many of the specific measures that have been proposed to stimulate technological changes.

The Reagan administration pushed through Congress some very large tax cuts in 1981, the idea being to shift the aggregate supply curve to the right.

The Clinton administration advocated direct, purposeful investments in commercially relevant technologies. This was contrary to the views of its predecessor, the Bush administration.

Concepts for Review

Productivity
Research and development
Innovation
U.S. technological lead

Completion Questions

1. During periods of recovery and prosperity, the U.S. economic growth rate was (high, low) _____; during depressions, it was (high, low) _____.

2. By 1840, the United States ranked fourth in per capita income, behind _____, _____, and _____.

3. In the United States, the federal government is the source of about _____ of all R and D funds, which have been heavily concentrated on _____ and _____ technology.

4. The increase in the proportion of youths and women in the U.S. labor force may have been responsible for _____ to _____ percentage points of the difference between the average rate of productivity increase in 1947–66 and that in 1966–73.

5. The reduction after 1973 in the rate of increase of the capital-labor ratio may have reduced the U.S. rate of productivity increase by up to _____ percentage points per year.

6. It is important to distinguish between a reduction in the rate of _____ in the United States and a reduction in the American _____ over other countries.

7. Total U.S. R and D expenditures, when inflation is taken into account, (increased considerably, decreased considerably, were essentially constant) _____ during 1966–77.

8. For public goods like defense and space, since the government must take the primary responsibility for their _____, it must also take primary responsibility for the promotion of _____ in relevant areas.

9. An R and D _____ allows a firm to reduce its income tax liability by an amount equal to a certain percentage of its R and D expenditures.

10. A(n) _____ allows a firm to reduce its income tax liability by a certain percentage of the increase in its R and D expenditures.

True-False

_____ 1. The bulk of R and D expenditures go for minor improvements rather than major advances.

_____ 2. The United States has grown more rapidly than any other industrialized country in the past twenty years.

_____ 3. The quality as well as the quantity of the population determines how much is produced.

_____ 4. In the past fifteen or twenty years, the U.S. birth rate has fallen, due partly to changes in attitudes toward women's role in society.

_____ 5. In recent years, fear has been expressed that, if the world economy continues to grow at current rates, we shall begin to run out of some basic raw materials.

_____ 6. It is generally accepted that we should curb our rate of growth to avoid running out of raw materials in the next twenty years.

_____ 7. Different government agencies have adopted different policies with respect to patents resulting from government contracts.

_____ 8. The government should focus its R and D support on economically beleaguered industries.

_____ 9. The government should concentrate its technological efforts on what is essentially commercial development.

_____ 10. A sound coupling of technology and marketing is one of the characteristics that is most significant in distinguishing the relatively successful innovators from the relatively unsuccessful ones.

_____ 11. Rapid technological change will always result in mass unemployment.

_____ 12. Measures that encourage investment are likely to encourage innovation as well.

Multiple Choice

1. If a nation's GDP is growing at 3 percent per year, how many years will it take for its GDP to double?

   a. 70
   b. 35
   c. 24
   d. 18
   e. 14

2. The slowdown of productivity growth in the United States:

   a. reduces the nation's rate of economic growth.
   b. helps to increase the inflation rate.
   c. makes some of our industries less competitive with foreigners.
   d. all of the above.
   e. none of the above.

3. The slowdown in productivity growth in the United States has been due in part to:

   a. increases in government regulations.
   b. increases in the proportion of women and teenagers in the labor force.
   c. reductions in the rate of growth of capital per worker.
   d. all of the above.
   e. none of the above.

4. The rate of return to society from investments in research and development is likely to exceed the rate of return from these investments to the firm or individual financing the research and development because:

   a. many of the benefits from the research accrue to firms and individuals other than the ones financing the R and D.
   b. research and development yield external economies.
   c. the risks to society from research and development are less than the risks to the firms carrying out the research and development.
   d. all of the above.
   e. none of the above.

5. From 1950 to 1964, the nation with the highest growth rate, among the following four, was:

   a. United States.
   b. Germany.
   c. Canada.
   d. Japan.

6. The factor listed below that has been least important in determining the rate of economic growth in the United States is:

   a. increases in capital.
   b. investment in education.
   c. technological change.
   d. the size of the national debt.

7. Which of the following tends to reduce the economic growth rate?

    a.   increased immobility of resources
    b.   growth of monopolies that prevent efficient allocation of resources
    c.   increased unemployment
    d.   all of the above
    e.   none of the above

8. Increases in the rate of technological change result in increases in aggregate unemployment:

    a.   always and necessarily.
    b.   when total spending rises too slowly.
    c.   when total spending rises rapidly and resources are already fully employed.
    d.   all of the above.
    e.   none of the above.

Discussion and Extension Questions

1. Writing in the *New York Times*, Edwin Dale pointed out that a communique of the Organization for Economic Cooperation and Development said that "the steady economic growth needed to restore full employment and satisfy rising economic and social aspirations will not prove sustainable unless all member countries make further progress toward eradicating inflation." Using the concepts developed in this and previous chapters, explain in your own words what this passage means, and indicate whether you agree and why or why not.

2. "Economic growth is an archaic social objective. We have plenty of goods and services. Why should we strive for more?" Comment and evaluate.

3. Is America's technological lead relatively new, or something that has existed for a century or more? Is it true that independent inventors play practically no role at all today in the process of technological change? Discuss.

4. According to M.I.T.'s study of *The Limits to Growth*, continued economic growth is likely to mean that we will run out of raw materials in the reasonably near future. Does this seem likely? Why or why not?

5. What aspects of the American economy have not been conducive to economic growth? What are the principal arguments used today in favor of rapid economic growth? What are the principal arguments used today against rapid economic growth? What policies can the government adopt to increase the rate of economic growth?

6. Must increases in the rate of technological change result in increases in aggregate unemployment? Why or why not?

7. If GDP in the year 2000 is much higher than it is today, will this mean that all our material problems will be solved? Why or why not?

Problems

1. Output per hour of labor increased by 4 percent per year in the chemical industry in country Z between January 1, 1989, and January 1, 1994.

   a. In 1994, the chemical industry's employment (in hours of labor) was equal to what it had been in 1989. How big was the percentage change in chemical output between 1989 and 1994?

   b. Suppose that the chemical industry's employment (in hours of labor) was 10 percent less in 1994 than in 1989. How big was the percentage change in chemical output between 1989 and 1994?

   c. Suppose that the government of country Z dictates that chemical output is to remain constant (at its 1994 level) from 1994 to 1999. If output per hour of labor increases by 4 percent per year from 1994 to 1999, and if the industry's 1994 employment is 100 million hours, how many hours of labor will the industry employ in 1995? 1996? 1997? 1998? 1999? Plot the number of hours employed each year in the graph below.

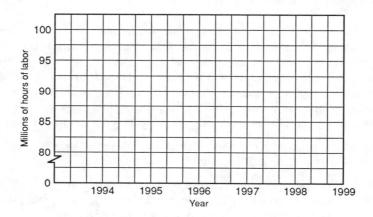

   d. What will happen to the workers that no longer are needed in the chemical industry?

2. Economic growth in Palmerland, the golfer's paradise, is spurred by the production of a new supersonic golf cart. Suppose that this technological change results in an increase in full-employment GDP from $1,000 million to $1,100 million. (Net exports in Palmerland equal zero.)

   a. If the $C + I + G$ line is as shown on the next page, what will be the immediate effect on unemployment of this technological change?

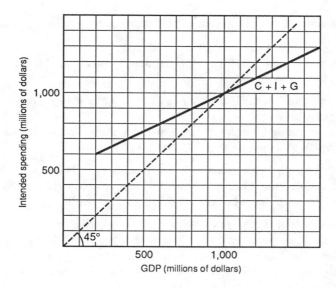

b. In what direction must the $C + I + G$ line be pushed in order to attain full employment? By how much must it be pushed? Draw the new $C + I + G$ line in the graph above.

c. What kinds of policies might the government of Palmerland adopt to push the $C + I + G$ line in the direction indicated in part b?

3. Suppose that the real GDP of country Y was $800 million in 1993. If it increases at a compound rate of 5 percent per year, what will its real GDP be in 1994? 1995? How long will it take before its GDP equals $1 billion?

4. Economy X's productive capacity is growing at 5 percent per year. In 1994 economy X had the capacity to produce $100 billion of GDP. Aggregate demand each year is also shown below. All amounts are in billions of constant dollars.

Year	Aggregate demand	Productive capacity	Actual GDP
1994	95	100	_____
1995	100	_____	_____
1996	107	_____	_____

a. Fill in the blanks above.
b. Is the rate of growth of actual GDP between 1994 and 1995 as big as it could be? Why or why not?
c. Between 1995 and 1996 is the rate of increase of actual GDP as big as it could have been? Why or why not?
d. Between 1995 and 1996 is the rate of increase of actual GDP bigger or

smaller than the rate of increase of productive capacity? How is this possible?

5. Suppose that the United States has 1 billion tons of iron ore, and that it uses 10 million tons of iron ore per year.

    a. Does this mean that the United States will run out of iron ore in 100 years? Why or why not?
    b. Does this mean that the United States will not be able to produce steel in 100 years? Why or why not?

6. According to the U.S. Department of the Interior, the world demand for bauxite (used to make aluminum) during 1974 to 2000 will be about 962 million tons. Identified world resources of bauxite are 6,310 million tons.

    a. Does this mean that the United States need not worry about the price of bauxite going up significantly in the next decade or so? Why or why not?
    b. Does this mean that the world as a whole need not worry about the price of bauxite going up significantly in the next decade or so? Why or why not?

7. According to the U.S. Bureau of Mines, potential total reserves of mercury in the United States would have been about 1.3 million flasks if the price of mercury were $1,000 per flask, but only about 140,000 flasks if the price were $200 per flask.

    a. How is it possible that the reserves of mercury are variable, not constant?
    b. Why are mercury reserves directly related to the price of mercury?
    c. According to William Baumol and Wallace Oates, "It is hard to believe that any resource whose price falls consistently without regulatory interference is really growing very scarce relative to prospective demand." Does this proposition seem reasonable in the case of mercury? Why or why not?
    d. Harold Barnett and Chandler Morse studied the unit cost of extraction of 13 minerals during 1870 and 1957 and found that the cost of each declined. Does this indicate a shortage of these minerals? Why or why not?

8. Suppose that both a haircut (a service) and a watchband (a manufactured good) can be produced by an hour of labor (and for simplicity, no other resources) in 1994.

    a. What will be the cost of a haircut and of a watchband in 1994, if the wage rate in both industries is $3 per hour?
    b. If technological change is greater in the production of watchbands than in the production of haircuts, with the result that labor productivity increases by 5 percent per year in watchband production but by only 1 percent per year in haircut production, what will be the cost of a haircut and of a watchband in 1995, if the wage rate in both industries increases by 3 percent per year?
    c. If labor productivity and wages increase at these rates, what will be the cost of a haircut and of a watchband in 1996?

d. Do you think that this simple model helps to explain why the costs of education, local government, and many other services have risen relative to the costs of manufactured goods in recent years? Why or why not?

ANSWERS

Completion Questions

1. high, low   2. England, France, Germany   3. half, defense, space   4. 0.2, 0.3
5. 0.5   6. technological change, technological lead   7. were essentially constant
8. production, technological change   9. tax credit   10. incremental R and D tax credit

True-False

1. True   2. False   3. True   4. True   5. True   6. False   7. True   8. False
9. False   10. True   11. False   12. True

Multiple Choice

1. c   2. d   3. d   4. d   5. d   6. d   7. d   8. b

Problems

1. a. $[(1.04)^5 - 1] \times 100$ percent, which is approximately 22 percent.
    b. $[.9 \times (1.04)^5 - 1] \times 100$ percent, which is approximately 10 percent.
    c.

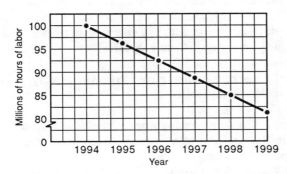

d. Presumably they will find employment in other industries.
2. a. Increased unemployment.
    b. Upward. To the point where it intersects the 45-degree line at $1,100 million.

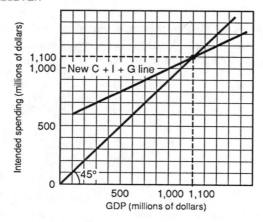

c. Increase the money supply, reduce interest rates, increase government spending, reduce taxes.

3. $1.05 \times \$800$ million $= \$840$ million. $(1.05)^2 \times \$800$ million $= \$882$ million. About 5 years.

4. a.

Year	Productive capacity	Actual GDP
1994	100	95
1995	105	100
1996	110	107

b. No, because in 1995 actual GDP is less than it could be if all capacity were utilized.

c. No, because in 1996 actual GDP is less than it could be if all capacity were utilized.

d. Bigger, because the rate of utilization of capacity is higher in 1996 than in 1995.

5. a. No, because more iron ore may be discovered in the future.
   b. No, because more iron ore may be discovered.

6. a. No, because bauxite is produced by only a small number of countries and they may enter into collusive agreements to drive up the price.
   b. Same answer as in part a.

7. a. Because if the price is higher, it pays to obtain mercury that is more difficult and costly to obtain.
   b. See part a.
   c. Yes, because if it were growing scarcer relative to demand, one would expect producers to have to resort to more costly methods to obtain it, and the price would rise.
   d. No, for the reason given in part c.

8. a. $3.
   b. $3.06 for a haircut and $2.94 for a watchband.
   c. $3.12 for a haircut and $2.89 for a watchband.
   d. Yes, because productivity has not appeared to have risen as rapidly in some of the service industries as in manufacturing.

CHAPTER 12

Deficits, Public Debt, and the

Federal Budget

Chapter Profile

At least three policies concerning the government budget have had serious proponents. First, the budget should be balanced each and every year. Second, the budget should be balanced over the course of the business cycle. Third, the budget should be set in a way that will promote full employment and stable prices whether or not this means that the budget is unbalanced over considerable periods of time.

The history of the past 50 years has seen enormous changes in the public's attitude toward the government budget. Fifty years ago, the prevailing doctrine was that the budget should be balanced each year. Now (although a balanced budget has more support than a few years ago) the attitude seems to be that the budget should be used as a tool to reduce unemployment and inflation.

Some of the popular misconceptions concerning budget deficits can be avoided by the use of the structural deficit, which shows the difference between government expenditure and tax revenue that would result if we had full employment. When the actual budget shows a large deficit but the structural deficit is very small, most economists feel that fiscal policy is not too expansionary.

When the government spends more than it receives in revenues, the government borrows money to cover the difference. It could simply print money for this purpose, but it has chosen to borrow a considerable proportion of what has been needed. The resulting debt is often called the national debt.

One reason why the public is concerned about deficits is that they may cause inflation if the government finances the deficit by increasing the money supply. Also, government budget deficits may crowd out private investment because government borrowing may push up the interest rate.

Despite much public worry about the size of the national debt, as a percentage of national output it was not much larger in 1994 than in 1939. There are important differences between government debt and private debt. Although the size of the debt is certainly of consequence, it is not true that it somehow leads to bankruptcy.

The spending decisions of the federal government take place in the context of the budgetary process. The president submits his budget, which is a statement of anticipated expenditures and revenues, to Congress, which votes appropriations. The Ways and Means Committee of the House of Representatives and the Senate Finance Committee play important roles in the federal tax legislative process.

Concepts for Review

Deficit	Crowding in	Balanced budget
Surplus	National debt	Structural deficit
Crowding out	Federal budget	

Completion Questions

1. Besides the crowding-out effect, there is the _____ effect.

2. The _____ is a statement of the government's anticipated expenditures and revenues.

3. The process of selling new bonds to get money to redeem old bonds when they fall due is called _____.

4. Borrowing is not the only method the government can use to finance a deficit. It can also create _____ to cover the difference between expenditures and revenues.

5. Suppose that tax receipts and government expenditures on goods and services are related in the following way to GDP (all figures are in billions of dollars):

GDP	Tax receipts	Government expenditures
800	200	260
900	230	260
1,000	260	260
1,100	300	260

If GDP is $900 billion, the government runs a (deficit, surplus)

_____ of $_____ billion. If the full-employment GDP is $1,100 billion, the structural deficit is $_____ billion. For this economy to achieve full employment, intended investment must

be $_____ billion (greater, less) _____ than intended saving at full employment. (This assumes that net exports are zero.) This is because, in equilibrium, *intended saving plus taxes must equal intended investment plus government expenditure.* (This follows from the material in Chapter 6.)

True-False

_____ 1. If the structural deficit is $10 billion, the equilibrium value of GDP must be above the full-employment level of GDP.

_____ 2. One disadvantage to society of a government debt may be the inflation caused by the deficits producing the debt.

_____ 3. If the government's actual deficit in one year is $10 billion and its actual deficit in another year is $20 billion, fiscal policy must be more expansionary in the latter year than in the former.

_____ 4. To the extent that the national debt is held by foreigners, we must send goods and services overseas to pay the interest on it.

_____ 5. World War II would have imposed a burden on subsequent generations whether or not the national debt was increased.

_____ 6. As the national debt grows, the transfer payments required to meet interest charges grow too, and these transfer payments are likely to encourage national output.

_____ 7. If buyers can be found for the government bonds that represent the national debt, there is no need to worry about the effects of the debt on a nation's income distribution.

_____ 8. When the actual budget shows a deficit but the structural deficit is very small, fiscal policy is probably too expansionary.

_____ 9. In recent years the national debt has become so large that bankruptcy is likely.

_____ 10. The size of the deficits required to eliminate excessive unemployment will always equal the size of the surpluses required to moderate the subsequent inflation.

_____ 11. A deficit occurs when the government spends more than it collects in receipts.

_____ 12. All the automatic stabilizers do is cut down on variations in unemployment and inflation, not eliminate them.

Multiple Choice

1. The most expansionary fiscal policy is:

   a. a surplus that is impounded.
   b. a surplus used to reduce the public debt.
   c. a deficit financed by new money.
   d. a deficit financed by borrowing from the public.
   e. a balanced budget.

2. The most anti-inflationary fiscal policy is:

   a. a surplus that is impounded.
   b. a surplus used to reduce the public debt.
   c. a deficit financed by new money.
   d. a deficit financed by borrowing from the public.
   e. a balanced budget.

3. If the national debt is held by foreigners,

   a. interest must be sent abroad.
   b. the debt may produce enough extra output to cover the interest payments.
   c. goods and services are sent overseas.
   d. none of the above.
   e. all of the above.

Discussion and Extension Questions

1. If a balanced budget for the federal government is not all that important for the economy, why have so many politicians promised to have a balanced budget?

2. Why is it important to distinguish between the actual deficit and the structural deficit? Answer in detail.

3. Evaluate the significance of a large national debt.

4. Describe the budgetary process and suggest why it is often difficult for the president to pass his budget.

5. Explain the concept of crowding out, and indicate how it differs from crowding in.

Problems

1. The following figures pertain to country Q's economy at various levels of GDP (all figures in millions of dollars):

Taxes	GDP	Disposable income	Intended consumption expenditure	Intended saving
25	1,000	975	898	77
30	1,100	1,070	983	87
38	1,200	1,162	1,066	96
50	1,300	1,250	1,145	105
67	1,400	1,333	1,220	113
90	1,500	1,410	1,289	121
120	1,600	1,480	1,352	128
158	1,700	1,542	1,408	134
205	1,800	1,595	1,456	139

Suppose that intended investment is 128 and government expenditures on goods and services are 27. Net exports equal zero.

a. What is the equilibrium level of GDP? What is the status of the government's budget at this value of GDP? (Hint: See Completion Question 5.)

b. Assume full employment to occur at GDP = 1,600. Assuming that changes in government expenditures are the country's only policy tool, how large must these expenditures be to move the economy to full employment? What will be the status of the government's budget once full employment is reached?

2. In the previous problem, suppose that intended investment increases to 143 and government expenditures on goods and services rise to 37.

a. Is equilibrium GDP the same as it was in the previous problem? What is the new level of equilibrium GDP? What is the status of the government's budget at this equilibrium value of GDP?

b. Assume full employment to occur at GDP = 1,600. How large must government expenditures be to move the company to full employment? When it gets there, will the sum of taxes and intended saving equal the sum of government expenditure and intended investment? Why or why not?

3. Consider the following model of an economy:

(1) $C_d = 1,000 + .9Y_d$
(2) $G = 600$
(3) $I_d = 390$
(4) $T = 400$
(5) $Y_d = GDP - T$
(6) $B = T - G$

where G equals government expenditure on goods and services, T equals taxes, B equals the government surplus (or deficit), C_d is intended consumption expenditures, Y_d is disposable income, and I_d is intended investment. All figures are in millions of dollars. Fill in the blanks below.

a. Equilibrium GDP = _____.

b. The multiplier for a change in G = _____.

c. The impact on GDP of a $1 increase in taxes = _____.

d. Savings at equilibrium GDP = _____.

e. If GDP at full employment is 15,000, savings at full employment =

_____.

f. If taxes remain constant, the level of government expenditure needed to

attain full employment = _____.

4. You are given the following information about an economy: GDP = $20 billion at full employment; GDP = $16 billion currently; taxes = .1(GDP); and government expenditures on goods and services = $1.8 billion.

a. Is the government running a surplus or a deficit? Is the budget too expansionary? Why or why not?

b. Suppose you learn that when GDP = $20 billion, intended saving = $1.8 billion and intended investment = $1.5 billion. If tax rates cannot be changed, and if government expenditures are altered to push the economy to full employment, will there be a surplus or deficit? How big? (Assume net exports equal zero.)

5. Consider an economy in which:

$$C_d = 500 + .9(Y_d) \qquad I_d = 500 \qquad G = 225 \qquad T = 250$$

where C_d equals intended consumption expenditure, Y_d equals disposable income, I_d equals intended investment, G equals government expenditure, and T equals taxes. All figures are in millions of dollars. Net exports equal zero.

a. What is equilibrium GDP?

b. The full-employment GDP = $10,400. President Earnest is most interested in getting the economy to full employment, but she also feels a driving need to balance the government's budget. How would you change fiscal policy (T and/or G) in an attempt to satisfy President Earnest's twin goals? Convince Ms. Earnest that your policy suggestions will work by using numerical values.

ANSWERS

Completion Questions
1. crowding-in   2. budget   3. debt refunding   4. money   5. deficit, 30, minus 40, 40, greater

True-False
1. False   2. True   3. False   4. True   5. True   6. False   7. False   8. False
9. False   10. False   11. True   12. True

Multiple Choice
1. c   2. a   3. e

Problems
1. a. Since intended investment plus government spending equals 155, this should also be the sum of intended saving plus taxes. This is the case when GDP = 1,300, so the equilibrium GDP is $1,300 million. The government runs a surplus of $23 million.
   b. $120 million. There will be a balanced budget.
2. a. No. The new equilibrium GDP is $1,400 million. The government runs a surplus of $30 million.
   b. $105 million. Yes, because this is a necessary condition for equilibrium (if net exports are zero).
3. a. $16.3 billion
   b. 10
   c. −$9
   d. $590 million
   e. $460 million
   f. $470 million
4. a. The government is running a deficit of $0.2 billion. Since it is running a structural surplus of $0.2 billion, the budget does not seem too expansionary.
   b. There will be a deficit of $0.3 billion.
5. a. GDP = 500 + .9(GDP − 250) + 500 + 225. Thus, .1GDP = 500 − 225 + 500 + 225 = 1,000, so the equilibrium value of GDP is $10,000 million.
   b. Ms. Earnest wants GDP = 10,400 and $T = G$. Thus, GDP = 500 + .9(GDP − G) + 500 + G = 10,400, which means that .1G = 10,400 − 500 − 500 − 9,360 = 40. Thus, both G and T should be set equal to $400 million.

CHAPTER 13

Monetary Policy, Interest Rates,

and Economic Activity

Chapter Profile

America's history has seen many sharp fluctuations in the price level. Generally, severe inflations have occurred because the government expanded the money supply far too rapidly. However, too small a rate of growth of the money supply can also be a mistake, resulting in excessive unemployment.

Most economists believe that the lower the interest rate, the greater the amount of money demanded. Thus increases in the quantity of money result in lower interest rates which result in increased investment (and other types of spending), which results in a higher GDP. Conversely, decreases in the quantity of money result in higher interest rates, which result in decreased investment (and other types of spending), which result in a lower GDP. This is the simple Keynesian approach.

The equation of exchange is $MV = PQ$, where M is the money supply, V is velocity, P is the price level, and Q is gross domestic product in real terms. The velocity of circulation of money is the rate at which the money supply is used to make transactions for final goods and services. Specifically, it equals GDP in money terms divided by the money supply.

If the velocity of circulation of money remains constant and if real gross domestic product is fixed at its full-employment level, it follows from the equation of exchange that the price level will be proportional to the money supply. This is the crude quantity theory, which is a reasonably good approximation during periods of runaway inflation, and works reasonably well in predicting long-term trends in the price level.

The monetarists, led by Milton Friedman, prefer the quantity theory to the Keynesian model. There have been many disagreements between the monetarists and the Keynesians, but both approaches agree that increases in the money supply will tend to increase nominal GDP while decreases in the money supply will tend to decrease nominal GDP.

As indicators of how tight or easy monetary policy is, the Fed has looked at the level of short-term interest rates, the rate of growth of the money supply, and the rate of growth of the monetary base. During the 1950s and 1960s, the Fed paid most attention to the first indicator; in the 1970s and early 1980s, the Fed increased the amount of attention paid to the last two.

The Federal Reserve is faced with many difficult problems in formulating and carrying out monetary policy. It must try to see where the economy is heading, and whether—and to what extent—it should tighten or ease money to stabilize the economy. This task is made very difficult by the fact that there is often a long—and highly variable—lag between an action by the Fed and its effect on the economy.

There is also considerable disagreement over the best way to measure how tight or easy monetary policy is.

There has been criticism of various kinds regarding the performance of the Federal Reserve. Often, the Fed is criticized for paying too little attention to the long lags between its actions and their effects on the economy. Some monetarists, led by Milton Friedman, believe that monetary policy would be improved if discretionary policy were replaced by a rule that the Fed should increase the money supply at some fixed, agreed-on rate, such as 4 or 5 percent per year.

A more sophisticated version of the quantity theory recognizes that real gross domestic product is often less than its full-employment value; consequently, Q is not fixed. Thus if velocity remains constant, gross domestic product in money terms should be proportional to the money supply. In fact, velocity has by no means remained stable over time. However, nominal GDP has been fairly closely related to the money supply, and the monetarists have asserted that velocity is predictable.

Concepts for Review

Transactions demand
Precautionary demand
Demand curve for money
Nominal GDP
Velocity of circulation of money

Monetary base
Equation of exchange
Crude quantity theory
Easy monetary policy
Tight monetary policy

Completion Questions

1. If the velocity of money is 5, and the money supply equals $200 billion, nominal GDP equals _____. If the velocity of money remains constant at 5, a $10 billion increase in the money supply results in a(n) _____ increase in nominal GDP, and a $5 billion decrease in the money supply results in a(n) _____ decrease in nominal GDP.

2. When William Malone pays $8 for a haircut, this is an example of the use of money as a _____. When Mary Malone keeps $400 in her checking account, this is an example of the use of money as a(n) _____. When John Malone announces that he receives $6 an hour as a lifeguard, this is an example of the use of money as a(n) _____.

3. A bond pays interest of $100 per year (indefinitely). If the interest rate is 5 percent, this bond is worth _____. If the interest rate is 10

percent, this bond is worth _____. An increase in the interest rate (reduces, increases) _____ the market price of the bond. An increase in the market price of the bond means a(n) (decrease, increase) _____ in the interest rate.

4. If the demand curve for money is a vertical line, the interest rate (does, does not) _____ influence the quantity of money demanded. One reason why such a demand curve for money seems (likely, unlikely) _____ is that there are _____ costs of holding money, and these costs increase as the interest rate (rises, falls) _____.

5. One of the most important costs of holding money is the loss of _____.

6. The _____ of money is the rate at which the money supply is used to make transactions for final goods and services.

7. The _____ assumes that full employment exists, and states that the price level must be proportional to the money supply.

8. The _____ shows the relationship between the interest rate and the quantity of money.

9. Excessive increases in the quantity of money may result in serious _____, while inadequate increases in the quantity of money may result in excessive _____.

10. The amount of money held by individuals and firms is inversely related to the _____.

11. The value of a dollar is equivalent to what a dollar will _____, which in turn depends on the _____ level. If all _____ doubled, the value of a dollar would be cut in half.

True-False

_____ 1. If the velocity of money is increasing at 2 percent per year and the economy's potential real GDP is growing at 3 percent per year, the money supply should grow at 6 percent to maintain a constant price level.

_____ 2. If the velocity of money is constant and the economy's potential real GDP is growing at 3 percent per year, the money supply should grow at 3 percent to maintain a constant price level.

_____ 3. During each war in which the United States has participated, there has been pronounced inflation followed by a postwar drop in prices.

_____ 4. The higher a person's income, the more money he or she tends to hold for transactions demand.

_____ 5. Over the past 50 years, nominal GDP has been uncorrelated with the money supply in the United States.

_____ 6. In the short run, if there is an increase in the money supply, there will be a tendency for the price level to fall.

_____ 7. The crude quantity theory sometimes works fairly well in predicting long-term trends in the price level and the course of runaway inflations.

_____ 8. The effect of an increase in the money supply is to decrease gross domestic product.

_____ 9. Basically, the value of currency depends on its acceptability by people and on its scarcity.

_____ 10. If all prices were reduced by 50 percent, the value of a dollar would double.

_____ 11. Holding GDP constant, the amount of money demanded by individuals and firms is inversely related to the interest rate, since the cost of holding money is the interest or profit forgone.

Multiple Choice

1. A reduction in the rate of interest is likely to result in:

   a. an increase in demand for capital goods.
   b. an increase in demand for consumer durable goods.
   c. an increase in demand for residential housing.
   d. all of the above.
   e. none of the above.

2. An increase in the quantity of money will *not* affect the interest rate if:

   a. the demand curve for money is upward sloping to the right.
   b. the demand curve for money is downward sloping to the right.
   c. the demand curve for money is horizontal.
   d. the demand curve for money is vertical.
   e. all of the above.

3. If the quantity of money supplied exceeds the quantity of money demanded,

   a. the interest rate will rise.
   b. the interest rate will rise, and GDP will rise too.
   c. the interest rate will fall.
   d. the demand curve for money will shift downward.
   e. the interest rate will be unaffected.

4. If next year's real GDP is expected to equal this year's, and if the velocity of money is expected to be 2 percent higher next year than this year, how big is the money supply expected to be next year if the price level is expected to be 3 percent higher than this year?

    a. The money supply is expected to be 1 percent above this year's level.
    b. The money supply is expected to equal its value this year.
    c. The money supply is expected to be 2 percent above this year's level.
    d. The money supply is expected to be 3 percent above this year's level.
    e. The money supply is expected to be 4 percent above this year's level.

5. The velocity of circulation of money is:

    a. nominal GDP $\div M$.   d. all of the above.
    b. $P \times Q \div M$.   e. none of the above.
    c. not a constant.

6. On the average, 1984 prices in the United States were about how many times what they were in 1964?

    a. about the same   d. 10 times as high
    b. 2 times as high   e. 20 times as high
    c. over 3 times as high

7. The money that people and firms keep to meet contingencies like illness or home and car repairs is called the _____ demand for money.

    a. transactions   d. investment
    b. precautionary   e. none of the above
    c. speculative

Discussion and Extension Questions

1. *Business Week* has quoted Allen Meltzer of Carnegie-Mellon University as saying, "Given anticipations, the level of capacity utilization in the economy makes little difference. An increase in the money supply in the 1930s would have had the same impact on prices as a similar increase in the 1960s." Explain what he means. Do you agree? Why or why not?

2. How and why does the increased used of credit cards affect the demand for money?

3. Is it always true that $MV = PQ$? Why or why not? To what extent is velocity constant over time? How does the more sophisticated quantity theory differ from the crude quantity theory?

4. Does the fact that velocity is not constant mean that the more sophisticated version of the quantity theory is useless? Why or why not?

5. Explain how a worried public, which begins to increase the speed with which it spends money, can create inflation without any increases in the money supply.

6. Suppose that a ceiling is placed on the interest rate. In what way, if any, would such a ceiling interfere with the effect of a reduction of the money supply on GDP?

Problems

1. In nation A, the price level during various years was as follows:

Year	Price level (1950 = 100)
1950	100
1960	120
1970	140
1980	200
1990	300

a. Plot the relationship between the price level and time in the graph below:

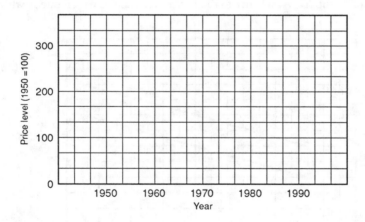

b. By what percentage did the value of money decline in nation A from 1980 to 1990? From 1950 to 1980?

c. If your grandfather invested in a 40-year, $1,000 bond in nation A in 1950, and if he held it until maturity in 1990, how much did he receive in principal in 1990 dollars? In 1950 dollars?

2. Suppose that in the nation of South Isthmus the relationship between the interest rate and the quantity of money demanded, holding GDP constant, is

$$i = 20 - 2M,$$

where i is the interest rate (in percentage points) and M is the quantity of money (in trillions of dollars).

   a.   What is the name often given to this relationship?

   b.   What is the interest rate in South Isthmus if the quantity of money demanded equals $5 trillion?

   c.   Suppose that GDP in South Isthmus increases. Will the relationship between i and M remain constant? If not, in what direction will it shift?

3. a.   If nominal GDP in South Isthmus increases by 20 percent between 1992 and 1994, while the money supply increases by 10 percent, what change occurs in the velocity of circulation of money?

    b.   If nominal GDP in South Isthmus increased by 20 percent between 1992 and 1994, while velocity increased by less than 20 percent, did the money supply increase during this period, or did it decrease?

4. a.   In South Isthmus, suppose that the quantity of money increased considerably during 1993. The graph below shows two investment functions, one of which was the one that existed before the increase in the money supply, the other being the one that existed after the increase in the money supply. According to the Keynesian model, which one is which?

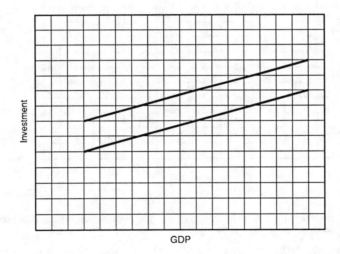

    b.   After the increase in the money supply, it was discovered that the crude quantity theory of money was applicable. The money supply was increased by 10 percent. How much did the price level increase during 1993?

5. Country Q's real GDP increased from 1992 to 1995 by 3 percent per year, and its velocity of money increased by 2 percent per year. Fill in the blanks below.

Year	Price Level (1992 = 100)	Money Supply (1992 = 100)
1992	100	100
1993	_____	101
1994	100	_____
1995	100	_____

6. The following data come from the *Economic Report of the President:*

Year	M-1 (billions of dollars)	M-2 (billions of dollars)	Nominal GDP (billions of dollars)
1967	187.4	350.0	814.3
1969	209.0	392.5	959.5
1971	234.0	471.9	1,097.2
1973	270.5	571.4	1,349.6
1975	295.2	664.7	1,585.9
1977	338.5	809.5	1,974.1

When *M-2* is used rather than *M-1*, was velocity more stable over time during 1967–77?

7. A bond pays interest of $100 per year (forever). The following table shows the price of the bond at selected interest rates. Fill in the blanks.

Interest rate (percent)	Price of bond (dollars)
1	_____
2	_____
_____	2,500
_____	2,000
10	_____
12 1/2	_____

8. Suppose that the quantity of money demanded in country X (denoted by M) is related in the following way to nominal GDP (denoted as Y) and the interest rate (denoted by i):

$$M = \frac{Y(30 - 2i)}{50},$$

where M and Y are in trillions of dollars and i is in percentage points.

    a.   Is the demand curve for money in this country a straight line?

    b.   Does an increase in GDP from 1 to 2 trillion dollars affect the slope of the demand-curve for money? If so, what is its effect?

    c.   If the interest rate exceeds 15 percent, do you think that this equation holds? Why or why not?

9. a.   Based on the data given in the previous problem, is the crude quantity theory of money valid in country X? Explain.

    b.   In country X, is velocity influenced by the interest rate? Explain.

    c.   Country X adopts a variety of devices to reduce the cost of transferring money balances from saving to checking accounts. Will this affect the validity of the equation in the previous problem? If so, what effect is it likely to have?

ANSWERS

Completion Questions

1. $1 trillion, $50 billion, $25 billion   2. medium of exchange, store of value, standard of value   3. $2,000, $1,000, reduces, decrease   4. does not, unlikely, opportunity, rises   5. interest or profit   6. velocity of circulation   7. crude quantity theory   8. demand curve for money   9. inflation, unemployment 10. interest rate   11. buy, price, prices

True-False

1. False 2. True 3. False 4. True 5. False 6. False 7. True 8. False 9. True 10. True 11. True

Multiple Choice

1. d 2. c 3. c 4. a 5. d 6. c 7. b

Problems

1. a.

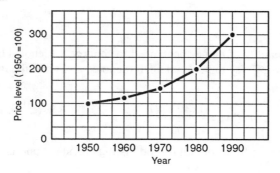

   b.   33 1/3 percent, 50 percent.
   c. $1,000, $333 1/3.
2. a.   Demand curve for money.
   b.   10 percent.
   c.   No. It will shift upward and to the right.
3. a.   It increases by about 9 percent.
   b.   It increased.
4. a.   The higher one is after the increase in the money supply; the lower one is before the increase in the money supply.
   b.   10 percent.
5. The 1993 price level was 100; the 1994 money supply was 102; and the 1995 money supply was 103.
6. Velocity based on M-1 and M-2 was as follows:

Year	Based on M-1	Based on M-2
1967	4.35	2.33
1969	4.59	2.44
1971	4.69	2.33
1973	4.99	2.36
1975	5.37	2.39
1977	5.83	2.44

Velocity was more stable when M-2 is used than when M-1 is used.
7. The complete table is:

Interest rate (percent)	Price of bond (dollars)
1	10,000
2	5,000
4	2,500
5	2,000
10	1,000
12 1/2	800

8. a.   Yes.
   b.   Yes. The slope changes from −.04 to −.08.
   c.   No, because if this equation holds, M is negative if i is greater than 15.
9. a.   No. Velocity equals $50 \div (30 - 2i)$, which means that velocity is not constant if the interest rate changes.
   b.   Yes. See part a.
   c.   The adoption of such devices may result in there being less money demanded at each level of Y and i than indicated by this equation.

CHAPTER 14

Controversies over Stabilization

Policy

Chapter Profile

The principal debate of the 1960s and 1970s was between the Keynesians and the monetarists. The Keynesians put more emphasis than did the monetarists on the federal budget; the monetarists put more emphasis than did the Keynesians on the money supply. In the late 1970s, supply-side economists came to prominence, their emphasis being on tax cuts to push the aggregate supply curve to the right.

The new classical macroeconomists like Robert Lucas also came to prominence in the 1970s. Based on their assumptions, the new classical macroeconomists conclude that the government cannot use monetary and fiscal policies to close recessionary and inflationary gaps in the ways described in earlier chapters, because the models presented in those chapters do not recognize that the expectations of firms and individuals concerning their incomes, job prospects, sales, and other relevant variables are influenced by government policies. If firms and individuals formulate their expectations rationally, they will tend to frustrate the government's attempts to use activist stabilization policies.

According to real business cycle models, put forth by some new classical macroeconomists like Edward Prescott, business fluctuations are due largely to shifts in the aggregate supply curve. Among the most important factors shifting the aggregate supply curve are new products, new methods of production, new sources of raw materials, and good or bad weather. Real business cycle theorists tend to ignore monetary policy and believe that changes in real GDP result in changes in the money supply, rather than the other way around.

The new Keynesians, like the old Keynesians, assume that prices and wages tend to be rigid in the short run, with the result that the quantity of output, more than price, tends to adjust to changes in aggregate demand. But whereas the old Keynesians merely assumed that wages and prices are sticky, the new Keynesians have developed theories that help to explain why such wage and price stickiness can be expected, given the rational behavior of individuals and firms.

According to the new Keynesians, prices tend to be sticky because of menu costs (costs incurred by firms when they change prices), and wages tend to be sticky because of long-term labor contracts. Based on the theory of implicit contracts, they conclude that wages are set based on long-term considerations. (Responding to workers' aversion to risk, firms maintain relatively rigid wages.)

The debate over the pros and cons of policy activism has been going on for decades. Opponents of policy activism tend to believe that activist monetary and fiscal policies to stabilize the economy are likely to do more damage than good. They have often favored a rigid policy rule stipulating that the money supply should grow at a constant rate. Policy activists, while admitting that discretionary monetary and fiscal policy have sometimes been destabilizing, are much more optimistic about the efficacy of such policies in the future.

Concepts for Review

Keynesians	New Keynesians
Monetarists	Supply shocks
Supply-side economics	Rigid policy rule
Rational expectations	Discretionary policy
New classical	Feedback policy rule
macroeconomists	Menu costs
Real business cycle models	Implicit contracts

Completion Questions

1. According to the Keynesians, although the money supply has an important influence on GDP, its impact on the _____ is what in turn affects spending. The Keynesians are more inclined than the monetarists to use the level of _____ to measure whether money is tight or easy. To the monetarists, the change in the quantity of _____, not the level of _____ rates, is most important.

2. According to some of the leading (Keynesians, monetarists) _____, a rule stipulating that the _____ should grow steadily at a rate fixed somewhere between 4 and 5 percent per year would be the most effective way to regulate the economy.

3. According to real business cycle theories, output fluctuations are due predominantly to shifts in the aggregate supply curve. Among the factors causing shifts in this curve are new _____, new _____ of production, and good or bad _____.

4. According to the new classical macroeconomists, high rates of unemployment (are, are not) _____ evidence of a gap between actual and _____ output that can be reduced; instead, output fluctuations result from _____ errors.

True-False

_____ 1. During the 1940s, 1950s, and early 1960s, the Keynesian view was definitely predominant, both here and abroad. But, by the mid-1960s, it was being challenged seriously by the monetarists, led by Professor Milton Friedman and his supporters.

_____ 2. According to Keynesians, the velocity of money is more predictable than the multiplier.

_____ 3. Both the new classical macroeconomists and the new Keynesians often assume that the expectations of people and firms conform to the theory of rational expectations.

_____ 4. Real business cycle models, in contrast to new Keynesian models, assume that prices and wages are flexible and markets clear.

_____ 5. According to real business cycle theories, changes in real GDP tend to cause changes in the money supply, rather than the other way around.

_____ 6. According to the new classical macroeconomists, prices can be sticky because of the existence of menu costs.

_____ 7. The new classical macroeconomists believe that fluctuations in aggregate demand are due principally to erratic and unpredictable government policy.

_____ 8. According to Robert Lucas, people come to learn the way in which policy is made, and only unanticipated government policy changes can have a substantial effect on output or employment.

_____ 9. According to Lucas, excess unemployment is essentially voluntary.

_____ 10. Critics claim that the new classical macroeconomics neglects the inertia in wages and prices and is inconsistent with the evidence.

Multiple Choice

1. The reason why some leading monetarists favor a growth rate of M of 4 to 5 percent per year is that:

   a. this has been the rate of increase of M in the past.
   b. this has been the rate of increase of V in the recent past.
   c. this has been the average rate of increase of real output.
   d. this has been the average rate of increase of potential real output.
   e. none of the above.

2. According to the Keynesians:

   a. prices are relatively inflexible downward.
   b. the length of time required for the economy to get itself out of a severe recession would be very long.

c. business spending represents a substantial source of instability.
d. governments can be trusted to establish responsible economic policies.
e. all of the above.

3. Real business cycle theorists believe that:

a. supply shocks are important causes of business fluctuations.
b. prices and wages respond flexibly to changing economic conditions.
c. both business fluctuations and economic growth stem from factors that shift the long-run aggregate supply curve.
d. all of the above.
e. none of the above.

4. The new Keynesians believe that prices and/or wages tend to adjust slowly because of:

a. menu costs.
b. long-term contracts.
c. implicit contracts.
d. all of the above.
e. none of the above.

5. Milton Friedman's suggestion that the money supply be set so that it grows at a fixed, agreed-on percentage rate is a(n):

a. rigid policy rule.
b. feedback policy rule.
c. discretionary policy.
d. all of the above.
e. none of the above.

Discussion and Extension Questions

1. Do the monetarists agree that fiscal policy works as the Keynesians assert? If not, what are the differences between their views?

2. "Skeptics [of real business cycle models] doubt that any conceivable supply shock could explain why output fell one-third in the Great Depression of the 1930s." Do you agree? Why or why not?

3. Do you tend to agree with the policy activists or with their critics? Explain your own position on this issue.

4. Paul Volcker, former chairman of the Federal Reserve, in testimony before a congressional committee, "downplayed the significance of M-1 altogether, calling it a 'useful' measure rather than a firm guideline." Do you think that Volcker is a monetarist? Why or why not?

5. Assuming that you were a new classical macroeconomist, what policy recommendations would you make to stabilize the economy?

6. According to Franco Modigliani, "the most glaring flaw of the [new classical macroeconomics] . . . is its inconsistency with the evidence: if it were valid, deviations of unemployment from the natural rate would be small and transitory—in which case Keynes' *General Theory* would not have been written." What does he mean? Do you agree? Why or why not?

7. From the point of view of the new classical macroeconomics, criticize both the Keynesian and monetarist policy recommendations to stabilize the economy.

Problems

1. Suppose that the quantity of money demanded (M_d) depends on GDP and the interest rate (i) in the following way:

$$M_d = .4\text{GDP} - 2i,$$

where M_d and GDP are measured in billions of dollars and i is measured in percentage points.

   a. If GDP = $100 billion and i = 8, what is the quantity of money demanded?
   b. If the quantity of money demanded equals the quantity of money supplied when GDP = $100 billion and i = 8, what does velocity equal under these circumstances?
   c. Suppose that the monetary authorities increase the money supply from $24 billion to $30 billion, with the result that GDP increases to $110 billion and that the interest rate falls to 7 percent. What now is the quantity of money demanded? Does the quantity of money demanded equal the quantity of money supplied?
   d. Under the circumstances described in part c, what change, if any, occurs in the velocity of money?
   e. Suppose that the fiscal authorities carry out an expansionary fiscal policy, with the results that GDP increases to $115 billion and that the interest rate rises to 8 percent. The money supply remains at $30 billion. What now is the quantity of money demanded? Does the quantity of money demanded equal the quantity of money supplied?
   f. Under the circumstances described in part e, what change, if any occurs in the velocity of money?
   g. A Keynesian economist claims that velocity is not constant in this economy. Is he correct?
   h. A monetarist economist claims that velocity is predictable in this economy. Is she correct? If so, how can it be done?
   i. Why is it useful to try to predict the velocity of money?

2. In Muppetland, suppose that real output (Q) is related in the following way to the price level (P):

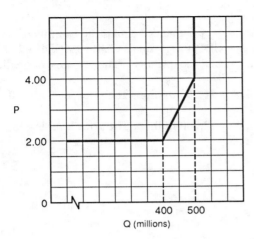

Q (millions)

Muppetland's leading economist says that velocity equals 5.

a. If the money supply is $270 million, what is (1) equilibrium nominal GDP, (2) the price level, (3) real output?

b. If the money supply increases to $400 million, what is (1) equilibrium nominal GDP, (2) the price level, (3) real output?

ANSWERS

Completion Questions
1. interest rate, interest rates, money, interest   2. monetarists, money supply
3. products, methods, weather   4. are not, potential, random forecasting

True-False
1. True   2. False   3. True   4. True   5. True   6. False   7. True   8. True
9. True   10. True

Multiple Choice
1. d   2. e   3. d   4. d   5. a

Problems
1. a. $24 billion.
   b.   4.17.
   c. $30 billion. Yes.

d. Velocity equals 3.67.
e. $30 billion. Yes.
f. Velocity equals 3.83.
g. Yes.
h. So long as the quantity of money demanded equals the quantity of money supplied, velocity (= GDP ÷ M_d) equals GDP ÷ (.4GDP − 2i).
i. Because if we know velocity and the quantity of money, we can predict nominal GDP.

2. a. Equilibrium nominal GDP is $1,350 million. The price level is 3.00. Real output is 450 million.
   b. Equilibrium nominal GDP is $2,000 million. The price level is 4.00. Real output is 500 million.

CASE 2

Promoting Technology and Economic Growth

COUNCIL OF ECONOMIC ADVISERS

Technological progress fuels economic growth. It creates new industries and reinvigorates old ones. It can enable small businesses to do high-quality design and manufacturing work that previously required the resources of big business. It can help big businesses achieve the speed, flexibility, and closeness to customers that once were a defining characteristic of small business. Technology helps to make our work force more productive and, in doing so, improves the Nation's standard of living. Every recent generation has seen its dreams turn into technological marvels, new products from new industries that have transformed the way we live and work: from the telephone, radio, airplanes, and x-rays, to television, xerography, computers, and magnetic resonance imaging equipment. Advances in technical know-how have accounted for at least one-quarter of our Nation's economic growth over the past half-century.

During the past two decades, powerful trends have altered the environment for American technology development. Commercial technology has become increasingly science-based and interdisciplinary. International competition has intensified as other nations have advanced in wealth and technological sophistication. The Nation's defense capability has become increasingly dependent on technologies developed and applied first in commercial markets. A microelectronics-based revolution in production has transformed the organization of office and factory work, increasing the need for a well-trained and flexible work force.

By the end of the 1980s, many analysts believed that these trends required a reexamination of the existing approaches of government and industry for supporting technology development and diffusion. Accordingly, in its first year the Administration has supported tax incentives for investments in research and development (R&D) and new businesses, liberalized export controls, shifted Federal resources toward basic research and civilian technology, invested in worker skills, and promoted defense conversion. In addition, the Administration's technology initiatives, such as the promotion of the National Information Infrastructure discussed above, the Partnership for a New Generation of Vehicles, and the creation of a Manufacturing Extension Partnership, rely on an alliance of government and industry. They also require rigorous attention to the economic rationales for cooperative efforts and then to the details of project design and assessment, to ensure that market failures are corrected, not made worse, by government action.

This article comes from the *Economic Report of the President* (Washington, D.C.: Government Printing Office, 1994, pp. 189–198).

Principles of Technology Policy

The Administration's technology initiatives aim to promote the domestic development and diffusion of growth- and productivity-enhancing technologies. They seek to correct market failures that would otherwise generate too little investment in R&D, with programs that avoid "government failure."

THE ECONOMICS OF APPROPRIABILITY

New technologies often fail to attract sufficient private sector investment because their technical risk is high or because of limited appropriability—that is, the new technologies create economic and social benefits beyond what the investment firms can capture for themselves. Indeed, despite intellectual property protection, the social returns to innovation have been estimated to exceed the private returns by between 35 and 60 percent.

The most important innovations generate spillover benefits for interconnected sectors, creating economic gains well beyond any that eventually accrue to their inventors. These innovations include risky "pathbreaking" technologies that pay off in the creation of new industries (or the transformation of existing industries), and lower risk "infratechnologies" that can enhance the productive performance of a broad spectrum of firms and industries but that receive low levels of investment because of barriers to appropriability and implementation. For example, the development of refrigerated steamships at the end of the nineteenth century increased the availability of perishable agricultural products throughout the world. Most of this benefit ultimately accrued to farmers and consumers rather than to the inventors of refrigerated steamships. Similarly, the principle of interchangeable parts in manufacturing, originally developed for the production of firearms, soon was adopted for use in the fabrication of clocks, hardware, sewing machines, and other manufactured products.

The appropriability problem is not limited to basic research, but frequently extends to so-called precommercial technology development and eventual commercial applications. Indeed, technological progress is full of feedbacks where developments downstream alter the course of behavior upstream, as well as the degree of ultimate market success. A sharp distinction between basic research and precommercial development activities is difficult to draw. Investments that are necessary to the utilization and adoption of research results—investments in information gathering, work force training, or the integration of new production equipment into automated systems—can also create spillover benefits that the investing firm cannot perfectly appropriate. In addition, new manufacturing processes that lower cost or improve quality may not be patentable, and new ideas embodied in computer software can often be imitated rapidly without violating the originator's intellectual property rights. In all of these cases, public actions can offset the effects of underinvestment by the private sector that is caused by limitations on appropriability.

AVOIDING "GOVERNMENT FAILURE"

The goal of technology policy is not to substitute the government's judgment for that of private industry in deciding which potential "winners" to back. Rather, the point is to correct a genuine and significant market failure—underinvestment in basic research and in precommercial R&D resulting from the divergence between private and social returns to those activities. A complementary goal is to design the technology investments that the government itself makes in public goods—national security, public health, education, a clean environment, an efficient transportation system—in ways that maximize the potential external benefits for the Nation's commercial technology base. In both cases, technology policy enhances the Nation's economic and social welfare.

Investments in R&D are risky. Like all risky investments, public or private, government-supported explorations sometimes drill dry holes—such as the efforts during the 1960s and 1970s to develop synthetic fuels, a supersonic transport, and a fast breeder reactor. Yet even research that never delivers an enormous economic payoff for itself often contributes useful technical knowledge and lessons for the future. And when the drilling strikes oil, as with government support of R&D for computers and integrated circuits, jet engines and airframes, and biotechnology and medical equipment, the initial gusher can generate an entire field of newly productive, wealth-enhancing, job-creating economic activity. For this reason, the success of government R&D policy must be measured by the rate of return on the entire portfolio of R&D investments supported by the public.

We can learn from both the gushers and the dry holes about how to design programs to promote investments in basic and precommercial R&D to maximize their prospects for success. Federal R&D investment programs leading to successful commercial products tend to share certain design features: They are insulated from the demands of distributional politics; they subject potential projects to rigorous technical and economic evaluation; and they recognize that product specifications must be developed with an eye toward manufacturability and a balance between product performance and cost that will be acceptable to commercial customers. Accordingly, the Administration's efforts to promote innovative technology contain design features that are meant to limit the possibility of "government failure" in the implementation of technology policy:

- To ensure that R&D funded by the government in cooperative ventures with the private sector has direct market applications, participating firms must bear a significant share of program costs. In most cases, the Administration's technology partnerships require that private firms cover at least 50 percent of the costs.
- To ensure that both the timing and content of government investments in technology-based infrastructure impart maximum leverage on industry's competitive efforts, research frameworks for collaborative R&D should be initiated and designed by private industry and should be closely coordinated with industry investment patterns.
- To insulate publicly supported R&D efforts from political pressures exerted on behalf of special interests, evaluations of competing R&D proposals should be conducted by independent experts in the relevant scientific, technological, and economic fields. Political considerations should not be allowed to influence a project's technical objectives, the location of R&D facilities, or the way that management of the project is structured.
- Investments in a broad array of technical fields, including materials sciences, manufacturing product and process technologies, biotechnology and biomedical

sciences, and telecommunications and computer-related technologies, should compete for a finite flow of funds. This competition will help to ensure that expanded Federal support for precommercial R&D does not get captured by the champions of any particular technology or by any particular set of firms.

- Government investments in basic and precommercial R&D should be reviewed while in progress to determine whether funding should continue. Such reviews are difficult because the success of an R&D project is often not apparent for many years, but rigorous assessments can nevertheless be made by independent expert panels at regular intervals.

A NEW APPROACH

An enduring American approach to promoting technology development and diffusion evolved just after the Second World War. The United States channeled public investment into basic research at universities and government laboratories, then supported the initial application of the results in products and production processes procured by public agencies. New technologies first developed for (and procured by) the Department of Defense, the Department of Energy, or the National Aeronautics and Space Administration (NASA), or supported by the National Science Foundation or the National Institutes of Health (NIH), would then diffuse, or "spin off," into commercial use. In this manner, the Federal Government supported the development and diffusion of jet aircraft and engines, semiconductor microelectronics, computers and computer-controlled machine tools, pharmaceuticals and biotechnology, advanced energy and environmental technologies, advanced materials, and a whole host of other commercially successful technologies.

This system worked well as long as military systems represented the leading-edge applications of new industrial technologies and as long as foreign competitors, with direct support from their own governments, did not pose a significant competitive challenge. In many areas of basic research supported outside the defense establishment, including biomedical research and the development of pharmaceuticals, biotechnology, and medical diagnostic devices, the system continues to work well. But the circumstances that allowed the United States to rely primarily on a defense-led model have changed. With the end of the cold war, demand for new defense systems is now less than it was. Commercial product spinoffs from military research have also diminished from their heyday of the 1950s and 1960s, and American companies face intense international competition from increasingly capable foreign firms. On the other hand, these changes also create exciting new opportunities: Innovative defense technologies are now more likely to emerge first in commercial products and production techniques, and American companies are taking advantage of expanded opportunities in foreign markets. Accordingly, the Administration's technology initiatives are shifting the composition of Federal R&D from military to civilian concerns, and the composition of military R&D toward the development of so-called dual-use technologies—those with applications to both military and commercial products.

The Administration's Technology Initiatives

The Administration's investments in growth- and productivity-enhancing technologies encompass a wide range of physical and human resource priorities. They finance basic research and leverage private funds for technology development and commercialization. They promote the diffusion and adoption of advanced manufacturing technologies by U.S. industry. They facilitate defense conversion by easing defense suppliers into civilian markets, focusing military R&D on dual-use technologies, and freeing the Pentagon to purchase commercial products and processes. They seek to promote the development of a national telecommunications infrastructure for the information age. Finally, they create partnerships with industry and academia to ensure that the government's investments to solve pressing problems in energy, transportation, and the environment simultaneously work to promote the Nation's economy and overall standard of living.

BASIC RESEARCH

The Administration worked with the Congress to increase budget authority for basic research in all categories to $13.8 billion in fiscal year 1994. This includes a 7.2-percent increase in the National Science Foundation's budget to a total of $1.9 billion. The National Science Foundation will continue to provide strong support for fundamental research critical to manufacturing, advanced materials, environmental technologies, and biotechnology. It has also doubled its support for modernizing academic research facilities and instrumentation. In addition, basic space science research is continuing at NASA, representing an investment of $1.9 billion in fiscal 1994. The Department of Defense has been appropriated $1.2 billion for basic research in fiscal 1994; the Department of Energy will support an additional $1.7 billion in basic research, in areas including materials science, chemical science, engineering and geoscience, high-energy nuclear physics, and nuclear fusion. Finally, the Administration continues to support basic research conducted through the National Institutes of Health, which account for over 40 percent of federally sponsored basic research. NIH is projected to spend nearly $6 billion for basic research in fiscal 1994, exceeding last year's level by almost $300 million (or 5 percent).

TECHNOLOGY

Through the Commerce Department's Advanced Technology Program and through the hundreds of cooperative research and development agreements that have been signed between private firms and researchers at many of America's 726 Federal laboratories, the government is investing in industrial projects to develop and to promote commercialization of technologies with high payoff potential. The Nation's antitrust laws have also been clarified to avoid discouraging beneficial private research collaborations.

The Advanced Technology Program (ATP). The ATP is administered by the Commerce Department's National Institute of Standards and Technology (NIST). In four competitions completed over the past 4 years, the ATP has made 89 awards to

66 companies and 23 joint ventures. The projects receiving awards have included ventures to develop a way to control personal computer programs through "natural language" instructions; a pen-based character-recognition system for the Chinese language, with the goal of enhancing software exports to Chinese-speaking companies; and a technology for preserving patients' bone marrow during chemotherapy.

The ATP is designed to avoid government failure. Government acts as the catalyst, but the ATP relies on industry to define and carry out its R&D projects. Independent expert panels select projects through rigorous competitions based on both technical and business merit. The ATP provides technology development funds under cooperative research agreements. It requires single-company applicants to pay their own indirect costs, and joint ventures to provide matching funds. In general, award recipients may patent inventions or copyright software developed under an ATP award, but the government retains a nonexclusive license.

The total of ATP awards plus private sector funds over the life of the first 89 awards amounts to over $500 million. The Administration has proposed to increase the ATP budget from $68 million in 1993 to $750 million in 1997, and $200 million has been appropriated for the program in 1994. In addition to announcing about 100 new awards to industry in fiscal 1994, the ATP will embark on a set of "strategic" program competitions. These competitions will focus on particular technology areas recommended by industry as having especially significant potential to generate large economic and social payoffs.

Cooperative Research at Government Laboratories. The Nation's 726 Federal laboratories, especially the three large, multiprogram nuclear weapons laboratories (Los Alamos and Sandia in New Mexico and Lawrence Livermore in California), offer a repository of vast technical expertise that can be leveraged to enhance the competitive performance of American industry. As part of its plan to alter the balance between military and civilian objectives in the Federal R&D budget, the Administration has authorized the weapons labs to redirect at least 10 to 20 percent of their defense program budgets to commercial technology-transfer activities with industry. The Department of Energy's 31 laboratories, which employ over 23,000 scientists and engineers and perform $6 billion in civilian and military research annually, already have in place over 650 cooperative research and development agreements (CRADAs) with private firms, totaling $1.4 billion in combined public and private funds. CRADAs are also used to structure public-private partnerships involving laboratories at NIST and the Department of Defense. A similar program is in place at NASA.

Using CRADAs, Federal laboratories have already begun or strengthened jointly financed collaborations with companies and industry consortia in a number of research and production prototyping projects. These have covered semiconductor production equipment, flat panel display technology, new technologies for textile manufacturing, the investigation of new polymer blends, biosensors, new aerospace alloys, and microscopic-sized machines known as microelectromechanical systems. These partnerships may begin a longer term process of redirecting the defense-oriented labs' missions toward civilian needs—ranging from the development of energy-efficient and environmentally sustainable industries to the invention of new medical, manufacturing, and transportation technologies—while utilizing the labs' expertise in such fields as high-performance computing, communications, and new materials.

Collaboration in Research and Development. Competition promotes R&D, but collaboration can also promote both research and the effective commercialization of research results. When firms have complementary skills or information, an R&D joint venture among them may speed the development and commercial adoption of a new technology. And when firms have similar skills or information, an R&D joint venture may avoid costly duplication of effort. Yet allowing collaboration in R&D risks facilitating undesirable cooperation in the firms' other activities. For example, it may make it easier to engage in price fixing or other anticompetitive practices in the sale of the products manufactured by the firms collaborating on research. This risk is small if collaboration is limited to early-phase R&D, however.

The Congress balanced these concerns in 1984 when it passed legislation guaranteeing that collaborative research would violate the antitrust laws only if the collaboration were found unreasonable. That legislation also provided that research joint ventures could register with the government and thereby limit their antitrust exposure to actual damages, rather than face the usual treble damage penalty for antitrust violations. Legislation enacted in 1993 extends these protections to production joint ventures, thereby removing a barrier to collaborative efforts to implement new manufacturing techniques and production processes. Because these aspects of the production process can be understood as research into product commercialization, this extension serves a purpose similar to that of the 1984 legislation.

DEVELOPMENT AND DIFFUSION OF ADVANCED MANUFACTURING TECHNOLOGY

Anecdotal examples abound of technologies developed in the United States, such as numerically controlled machine tools, that were commercially exploited first or more successfully abroad. These anecdotes point to market failures other than imperfect appropriability that also contribute to insufficient adoption and utilization of research results. For example, firms may face unnecessarily high transactions costs for obtaining information, and firms with good ideas but limited sources of collateral or internal finance may find themselves unable to raise funds in the capital markets.

The effort to commercialize a new technology often presents firms with an array of organizational challenges: New manufacturing processes and distribution channels must be developed, workers must be retrained, and new suppliers and perhaps even new customers must be identified. In meeting these challenges, firms develop a great deal of valuable information—from manufacturing know-how to marketing insights—some of which cannot be protected as intellectual property or trade secrets.

On the other hand, firms sometimes have difficulty gaining access to other types of technological know-how developed inside other companies and the ways different firms have met implementation challenges. Adoption of advanced manufacturing technology is typically a "systems" problem. Suppliers must be able to sell components that fit into complex automated production systems. Buyers must be assured of compatibility among machines, robots, transfer lines, and the like, or they will not adopt the technology.

To help remedy these market failures, and so promote more rapid and extensive commercialization and diffusion of important new technologies, the Administration is expanding NIST's Manufacturing Extension Partnership (MEP) program. Manufacturing Technology Centers (MTCs) form the backbone of the program. MTCs offer impartial advice to small and medium-sized manufacturers from people with extensive industrial experience. This advice is backed by hands-on technical assistance. MTCs will be linked among themselves to a set of smaller Manufacturing Outreach Centers (MOCs), geared to areas with smaller concentrations of industry. MOCs will be affiliated with technical colleges, vocational schools, and State technical assistance centers. Together MTCs and MOCs will help firms to identify, evaluate, install, adapt, and then commercially exploit appropriate advanced technology in their manufacturing and business operations. The Administration anticipates that 100 centers will be established nationwide by 1997, up from 7 at the outset of this Administration.

Linkages have also been formed between the MEP and other Federal agencies with roles to play in the delivery of technical assistance, work force training, and small business support services. These agencies include the Department of Energy, NASA, the Small Business Administration, and the Department of Labor. In addition, the Department of Energy dedicated over $400 million to advanced manufacturing-related technologies in fiscal 1993 and has under way or in negotiation more than 115 advanced manufacturing cooperative projects involving over 60 companies. One of these is the AMTEX Partnership, a model collaboration between the Department of Energy's national laboratories and the American textile industry. Finally, the deployment portion of the Administration's defense conversion Technology Reinvestment Project (discussed below) includes an additional $87 million for manufacturing extension programs.

Discussion Questions

1. Why should the government support research and development benefiting industry? In a capitalistic system, shouldn't firms pay for research and development if they benefit from it?

2. Is it realistic to believe that political factors can be expunged from the process by which researchers are chosen, fields are picked for support, and contracts are let to particular firms and individuals? Won't members of Congress fight to get R and D funds for their own constituents?

3. Why did the Clinton administration want to push military research and development toward the development of technologies with applications to both military and commercial products?

4. The Commerce Department's Advanced Technology Program relies on industry to define and carry out its R and D projects. Independent expert panels select the projects. What criteria should these panels use in making this selection? Why?

5. The Manufacturing Technology Centers offer impartial advice to small and medium-sized manufacturing firms from people with extensive industrial experience. How will one be able to tell whether such centers have been successful?

CHAPTER 15

The Business Firm: Organization,

Motivation, and Optimal Input

Decisions

Chapter Profile

There are three principal types of business firms: proprietorships, partnerships, and corporations. The corporation has many advantages over the other two—limited liability, unlimited life, and greater ability to raise large sums of money. Nonetheless, because the corporation also has disadvantages, many firms are not corporations.

As a first approximation, economists generally assume that firms attempt to maximize profits. In large part, this is because it is a close enough approximation to reality for many of the most important purposes of economics. Also, economists are interested in the theory of the profit-maximizing firm because it provides rules of behavior for firms that do want to maximize profits.

To summarize the characteristics of existing technology at a given point in time, the economist uses the concept of the production function, which shows the maximum output rate of a given commodity that can be achieved from any specified set of usage rates of inputs.

Inputs can be classified into two categories: fixed and variable. A fixed input is one whose quantity cannot be changed during the period of time under consideration. A variable input is one whose quantity can be changed during the relevant period. Whether an input is considered variable or fixed depends on the length of the period under consideration. The longer the period, the more inputs are variable, not fixed. The short run is defined as the period of time in which some of the firm's inputs (generally its plant and equipment) are fixed. The long run is the period of time in which all inputs are variable.

The average product of an input is the firm's total output divided by the amount of input used to produce this amount of output. The marginal product of an input is the addition to total output due to the addition of the last unit of input, the quantity of other inputs used being held constant.

The law of diminishing marginal returns states that if equal increments of an input are added (and the quantities of other inputs are held constant), the resulting increments of product will decrease beyond some point; that is, the marginal product of the input will diminish.

To minimize its costs, a firm must choose its input combination so that the marginal product of a dollar's worth of any one input equals the marginal product of a dollar's worth of any other input used. Put differently, the firm should combine inputs so that for every input used, the marginal product of the input is proportional to its price. As an illustration, we showed in the section "Exploring Further" how this sort of model can be used to determine the optimal combination of fertilizer and land in the production of Kansas corn.

Concepts for Review

Proprietorship
Partnership
Corporation
Profits
Technostructure
Input
Production function

Variable input
Short run
Long run
Average product
Marginal product
Law of diminishing marginal returns
Fixed input

Completion Questions

1. The _____ of an input is the change in total output due to the addition of the last unit of input.

2. The average product of an input is the firm's _____ divided by the _____.

3. A firm will minimize cost by combining inputs so that, for every input used, the _____ of the input is proportional to the input's _____.

4. Marginal product must exceed average product when the latter is (decreasing, increasing) _____, it must equal average product when the latter reaches a (maximum, minimum) _____, and it must be less than average product when the latter is (decreasing, increasing) _____ .

5. An inefficient combination of inputs is one that includes (less, more) _____ of at least one input, and as much of other inputs, as some other combination of inputs that can produce the same _____. Inefficient combinations generally (can, cannot) _____ minimize costs or maximize profits.

6. The firm will minimize cost by combining inputs in such a way that the (average product, marginal product) _____ of a dollar's worth of any one input equals the (average product, marginal product) _____ of a dollar's worth of any other input used.

7. If the marginal product of the first unit of labor equals 2 units of output, and if the marginal product of the second unit of labor equals 3 units of output, the total output produced with 2 units of labor equals _____ units of output. This answer will remain valid only if the quantities of other _____ are held constant and if there is no change in _____.

8. If the marginal product of the eighth unit of labor equals the marginal product of the ninth unit of labor, and if total output with 7 units of labor is 80 and total output with 9 units of labor is 90, the marginal product of the eighth unit of labor equals _____.

9. The average product of labor equals $3L$, where L is the number of units of labor employed per day. The total output produced per day if 4 units of labor are employed per day is _____. The total output produced per day if 5 units of labor are employed per day is _____. The marginal product of the fifth unit of labor employed per day is _____.

True-False

_____ 1. If the average product of labor equals $6/L$, where L is the number of units of labor employed per day, total output is the same regardless of how much labor is used per day.

_____ 2. If the third unit of labor adds more to output than the second unit of labor, the average product of labor when three units of labor are employed cannot equal the average product of labor when two units of labor are employed.

_____ 3. If the average product of labor equals 4 when the number of units of labor employed per day is between 1 and 6, the marginal product of labor also equals 4 when the amount of labor used is within this range.

_____ 4. If the average product of labor equals $5L$, where L is the number of units of labor employed per day, the law of diminishing marginal returns is violated.

_____ 5. In production processes, both the average product of the variable input and the marginal product usually rise, fall, and then rise again to infinity.

_____ 6. The law of diminishing marginal returns indicates that, if equal increments of an input are added (and quantities of others are held constant), the marginal product of the input will diminish beyond some point.

_____ 7. The long run refers to a period when all inputs are variable and none is fixed.

_____ 8. The average product of an input is the addition to total output due to the addition of the last unit of input, the quantity of other inputs used being held constant.

_____ 9. The marginal product curve intersects the average product curve when the latter is a maximum.

_____ 10. If technology changes, the law of diminishing marginal returns can predict the effect of an additional unit of input.

_____ 11. The law of diminishing marginal returns is not applicable to cases where there is a proportional increase in all inputs.

_____ 12. If the price of a unit of capital is equal to the price of a unit of labor, a cost-minimizing firm will choose a combination of inputs where the marginal product of capital minus the marginal product of labor equals zero.

_____ 13. If a nonzero amount of output results when no labor is used, this violates the law of diminishing marginal returns.

_____ 14. If the price of a unit of capital is double the price of a unit of labor, a cost-minimizing firm will choose a combination of inputs where the marginal product of capital minus the marginal product of labor equals the marginal product of labor.

_____ 15. If labor can be obtained free, a cost-minimizing firm will choose a combination of inputs where the marginal product of capital minus the marginal product of labor equals the marginal product of capital.

Multiple Choice

1. If the marginal product of capital is negative:

   a. more capital results in less output.
   b. more capital does not affect output.
   c. more capital increases output but at a decreasing rate.
   d. more capital increases output at an increasing rate.
   e. none of the above.

2. If labor is the only input, a cost-minimizing firm, if it can hire all the labor it wants at $8 per hour, and if it must produce 10 units of output per day, will:

   a. maximize the amount of output from the labor it hires.
   b. minimize the amount of labor used to produce the 10 units per day.
   c. operate at a point on the production function.
   d. all of the above.
   e. none of the above.

3. Between 1 and 2 units of labor, what is the marginal product of labor if the average product of labor is 20 bushels for 1 unit of labor and 25 bushels for 2 units of labor?

   a. 20 bushels
   b. 25 bushels
   c. 30 bushels
   d. 40 bushels
   e. 50 bushels

4. Which of the following statements about the law of diminishing marginal returns is *not* true?

   a. It is an empirical generalization.
   b. It assumes that technology remains fixed.
   c. No inputs are fixed in quantity.
   d. It must be possible to vary the proportions in which various inputs are used.
   e. It holds in both agriculture and industry.

5. Based on its production function alone, a firm can determine:

   a. what input combination to use.
   b. what amount of output to produce.
   c. what price to charge.
   d. all of the above.
   e. none of the above.

6. Firm A is run by a big-time spender who wants to maximize the amount that he produces, regardless of the amount that it costs. Firm A should:

   a. increase its employment of labor indefinitely.
   b. increase its employment of capital indefinitely.
   c. increase its employment of labor until the marginal product of labor is zero.
   d. increase its employment of capital until the marginal product of capital is zero.
   e. both (a) and (b).
   f. both (c) and (d).

7. If the average product of labor equals $4 + \sqrt{L}$, where L is the amount of labor employed per day:

    a. labor is always subject to diminishing marginal returns.

    b. labor is subject to diminishing marginal returns only when L is greater than 4.

    c. labor is not subject to diminishing returns.

    d. labor is not subject to diminishing returns when L is greater than 4.

    e. none of the above.

Discussion and Extension Questions

1. "Any fool knows that a firm should not operate at a point where there are rising marginal returns." Comment and evaluate.

2. Suppose that capital and labor are a firm's only inputs. If the price of capital is held constant, how can we determine how many units of labor the firm will hire at various prices of labor, if the output of the firm is held constant? Show that the amount of labor that the firm will hire is inversely related to the price of labor.

3. Is the production function for an auto firm the same in the long run as in the short run? Why or why not?

4. Is General Motors' production function the same as Ford's? Is General Motors' production function the same as the production function of an automobile manufacturer in Argentina? Explain.

5. Do firms have detailed and reliable information concerning the quantity of output that they will receive from each and every combination of inputs? Or do they have such information only concerning those input combinations that are close to those that they have used or experimented with? Explain.

6. Do firms take their production functions as given, or do they engage in various kinds of activities to alter their production functions? If the latter is the case, what are some names commonly used to designate activities of this sort? Give some examples of cases where firms altered their production functions.

7. Is it commonly true that activities carried out by one firm alter another firm's production function? If so, is this commonly true even though the firms are in different industries? Explain, and give examples to buttress your answer.

Problems

1. Suppose that the production function for a 1-acre wheat farm is as follows:

Number of units of labor	Bushels of wheat produced per year
1	50
2	90
3	120
4	145
5	165

   a.   What is the average product of labor when 1 unit of labor is used?

   b.   What is the marginal product of labor when between 2 and 3 units of labor are used?

   c.   Does the law of diminishing marginal returns seem to hold? Why or why not?

2. Suppose that the production function for a car wash is as follows:

Hours of labor per day	Cars washed per day	Average product of labor		Marginal product of labor
0	0	_____		
1	2	_____		_____
2	5	_____		_____
3	7	_____		_____
4	8	_____		_____

   a.   Fill in the blanks in the table above.

   b.   Why don't we compute the average product of labor when there are zero hours of labor?

3. Suppose that the marginal product of labor is as shown below:

Quantity of labor per day		Marginal product of labor	Total output per day
0		3	0
1		5	—
2		8	—
3		—	—
4		2	23
5			—

   a.   Fill in the blanks.

b. Does this case conform to the law of diminishing marginal returns? Why or why not?

4. Suppose that the average product of capital is as shown below:

Quantity of capital used per day	Average product of capital		Marginal product of capital
1	3		_____
2	8		_____
3	8		_____
4	6		_____
5	4		

a. Fill in the blanks.
b. What is the maximum amount of capital that this firm will use per day? Why?

5. The average product of labor equals 6, regardless of how much labor is used.

a. What is the marginal product of the first unit of labor?
b. What is the marginal product of the fiftieth unit of labor?
c. By how much will output increase if labor is increased by 200 units?
d. By how much will output fall if labor is reduced by 100 units?
e. Does this case conform to the law of diminishing marginal returns? Why or why not?
f. Does this case seem realistic? Why or why not?

6. A firm uses two inputs, labor and capital. The price of capital is $5 per unit; the price of labor is $7 per unit; and the marginal product of capital is 15.

a. Is the firm minimizing cost if the marginal product of labor is 20? Why or why not?
b. If the firm is not minimizing cost, should it use more or less labor relative to capital? Why?
c. If the marginal product of labor is 23, is the firm minimizing cost? Why or why not?
d. If the firm is not minimizing cost, should it use more or less labor relative to capital? Why?
e. If the marginal product of labor is 21, is the firm minimizing cost? Why or why not?

7. A firm has two plants, A and B. Both produce the same product. The price of capital is the same at both plants, and the price of labor is the same at both plants. The marginal product of labor is 6 at plant A and 15 at plant B.

a. Can you tell whether each plant is minimizing cost? Why or why not?
b. If the marginal product of capital is 20 at plant A and 40 at plant B, is each plant minimizing cost? Why or why not?

    c.   If the marginal product of capital is 40 at plant A, what must the marginal product of capital be at plant B, if each plant is minimizing cost?

    d.   If the marginal product of capital is 40 at point A, and each plant is minimizing cost, can you tell what the price of capital and the price of labor are?

    e.   If the marginal product of capital is 40 at plant A, what is the ratio of the price of labor to the price of capital?

ANSWERS

Completion Questions

1. marginal product   2. total output, quantity of input used   3. marginal product, price   4. increasing, maximum, decreasing   5. more, output, cannot   6. marginal product, marginal product   7. 5, inputs, technology   8. 5   9. 48, 75, 27

True-False

1. True   2. False   3. True   4. True   5. False   6. True   7. True   8. False   9. True   10. False   11. True   12. True   13. False   14. True   15. True

Multiple Choice

1. a   2. d   3. c   4. c   5. e   6. f   7. a

Problems

1. a. 50 bushels of wheat per unit of labor.

    b. 30 bushels of wheat.

    c. Yes, because as more labor is used, the marginal product of labor declines.

2. a.

Average product of labor	Marginal product of labor
—	
2	2
2 1/2	3
2 1/3	2
2	1

b. Because it would mean dividing zero by zero, since both output and labor are zero.

3. a.

Marginal product of labor		Total product per day
		0
3		
		3
5		
		8
8		
		16
7		
		23
2		
		25

b. Yes, because marginal product eventually falls as more labor is applied.

4. a.

Marginal product
of capital

13
8
0
−4

b.   3 units, because capital's marginal product is not positive when more capital is used.

5. a. 6.
   b. 6.
   c. 1,200.
   d. 600.
   e. No, because the marginal product of labor is the same regardless of how much labor is used.
   f. No, because it violates the law of diminishing marginal returns.

6. a. No, because the ratio of the marginal product of capital to its price does not equal the ratio of the marginal product of labor to its price.
   b. It should use less labor because the ratio of labor's marginal product to its price is lower than the ratio of capital's marginal product to its price.
   c. No, for the same reason as in part a.
   d. It should use more labor because the ratio of labor's marginal product to its price is higher than the ratio of capital's marginal product to its price.
   e. Yes, because the ratio of labor's marginal product to its price equals the ratio of capital's marginal product to its price.

7. a. You cannot tell because not enough information is given.
   b. No, because, since the prices of capital and labor are the same at both plants, the ratio of the marginal product of labor to the marginal product of capital must be the same at both plants, if each plant is minimizing cost.
   c. 100.
   d. No.
   e. 3/20.

CHAPTER 16

Getting Behind the Demand and

Supply Curves

Chapter Profile

Utility is a number that represents the level of satisfaction derived by the consumer from a particular market basket. Market baskets with higher utilities are preferred over market baskets with lower utilities.

The model of consumer behavior recognizes that preferences alone do not determine the consumer's actions. Choices are dictated by the size of the consumer's money income and the nature of commodity prices. These factors, as well as the consumer's preferences, determine choice.

If consumers maximize utility, their income is allocated among commodities so that for every commodity purchased, the marginal utility of the commodity is proportional to its price. In other words, the marginal utility of the last dollar spent on each commodity is made equal for all commodities purchased.

The individual demand curve shows the quantity of a good demanded by a particular consumer at various prices of the good. The individual demand curve for practically all goods slopes downward and to the right. Its location depends on the consumer's income and tastes and the prices of other goods.

To derive the market demand curve, we obtain the horizontal sum of all the individual demand curves of the people in the market. Since individual demand curves for a commodity almost always slope downward to the right, it follows that market demand curves too almost always slope downward to the right.

The cost of a certain course of action is the value of the best alternative course of action that could have been pursued instead. This is the doctrine of opportunity, or alternative, cost.

Three kinds of total cost functions are important in the short run—total fixed cost, total variable cost, and total cost. In addition, there are three kinds of average cost functions (corresponding to each of the total cost functions)—average fixed cost, average variable cost, and average total cost.

Marginal cost—the addition to total cost due to the addition of the last unit of output—is of enormous significance in the firm's decision-making process. Because of the law of diminishing marginal returns, marginal cost tends to increase beyond some output level.

The firm's long-run average cost curve shows the minimum average cost of producing each output level when any desired type or scale of plant can be built. The shape of the long-run average cost curve is determined in part by whether there are increasing, decreasing, or constant returns to scale.

Suppose that a firm increases the amount of all inputs by the same percentage. If output increases by more than this percentage, this is a case of increasing returns to scale. If output increases by less than this percentage, this is a case of decreasing returns to scale. If output increases by this same percentage, this is a case of constant returns to scale.

Concepts for Review

Model of consumer behavior	Total fixed cost
Marginal utility	Total variable cost
Law of diminishing marginal utility	Total cost
Equilibrium market basket	Average fixed cost
Individual demand curve	Average variable cost
Opportunity cost	Average total cost
Alternative cost	Marginal cost
Implicit costs	Long-run average cost function
Cost functions	Increasing returns to scale
Short run	Decreasing returns to scale
Long run	Constant returns to scale

Completion Questions

1. Economists assume that the consumer attempts to _____ utility.

2. If the prices of goods X and Y are both $2 per unit, and the marginal utility of good X is twice that of good Y, the consumer should buy (less, more) _____ of good X and (less, more) _____ of good Y.

3. If average fixed cost is triple average variable cost, and if average total cost is $40, average fixed cost equals _____ and average variable cost equals _____. If marginal cost equals $20, average variable cost is (rising, falling) _____, and average total cost is (rising, falling) _____.

4. Total cost at a given output is the sum of _____ and _____.

5. Average fixed cost is the firm's total fixed cost divided by its _____.

6. The addition to total cost resulting from the addition of the last unit of output is called _____.

7. Total fixed cost is the total expenditure per period of time by the firm for

   _____ inputs. Since the quantity of the _____ inputs is unvarying (by definition), the total fixed cost will be (the same, different) _____ for various levels of the firm's output. Among the firm's fixed costs in the short run are _____ taxes and _____ on bonds issued in the past.

8. Total variable cost is the total expenditure per period of time on

   _____ inputs. Due to the law of diminishing marginal returns, total variable cost (decreases, increases) _____ first

   at a(n) (decreasing, increasing) _____ rate, then at a(n)

   (decreasing, increasing) _____ rate.

9. Average total cost is total cost divided by _____. It equals

   average _____ cost plus average _____ cost; and beyond a point, it increases as output _____ because of the law of diminishing marginal returns.

10. Marginal cost is the addition to total cost resulting from the _____

    ___ of the last unit of output. Beyond a point, it _____ as output increases because of the law of diminishing marginal returns.

11. If the marginal cost of producing the first unit of output is $20, if the marginal cost of producing the second unit of output is $25, and if the marginal cost of producing the third unit of output is $30, the total variable

    cost of producing 3 units of output is _____. The average

    variable cost of producing two units of output is _____.

    Average variable cost (rises, falls) _____ when output increases from 1 to 3 units.

12. If the average fixed cost of producing 10 units of output is $10, the average

    fixed cost of producing 20 units is _____. If the marginal cost of each of the first 20 units of output is $5, the average variable cost of

    producing 20 units is _____. And the average total cost of

    producing 20 units is _____.

True-False

_____ 1. If there are diminishing marginal returns from the variable input, total variable cost will ultimately increase at an increasing rate.

_____ 2. If marginal cost always increases with increases in output, so must average variable cost always increase with increases in output.

_____ 3. If average variable cost always equals $10 when output is less than 100 units, marginal cost is less than $10 when output is in this range.

_____ 4. There is sometimes a marked difference between social and private costs of producing a given commodity.

_____ 5. Average fixed cost must increase in the short run with increases in output.

_____ 6. Since price is not usually influenced by amount sold, total revenue is equal to output.

_____ 7. Average cost is at a minimum only when it is lower than marginal cost.

_____ 8. If a payment is made to a supplier (other than the firm's owner), this is an explicit cost.

_____ 9. The total cost curve differs by a constant amount (equal to total fixed cost) from the total variable cost curve.

_____ 10. Cost functions are used very extensively by firms and other groups to estimate the effect of the sales rate on costs.

_____ 11. One of the principal determinants of the shape of the long-run average cost function is the law of diminishing marginal returns.

_____ 12. In the long run a firm's fixed costs in industries like steel and autos may amount to tens of millions of dollars per year.

_____ 13. When a firm is experiencing diminishing marginal returns to its variable input, marginal cost is increasing.

Multiple Choice

1. Suppose that Mary Murphy's total utility from various quantities of good X and good Y are as follows:

Good X			Good Y	
Quantity	Total utility		Quantity	Total utility
0	0		0	0
1	10		1	30
2	30		2	50
3	40		3	60
4	45		4	65
5	48		5	67
6	50		6	68

For good X, diminishing marginal utility occurs:

    a.   at some, but not all quantities consumed.
    b.   at quantities exceeding 2.
    c.   at larger quantities than those where increasing marginal utility occurs.
    d.   all of the above.
    e.   none of the above.

2. In the previous question, the price of good X equals the price of good Y, and Ms. Murphy's income allows her to buy 6 units of good X. Under these circumstances, her optimal market basket is:

    a.   4 units of good X and 2 units of good Y.
    b.   3 units of good X and 3 units of good Y.
    c.   2 units of good X and 4 units of good Y.
    d.   5 units of good X and 1 unit of good Y.
    e.   none of the above.

3. In question 1, if good X's price is $5, the marginal utility of the last dollar spent on good X is 4 if Ms. Murphy consumes:

    a.   1 unit of good X and 1 unit of good Y.
    b.   2 units of good X and 2 units of good Y.
    c.   3 units of good X and 3 units of good Y.
    d.   all of the above.
    e.   none of the above.

4. In question 1, if good X's price is $5 and good Y's price is $10, and Ms. Murphy has $35 to spend on good X and good Y combined, she should purchase:

    a.   a market basket where the marginal utility of the last dollar spent on good X equals 2.
    b.   2 units of good Y and 3 units of good X.
    c.   a market basket where the marginal utility of the last dollar spent on good Y equals 2.
    d.   all of the above.
    e.   none of the above.

5. John Jones has 8 hours to spend during which he can either play tennis or read. The marginal utility he obtains from an hour of reading is 8 utils. The total utility he obtains from 1, 2, 3, 4, and 5 hours of tennis is as follows:

Hours	Total utility
1	20
2	33
3	40
4	40
5	35

If he maximizes utility (and if he can allocate only an integer number of hours to each activity), he will spend:

a. 3 hours playing tennis and 5 hours reading.
b. 2 hours playing tennis and 6 hours reading.
c. 4 hours playing tennis and 4 hours reading.
d. 1 hour playing tennis and 7 hours reading.
e. none of the above.

6. Firms A and B have identical total variable cost functions, but firm A's total fixed costs are $10,000 per month higher than firm B's.

a. The two firms have identical marginal cost curves.
b. Firm A's marginal cost curve is parallel to, but higher than, firm B's marginal cost curve.
c. Firm A's marginal cost curve is parallel to, but lower than, firm B's marginal cost curve.
d. Firm A's marginal cost curve is higher than that of firm B.
e. None of the above.

7. Suppose that firm C's total costs per month equal $50,000 + $10Q, where Q is the number of units of output produced per month. If firm C produces 100 units of output per month, its average fixed cost and average variable cost are:

a. $500 and $20.
b. $510 and $10.
c. $490 and $10.
d. $500 and $10.
e. none of the above.

8. Under the circumstances described in the previous question, increases in output result in:

a. decreases in average total cost and no change in marginal cost.
b. decreases in average variable cost and no change in average total cost.
c. decreases in average fixed cost and increases in average variable cost.
d. decreases in average fixed cost and increases in marginal cost.
e. none of the above.

9. If marginal cost is less than average cost, then with increased inputs the average cost of production will tend to:

a. rise.
b. drop.
c. stay the same.
d. none of the above.
e. all of the above.

10. In measuring long-run cost functions, it has generally been found that in most industries for which we have data:

    a. the long-run average cost curve tends to be L-shaped.
    b. the marginal cost tends to be constant at all output levels above zero.
    c. the total, average total, and marginal cost functions tend to be W-shaped.
    d. the shape of the long-run average cost curve is influenced by fixed costs.
    e. long-run average costs increase at all output levels.

Discussion and Extension Questions

1. The State of Virginia reimburses its employees when personal cars are used for state business. What costs should the state regard as the relevant ones? Why?

2. Universities frequently ask for student opinion about instructors and courses. The usual method is to distribute a questionnaire in class toward the end of a term. What are the costs of such programs? Be sure to think through what economists mean by costs. Try to formulate an actual dollar cost at your institution. Do you think such surveys are worth the costs?

3. If a large increase in the demand for economists by business firms and governmental agencies increases the salaries of such people, how can one also say that it has increased the cost of having an economist at a university?

4. "Statistical studies have shown that total cost is generally a linear function of output. This has embarrassed some economists, who insist that marginal cost must rise. In fact, marginal cost does not rise as output increases." Discuss and evaluate.

5. Consulting firm X claims that the minimum point on the long-run average cost curve occurs at an output level of 1,000 tons of output per week in a certain industry. As evidence for this claim, they say that firms of this size reap the biggest profits. Is this conclusive evidence? Why or why not?

6. "The concept of marginal cost is a purely academic concept. In the real world, no one can possibly tell what the value of marginal cost is." Comment and evaluate.

7. What is the cost of a certain course of action? Be specific.

8. Why does the marginal cost curve intersect both the average variable cost curve and the average total cost curve at their minimum points? Can there be cases where this is not true?

9. Suppose that two firms have exactly the same marginal cost curve, but their average fixed cost curve is not the same. Will their average variable cost curve be the same?

10. According to the *New York Times*, the cost of producing a barrel of oil from shale was thought by experts to be about $4.40 in 1972, about $10 in 1978, and about $25 in 1979. What factors can account for such great increases? Did productivity decrease in the industry? Did input prices change?

Problems

1. Suppose that the Chicago plant of the Bolton Press Company has the following cost structure: (1) its fixed costs are $1,000 per month; (2) its variable costs are shown below.

   a. Fill in the blanks indicated below:

Output (presses per month)	Total fixed cost (dollars)	Total variable cost (dollars)	Total cost (dollars)
0	_____	0	_____
1	_____	500	_____
2	_____	1,000	_____
3	_____	2,000	_____
4	_____	3,500	_____
5	_____	5,000	_____

   b. Fill in the blanks below. These blanks indicate the average cost functions of the Chicago plant of the Bolton Press Company.

Output (presses per month)	Average fixed cost (dollars)	Average variable cost (dollars)	Average total cost (dollars)
1	_____	_____	_____
2	_____	_____	_____
3	_____	_____	_____
4	_____	_____	_____
5	_____	_____	_____

c.   Fill in the blanks below:

Output (presses per month)	Marginal cost (dollars)
0 to 1	_____
1 to 2	_____
2 to 3	_____
3 to 4	_____
4 to 5	_____

2. Suppose that the Wilson Press Company's short-run total cost function is as follows:

Output (number of units per year)	Total cost (dollars per year)
0	20,000
1	20,100
2	20,200
3	20,300
4	20,500
5	20,800

a.   What are the firm's total fixed costs?
b.   What are its total variable costs when it produces 4 units per year?
c.   What is the firm's marginal cost when between 4 and 5 units are produced per year?
d.   Does marginal cost increase beyond some output level? Why?

3. Farm A is a profit maximizing, perfectly competitive producer of wheat. It produces wheat using 1 acre of land (price = $1,000) and varying inputs of labor (price = $500 per person-month). The production function is as follows:

Number of person-months (per month)	Output per month (in truckloads)
0	0
1	1
3	2
7	3
12	4
18	5
25	6

Show that the production of Farm A is subject to increasing marginal cost.

4. Suppose that you are given the production function, the price of the variable input, and the total fixed costs of the ABC Company. These data are shown below. Fill in the blanks.

Number of units of variable input	Number of units of output produced	Average product	Marginal product	Price of unit of variable input	Total variable cost	Average variable cost	Total fixed cost	Total cost	Average total cost	Marginal cost
							(dollars)			
0	0	—		2	—	—	100		—	—
1	4	—	>—	2	—	—	100		—	—	>—
2	9	—	>—	2	—	—	100		—	—	>—
3	15	—	>—	2	—	—	100		—	—	>—
4	22	—	>—	2	—	—	100		—	—	>—
5	30	—	>—	2	—	—	100		—	—	>—
6	37	—	>—	2	—	—	100		—	—	>—
7	43	—	>—	2	—	—	100		—	—	>—
8	48	—	>—	2	—	—	100		—	—	>—
9	52	—	>—	2	—	—	100		—	—	>—

5. A firm can build plants of three types: D, E, and F. The short-run average cost curve with each type is given below:

Type D		Type E		Type F	
Output	Average cost (dollars)	Output	Average cost (dollars)	Output	Average cost (dollars)
20	10	80	6	140	3.00
40	8	100	4	160	2.00
60	6	120	2	180	0.50
80	4	140	1	200	0.40
100	6	160	1	220	0.75

a. Draw the firm's long-run average cost curve in the graph below.

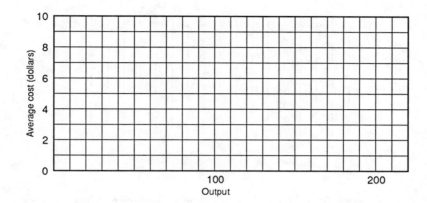

b. What is the minimum price at which the firm will stay in the industry?

6. Firm S hires a consultant to estimate its long-run total cost function. The consultant, after a long study, concludes that for firm S long-run cost equals $2 million + $4 × Q, where Q is annual output.

   a. What does this equation imply about the long-run total cost of producing nothing? Is this reasonable? Why or why not?
   b. What is the minimum value of long-run average cost?
   c. What size of plant results in the minimum value of long-run average cost? Is this reasonable? Why or why not?

7. Firm P's total cost curve is shown below:

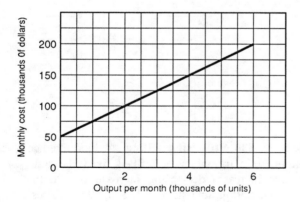

a. Draw the firm's marginal cost function in the graph below.

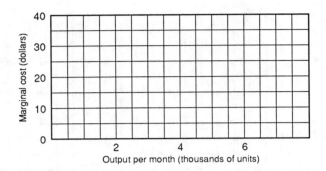

b. Suppose that it is impossible for firm P to produce more than 6,000 units of output per month. What is marginal cost at outputs above 6,000?

8. Based on the graph in the previous problem, fill in the blanks in the table below for firm P.

Output (thousands)	Average fixed cost (dollars)	Average variable cost (dollars)	Average total cost (dollars)
1	_____	_____	_____
2	_____	_____	_____
3	_____	_____	_____
4	_____	_____	_____
5	_____	_____	_____
6	_____	_____	_____

ANSWERS

Completion Questions

1. maximize   2. more, less   3. $30, $10, rising, falling   4. total fixed cost, total variable cost   5. output   6. marginal cost   7. fixed, fixed, the same, property, interest   8. variable, increases, decreasing, increasing   9. output, fixed, variable, increases   10. addition, increases   11. $75, $22.50, rises   12. $5, $5, $10

True-False
1. True 2. True 3. False 4. True 5. False 6. False 7. False 8. True
9. True 10. True 11. False 12. False 13. True

Multiple Choice
1. d 2. b 3. b 4. d 5. b 6. a 7. d 8. a 9. b 10. a

Problems

1. a.

Total fixed cost (dollars)	Total cost (dollars)
1,000	1,000
1,000	1,500
1,000	2,000
1,000	3,000
1,000	4,500
1,000	6,000

b.

Average fixed cost (dollars)	Average variable cost (dollars)	Average total cost (dollars)
1,000	500	1,500
500	500	1,000
333	667	1,000
250	875	1,125
200	1,000	1,200

c.

Marginal cost (dollars)
500
500
1,000
1,500
1,500

2. a. $20,000.
   b. $500.
   c. $300.
   d. Yes. The law of diminishing marginal returns.

3. Since the services of each person cost $500 per month, the total variable cost of each output level is (per month):

Output	Total variable cost (dollars)
0	0
1	500
2	1,500
3	3,500
4	6,000
5	9,000
6	12,500

Thus marginal cost is $500 between 0 and 1 units of output, $1,000 between 1 and 2 units of output, and so forth. Clearly, marginal cost increases as output increases.

4.

Average product	Marginal product	Total variable cost	Average variable cost	Total cost	Average total cost	Marginal cost
				(dollars)		
—		0	—	100	—	
4	4	2	1/2	102	25 1/2	0.50
4 1/2	5	4	4/9	104	11 5/9	0.40
5	6	6	6/15	106	7 1/15	0.33
5 1/2	7	8	8/22	108	4 10/11	0.29
6	8	10	1/3	110	3 2/3	0.25
6 1/6	7	12	12/37	112	3 1/37	0.29
6 1/7	6	14	14/43	114	2 28/43	0.33
6	5	16	1/3	116	2 20/48	0.40
5 7/9	4	18	18/52	118	2 14/52	0.50

5. a.

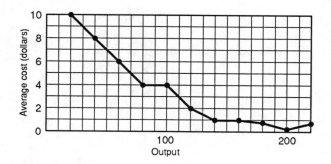

b. $0.40.
6. a. It implies it equals $2 million. No, because there are no fixed costs in the long run.
   b. $4.
   c. An infinite size of plant. No, because one would expect that eventually the long-run average cost function would turn up.
7. a.

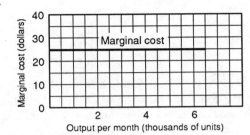

Output per month (thousands of units)

   b. Infinite.
8.

Average fixed cost (dollars)	Average variable cost (dollars)	Average total cost (dollars)
50	25	75
25	25	50
16 2/3	25	41 2/3
12 1/2	25	37 1/2
10	25	35
8 1/3	25	33 1/3

CHAPTER 17

Market Demand and Price

Elasticity

Chapter Profile

The market demand curve, which is the relationship between the price of a commodity and the amount of the commodity demanded in the market, is one of the most important and frequently used concepts in economics. The shape and position of a product's market demand curve depend on consumers' tastes, consumer income, the price of other goods, and the number of consumers in the market.

The price elasticity of demand, defined as the percentage change in quantity demanded resulting from a 1 percent change in price, measures the sensitivity of the amount demanded to changes in price. Whether a price increase results in an increase or decrease in the total amount spent on a commodity depends on the price elasticity of demand.

The market demand curve for a commodity is not the same as the demand curve for the output of a single firm that produces the commodity, unless the industry is composed of only one firm. In general, the demand curve for the output of a single firm will be more elastic than the market demand curve for the commodity. Indeed, if there are many firms selling a homogeneous commodity, the individual firm's demand curve becomes horizontal.

The income elasticity of demand, defined as the percentage change in quantity demanded resulting from a 1 percent increase in total money income, measures the sensitivity of the amount demanded to changes in total income. A commodity's income elasticity of demand may be positive or negative. Luxury items are generally assumed to have higher income elasticities of demand than necessities.

The cross elasticity of demand, defined as the percentage change in the quantity demanded resulting from a 1 percent change in the price of another commodity, measures the sensitivity of the amount demanded to changes in the price of another commodity. If the cross elasticity of demand is positive, two commodities are substitutes; if it is negative, they are complements.

*American agriculture has been plagued by relatively low incomes. Until 1973, the demand for farm products grew slowly, while rapid technological change meant that the people and resources currently in agriculture could supply more and more farm products. Because people and resources did not move out of agriculture as rapidly as the price system dictated, farm incomes tended to be relatively low.

---

*The starred items pertain to material covered in the section "Exploring Further."

*In response to political pressures from the farm blocs, the government set in motion a series of programs to aid farmers. A cornerstone of these programs was the concept of parity, which said that the prices farmers receive should increase at the same rate as the prices of the goods and services farmers buy. The government instituted price supports to keep farm prices above their equilibrium level. But since the support prices exceeded the equilibrium prices, there was a surplus of the commodities that the government had to purchase and store. To help reduce these surpluses, the government tried to restrict the output of farm products and expand the demand for them.

*In 1973, farm prices increased greatly, due partly to very great increases in foreign demand for U.S. agricultural products. By 1975, many people felt that American agriculture no longer was suffering from over-capacity. But subsequently farmers complained bitterly of low prices and their need for government assistance. In the early 1990s optimism began to spread throughout many parts of agriculture, although many observers were concerned about government's large role in farming.

Concepts for Review

Market demand curve
Price elasticity of demand
Arc elasticity of demand
Price elastic
Price inelastic
Unitary elasticity

Income elasticity of demand
Cross elasticity of demand
Substitutes
Complements
Parity

Completion Questions

1. When income increases from $80 billion to $81 billion, the quantity demanded of good X increases from 3,000 to 3,050. The income elasticity of demand for good X equals _____. When computing the income elasticity of demand, the price of good X is held _____.

2. When the price of good X rises from $2.00 to $2.10, the quantity demanded of good X falls from 3,000 to 2,800. The price elasticity of demand for good X equals _____. The demand for good X is (elastic, inelastic) _____.

3. The total amount spent on a good is not affected by its price if the price elasticity of demand equals _____. The total quantity demanded of a good is not affected by its price if the price elasticity of demand equals _____.

*The starred items pertain to material covered in the section "Exploring Further."

4. If the government imposes a $1 tax on a commodity, it will obtain the most revenue from the tax if the commodity's price elasticity of demand equals _____. The largest burden of the tax is borne by consumers if the price elasticity of demand equals _____.

5. Whether a price cut results in an increase in the total amount spent on a commodity depends on the _____.

6. The total amount spent on a commodity is the _____ times _____.

7. If the demand for a commodity is price inelastic, then the price elasticity of demand is _____.

8. The income elasticity of demand is the percentage change in the quantity demanded resulting from _____ increase in total _____.

9. If the cross elasticity of demand is positive, two commodities are _____.

10. The demand for a commodity is _____ when the price increase or decrease results in no difference in the total amount spent on the commodity.

11. The _____ is the percentage change in quantity demanded resulting from a 1 percent change in price.

12. During a (long, short) _____ period, demand for a nondurable good is likely to be more sensitive to price than over a (long, short) _____ one. The longer the period, the (easier, harder) _____ it is for consumers to substitute one good for another.

13. The demand curve for the output of a particular firm is generally (less, more) _____ price elastic than the market demand curve for the commodity, because the products of other firms in the industry are close (substitutes, complements) _____ for the product of this firm.

True-False

_____ 1. An increase in the price of fishing licenses will reduce the quantity of fishing poles demanded.

_____ 2. An increase in the subway fare in Philadelphia will increase the ridership on buses in Philadelphia.

_____ 3. Holding constant the demand curve of a perfectly competitive firm, the total amount spent on the firm's product is proportional to the number of units of output it produces and sells.

_____ 4. The demand for an appendectomy is likely to be less price elastic than the demand for aspirin.

_____ 5. If the price elasticity of demand of product Y equals infinity, and if the government imposes a tax of $1 per unit on product Y, none of the tax will be shifted to consumers.

_____ 6. If the quantity demanded of product Z falls by 5 units whenever the price of product Z increases by 1 dollar, the price elasticity of demand for product Z is 5.

_____ 7. The consumer generally tends to respond to an increase in a commodity's price by reducing the amount of it he or she consumes.

_____ 8. If the demand for a commodity is price elastic, an increase in its price will lead to an increase in the total amount spent by consumers on the commodity.

_____ 9. A commodity's income elasticity of demand may be positive or negative.

_____ 10. The income elasticity of demand for food is very high.

_____ 11. The price elasticity of demand is expressed in terms of relative, not absolute, changes in price and quantity demanded.

_____ 12. The price elasticity of demand is a measure of the sensitivity of quantity demanded to the price of other commodities.

_____ 13. Since the market demand curve reflects what consumers want and are willing to pay for, when the market demand curve for wheat shifts upward to the right, this indicates that consumers want more wheat at the existing price.

_____ 14. The demand for a particular brand of oil is more price elastic than the demand for fuel as a whole.

_____ 15. The demand for a commodity is price elastic if the price elasticity of demand is less than 1.

_____ 16. If the demand for the commodity is price elastic, an increase in its price will lead to a decrease in the total amount spent by consumers on the commodity.

_____ 17. The demand for a commodity is price inelastic if the price elasticity of demand is greater than 1.

Multiple Choice

1. If $R = 30 + 2P$, where R is the total amount spent on good A and P is the price of good A, the price elasticity of demand for good A is:

   a. less than 1.
   b. 1.
   c. 2.

   d. more than 2.
   e. none of the above.

2. A representative of organized labor says that an increase in the wage rate would have no effect on the total amount of wages paid to labor. If this is true, the price elasticity of demand for labor is:

   a. less than 1.
   b. 1.
   c. 2.

   d. more than 2.
   e. none of the above.

3. The supply curve for product Q is a vertical line. The government establishes a floor under the price of product Q, this floor being $1 above the equilibrium price. The surplus of product Q will be greatest if the price elasticity of demand of product Q is:

   a. 0.25.
   b. 1.
   c. 1.25.

   d. 2.50.
   e. 3.00.

4. The amount of strawberries available on any given day is 3 tons in Baltimore and 5 tons in Philadelphia. The equilibrium price is the same in both cities, but the government establishes a price ceiling that is 50¢ per box below the equilibrium price of both cities. The price elasticity of demand for strawberries is 2 in Baltimore and 3 in Philadelphia. The size of the shortage in Baltimore is:

   a. .50 tons.
   b. $(1 - .50) \div 2 = .25$ tons.
   c. $2 \div (1 - .50) = 4$ tons.

   d. zero.
   e. indeterminate from the information given.

5. In the previous question, the relative size of the shortage in Baltimore:

   a. will exceed that in Philadelphia.
   b. will equal that in Philadelphia.
   c. will be less than that in Philadelphia.
   d. will be less than or equal to that in Philadelphia.
   e. may or may not be greater than that in Philadelphia.

6. (Advanced.) Along any straight-line demand curve, the price elasticity of demand:

   a. increases as price falls.
   b. decreases as price falls.
   c. remains constant as price falls.

   d. equals the slope of the line.
   e. first increases and then decreases as price falls.

7. The quantity of Velasquez paintings increases by 2 percent because a number of such paintings is discovered in a cave by Basque revolutionaries. If the price elasticity of demand for Velasquez paintings is 0.3, the result will be a reduction in the price of Velasquez paintings of:

    a. 0.3 percent.   d. 6 2/3 percent.
    b. 0.6 percent.   e. none of the above.
    c. 3 1/3 percent.

8. A 1 percent increase in the price of good X results in a 2 percent increase in the quantity demanded of good Y. A 1 percent increase in the price of good Y will result in an increase in the quantity demanded of good X that is:

    a. 2 percent.   d. less than 1/2 percent.
    b. 1/2 percent.   e. indeterminate from the
    c. more than 2 percent.   information given.

9. If two goods are substitutes, a decrease in the price of one of them will result in:

    a. a shift to the right in the other good's supply curve.
    b. a shift to the left in the other good's supply curve.
    c. a shift to the right in the other good's demand curve.
    d. a shift to the left in the other good's demand curve.
    e. an increase in the quantity demanded of the other good.

10. If two goods are complements, a decrease in the price of one of them will result in:

    a. a shift to the left in the other good's demand curve.
    b. a shift to the right in the other good's demand curve.
    c. a decrease in the quantity demanded of the other good.
    d. no change in the quantity demanded of the other good.
    e. none of the above.

11. In general, the individual demand curve will not remain fixed if there is a change in:

    a. preferences.   d. any of the above.
    b. income.   e. none of the above.
    c. prices of other goods.

12. If there are a great many firms selling a homogeneous product, an individual firm's demand curve becomes:

    a. of unitary elasticity. d. close to horizontal.
    b. price inelastic.   e. income elastic.
    c. cross elastic.

13. If the cross elasticity of demand is negative, two commodities are:

    a. complements.   d. negative elastomers.
    b. substitutes.   e. none of the above.
    c. positive elastomers.

14. If the income elasticity of demand for a product is zero and incomes increase considerably during a 10 year period, then the effect of this change in income on the product's sales should be:

    a. positive.
    b. negative.
    c. impossible to predict.

    d. none of the above.
    e. infinite.

15. The income elasticity of demand:

    a. must always be negative.
    b. must always be positive.
    c. can be positive or negative.

Discussion and Extension Questions

1. According to the *New York Times*, "Coffee drinking, drip or perk, isn't as popular as it once was. Per capita consumption has dropped from 3.12 cups a day in 1962 to 2.2 cups. . . . The decline hasn't kept prices down, though." Does the information given here prove that there has been a shift to the left in the demand curve for coffee? Why or why not?

2. In the fall of 1973 there was talk of a beef shortage; in the winter of 1974 there was talk of a gasoline shortage. Why did government officials talk more about rationing gasoline to solve the latter problem than about rationing beef to solve the former?

3. If a family budgets a fixed amount of money for certain expenditures during the coming year, such as $800 a month for food and $200 a month for clothing purchases, what is that family's price elasticity of demand for food? Clothing? Be careful!

4. How could a state government use the information that the price elasticity of demand for cigarettes is about 0.4 when considering an increase in the state cigarette tax as a means of providing additional revenue for the state? How might the information that New Hampshire has a per capita sales of cigarettes that is twice that of any neighboring state affect your decision to use the number 0.4 as your estimate of price elasticity in your calculations?

5. "If the demand curve for coffee is linear, the price elasticity of demand for coffee is the same at all prices." Discuss and evaluate.

6. "The theory of demand is based entirely on the supposition that individualism should reign supreme. Yet it is obvious that people often do not know what is good for them. Consequently, the state should play a greater role in determining what consumers should have." Comment and evaluate.

7. What are some ways that market demand curves can be measured? According to results obtained by Professor William Vickrey, the demand for passenger service on the New York subways is price inelastic. Does this mean that fare increases would result in greater revenues for the New York subways?

8. According to estimates made by agricultural economists, the price elasticity of demand for cotton is about 0.12. If this is the case, to what extent will the quantity demanded of cotton increase if the price of cotton is reduced by 1 percent?

9. What is meant by a market? How can one derive the market demand curve from the demand curves of the individuals comprising the market?

10. According to the Department of Agriculture, the income elasticity of demand for coffee is about 0.23. If incomes rise by 1 percent, what effect would this have on the quantity demanded of coffee?

11. Based on the information in Question 8 above, would you expect that the price elasticity of demand for the output of a single cotton producer is 0.12? If not, what would you guess its value to be?

Problems

1. Suppose that the relationship between the price of aluminum and the quantity of aluminum demanded is as follows:

Price (dollars)	Quantity
1	8
2	7
3	6
4	5
5	4

   What is the arc elasticity of demand when price is between $1 and $2? Between $4 and $5?

2. Suppose that the price elasticity of demand for gasoline is 0.50. About how big a price increase will be required to reduce the consumption of gasoline by 1 percent?

3. Suppose that the income elasticity of demand for automobiles is 2.5 in the United States and 3.0 in the United Kingdom. If incomes in the United States rise by 2 percent next year and incomes in the United Kingdom rise by 1 percent, what will be the effect in each country on the quantity of automobiles purchased?

4. If a 1.5 percent reduction in the price of Nike running shoes results in a 3.0 percent reduction in the quantity demanded of New Balance running shoes, what is the cross elasticity of demand for these two commodities? Are they substitutes or complements?

5. Suppose that the market demand curve for mink coats is as follows:

Price (dollars)	Quantity of mink coats
500	500
1,000	300
1,500	200
2,000	100

a. What is the price elasticity of demand for mink coats when the price is between $1,500 and $2,000?

b. What is the price elasticity of demand when the price is between $500 and $1,000?

c. According to the text, an increase in price results in increased total expenditures on a product if its price elasticity of demand is less than 1, and less total expenditure on a product if its price elasticity of demand is greater than 1. Show that this proposition is true if the price of mink coats is raised from $500 to $1,000.

d. Show that the proposition in part c is true if the price of mink coats is raised from $1,500 to $2,000.

6. Suppose that there are only 3 people in the market for sable coats—Mrs. Smith, Mrs. Kennedy, and Mrs. Jones. Suppose that their demand curves are as given below. Fill in the blank spaces for the market demand curve for sable coats.

Price of a sable coat (dollars)	Smith	Quantity demanded Kennedy	Jones	Market demand
500	3	2	5	_____
1,000	2	1	4	_____
1,500	2	1	3	_____
2,000	1	0	2	_____

7. (Advanced.) Prove that the price elasticity of demand at any price less than $5.00 will always be the same on D_1 as on D_2.

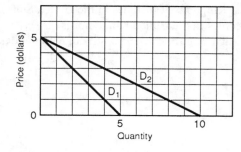

8. Every time the price of a pint of beer falls by a dime, Tom buys three more pints per week, but Jean buys five more. The price is now $1.00, and we observe Tom buying twenty-five pints per week while Jean is buying ten pints.

   a. Draw each person's demand curve for beer.

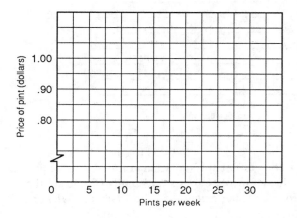

   b. Whose price elasticity of demand for beer is higher when the price is between $1.00 and $0.90 per pint?

9. Suppose the price elasticity of demand for zambowies is unity when the price is $40. Suppose further that when the price is $40, 100 zambowies are sold each week in Sommersville. Assuming no change in the elasticity for a small rise in zambowie prices, how many will be sold next week if price should rise to $42 per zambowie?

10. Suppose that the Brazilian government destroys a substantial portion of its coffee harvest in order to increase its revenue from coffee exports. What conditions are essential in order to make this type of policy economically beneficial for the country? Why would the conditions you identify increase export revenues?

11. a. Based on the diagram on the next page, which would be more expensive for the government:
     (1) set a minimum wage at $4.00 per hour and hire all the people the market will not hire at that wage; or
     (2) let the market determine an equilibrium wage ($3.00 per hour in the diagram) and pay everyone who works a subsidy of $1.00 to make up the difference between what the market will pay and what is deemed a fair wage ($4.00 per hour)?

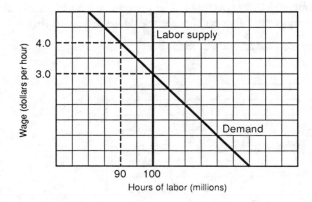

b. Would the answer be different if the demand for labor were price elastic with the result that an increase in the wage rate to $4.00 cut the quantity of labor demanded to a greater extent than shown above? Why or why not?

12. A firm estimates that the demand curves for its two products are given by

$$Q_1 = 200 - 2P_1 - 3P_2 \text{ and } Q_2 = 450 + 6P_1 - 2P_2,$$

where Q_1 is the quantity demanded of the first product, P_1 is its price, Q_2 is the quantity demanded of the second product, and P_2 is its price. Compute the following elasticities at $P_1 = \$2$ and $P_2 = \$2$:

a. Price elasticity of demand for the first product.
b. Cross elasticity of demand for the second product with respect to variation in the price of the first product.

ANSWERS

Completion Questions

1. 1.3, constant 2. 1.4, elastic 3. 1, zero 4. zero, zero 5. price elasticity of demand 6. quantity demanded, price 7. less than 1 8. a 1 percent, money income 9. substitutes 10. of unitary elasticity 11. price elasticity of demand 12. long, short, easier 13. more, substitutes

True-False

1. True   2. True   3. True   4. True   5. True   6. False   7. True   8. False
9. True   10. False   11. True   12. False   13. True   14. True   15. False
16. True   17. False

Multiple Choice

1. a   2. b   3. e   4. e   5. c   6. b   7. d   8. e   9. d   10. b   11. d   12. d
13. a   14. d   15. c

Problems

1.

$$-\frac{(Q_2-Q_1)}{\dfrac{Q_1+Q_2}{2}}\div\frac{(P_2-P_1)}{\dfrac{P_1+P_2}{2}}=-\frac{(7-8)}{\dfrac{8+7}{2}}\div\frac{(2-1)}{\dfrac{1+2}{2}}=\frac{3}{15}=0.20$$

$$-\frac{(Q_2-Q_1)}{\dfrac{Q_1+Q_2}{2}}\div\frac{(P_2-P_1)}{\dfrac{P_1+P_2}{2}}=-\frac{(4-5)}{\dfrac{5+4}{2}}\div\frac{(5-4)}{\dfrac{4+5}{2}}=\frac{9}{9}=1.00$$

2. 2 percent.
3. The quantity of automobiles demanded will increase by 3 percent in the United Kingdom and by 5 percent in the United States (assuming other factors are constant).
4. Plus two. Substitutes.

5. a.

$$-\frac{200-100}{150}\div\frac{1,500-2,000}{1,750}=\frac{100}{150}\div\frac{500}{1,750}$$

$$=\frac{2}{3}\div\frac{2}{7}=\frac{2}{3}\times\frac{7}{2}=\frac{7}{3}=2\,1/3$$

   b.

$$-\frac{500-300}{400}\div\frac{500-1,000}{750}=\frac{200}{400}\div\frac{500}{750}=\frac{1}{2}\div\frac{2}{3}=\frac{1}{2}\times\frac{3}{2}=\frac{3}{4}$$

   c. As indicated in part b, the price elasticity of demand is less than 1 in this range. Thus an increase in price should increase the total expenditure on the product. Looking at the figures, this is the case. When the price is $500, total expenditure is $250,000; when it is $1,000, total expenditure is $300,000.

   d. As indicated in part a, the price elasticity of demand is greater than 1 in this range. Thus an increase in price should decrease the total expenditure on the product. Looking at the figures in part a, this is the case. When the price is $1,500, total expenditure is $300,000; when it is $2,000, total expenditure is $200,000.

6. *Market demand*

    10
    7
    6
    3

7. Expressed in terms of calculus, the price elasticity of demand is $-\dfrac{dQ}{dP} \cdot \dfrac{P}{Q}$.

    If the demand curve is D_1, $\dfrac{dQ}{dP} = -1$; thus, $-\dfrac{dQ}{dP} \cdot \dfrac{P}{Q} = \dfrac{P}{Q} = \dfrac{P}{5-P}$. If the

    demand curve is D_2, $\dfrac{dQ}{dP} = -2$; thus, $-\dfrac{dQ}{dP} \cdot \dfrac{P}{Q} = \dfrac{2P}{Q} = \dfrac{2P}{10-2P} = \dfrac{P}{5-P}$.

    Since the price elasticity of demand equals $\dfrac{P}{5-P}$ in each case, it must be

    the same for both demand curves if the price is the same.

8. a.

    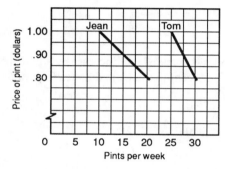

   b. For each person we can compute the arc elasticity of demand between

    $1.00 per pint and $0.90. For Tom it is $-\left(\dfrac{28-25}{26.5}\right) \div \left(\dfrac{90-100}{95}\right) = 1.08$.

    For Jean it is $-\left(\dfrac{15-10}{12.5}\right) \div \left(\dfrac{90-100}{95}\right) = 3.8$. Thus Jean's is higher.

9. About 95.

10. The price elasticity of demand must be less than one. Export revenues
    would increase because, if the price elasticity of demand is less than one,
    increases in price (and reductions in quantity) will increase revenue.

11. a. The cost of the first alternative would be 10 million × $4.00, or $40
    million. The cost of the second alternative would be 100 million × $1,
    or $100 million. Thus the second alternative would be more expensive.

    b. If the demand for labor were price elastic, the answer would be the op-
    posite. Let Q_1 be the quantity of labor demanded (in millions of hours)
    when the wage is $4.00. Under the first alternative, the cost to the
    government is $4.0 × (100 − Q_1) million. Under the second alternative,
    the cost is $100 million. If 4.0 × (100 − Q_1) > 100, the cost under the

first alternative would be higher. In other words, if $Q_1 < 75$, this is the case. If the demand for labor is price elastic, Q_1 will be less than 75, because an increase in the wage rate will reduce the total amount spent on labor.

12. a. If $P_2 = 2$, $Q_1 = 194 - 2P_1$. Thus, if $P_1 = 2$, $Q_1 = 190$. And if $P_1 = 2.02$, $Q_1 = 189.96$. Consequently, a 1 percent increase in price (from 2 to 2.02) results in about a 0.02 percent decrease (from 190 to 189.96) in quantity demanded, so the price elasticity of demand is about 0.02.

b. If $P_2 = 2$, $Q_2 = 446 + 6P_1$. Thus, if $P_1 = 2$, $Q_2 = 458$. And if $P_1 = 2.02$, $Q_2 = 458.12$. Consequently, a 1 percent increase in price (from 2 to 2.02) results in about a 0.03 percent increase (from 458 to 458.12) in quantity demanded, so the cross elasticity of demand is about +0.03.

CHAPTER 18

Economic Efficiency, Market Supply,

and Perfect Competition

Chapter Profile

Economists generally classify markets into four types—perfect competition, monopoly, monopolistic competition, and oligopoly. Perfect competition requires that the product of any seller be the same as the product of any other seller, that no buyer or seller be able to influence the price of the product, and that resources be able to switch readily from one use to another.

If it maximizes profit, a perfectly competitive firm should set its output rate in the short run at the level where marginal cost equals price, so long as price exceeds average variable cost. If there is no output rate at which price exceeds average variable cost, the firm should discontinue production.

The firm's supply curve coincides with its marginal cost curve for prices exceeding the minimum value of average variable cost. For prices that are less than or equal to the minimum value of average variable cost, the firm's supply curve coincides with the price axis.

As a first approximation, the market supply curve can be viewed as the horizontal summation of the supply curves of all of the firms producing the product. This assumes that increases or decreases in output by all firms simultaneously do not affect input prices.

Price and output under perfect competition are determined by the intersection of the market supply and demand curves. In the short run, price influences as well as rations the amount supplied.

In the long run, equilibrium is achieved under perfect competition when enough firms—no more, no less—are in the industry so that economic profits are eliminated. In other words, the long-run equilibrium position of the firm is at the point where its long-run average cost equals price. But since price must also equal marginal cost (to maximize profit), it follows that the firm must be operating at the minimum point on the long-run average cost curve.

In a perfectly competitive economy, prices are the signals that are used to guide the reallocation of resources in response to changes in consumer tastes, technology, and other factors.

Concepts for Review

Perfect competition	Firm's supply curve
Monopoly	Market supply curve
Monopolistic competition	Economic profits
Oligopoly	

Completion Questions

1. If a firm cannot affect the price of its product and it can sell any amount that it wants, the firm is said to be _____.

2. If a perfectly competitive firm's marginal cost of producing the Qth unit of output per month equals $5Q$ dollars, and if the price of a unit of output is $30, the firm, if it maximizes profit, should produce _____ units of output per month. If it does so, its profits per month will equal _____ if its fixed costs per month equal $100. If its fixed costs are $300 per month, the firm (would, would not) _____ be better off to shut down in the short run.

3. Maximum profit under perfect competition is achieved usually at the output rate where _____ equals _____.

4. A firm's _____ shows how much it will desire to produce at each price.

5. The _____ is the horizontal summation of the supply curves of all the firms producing the product, assuming that industry output does not influence input prices.

6. If there is an output rate where price exceeds average _____ cost, it will pay the firm to produce, even though price does not cover average _____ cost. If there is no such output rate, the firm is better off to produce _____.

7. Under perfect competition the firm's supply curve is exactly the same as the firm's _____ cost curve for prices above the minimum value of average _____ cost. For prices at or below the minimum value of average _____ cost, the firm's supply curve corresponds to the _____ axis, the desire to supply at these prices being uniformly _____.

8. In perfect competition, each firm has (no, little, much) _____ control over the price of its product.

9. A perfectly competitive firm is (likely, unlikely) _____ to advertise its product.

10. In the short run, _____ determines the amount of a product supplied. For instance, according to Hubert Risser of the University of Kansas, the short-run supply curve for bituminous coal is very price

(elastic, inelastic) _____ when output is within the range of existing capacity. In other words, if output is less than existing capacity, small

variations in price will result in (large, small) _____ variations in output.

11. Under perfect competition, long-run equilibrium requires that price equals the

(highest, lowest) _____ value of long-run average total costs. In other words, firms must be producing at the (maximum,

minimum) _____ point on their long-run average cost curves,

because to maximize their _____ they must operate where

price equals long-run (average, marginal) _____ cost. Also,

they must operate where price equals long-run _____ cost. But

if both these conditions are satisfied, long-run _____ cost

must equal long-run _____ cost—since both equal price. And

we know that long-run _____ cost equals long-run

_____ cost only at the point at which long-run average cost

is a (maximum, minimum) _____.

12. Firm X is a perfectly competitive firm that is in long-run equilibrium. The price of its product is $10 more than the value of its economic profit, which

means that the price of its product equals _____. Its long-run

average cost (equals, exceeds, is less than) _____ $10. Its

short-run marginal cost (equals, exceeds, is less than) _____

$10. In this situation firm X's economic profit (does, does not) _____ equal its accounting profit.

True-False

_____ 1. If the short-run marginal cost curve of each and every firm in an industry slopes upward and to the right, the industry's long-run supply curve must slope upward and to the right.

_____ 2. Firm Y, a perfectly competitive firm, is producing at an output rate where its marginal cost is $1 less than its average cost (which equals its price). To increase its profit firm Y should increase its output rate.

_____ 3. At all points where the total revenue curve lies below the total cost curve, profits will be negative.

_____ 4. If price is fixed, then increases in output will have little effect on the firm's profits.

_____ 5. The Golden Rule of Output Determination for a perfectly competitive firm is: Choose the output rate at which marginal cost is equal to price.

_____ 6. The firm will maximize profits by producing nothing if there is no output rate at which price exceeds average variable cost.

_____ 7. No industry, now or in the past, has met all of the requirements of perfect competition.

_____ 8. In the short run, output is set by demand alone.

_____ 9. Under perfect competition the product of any one seller must be the same as the product of any other seller.

_____ 10. A perfectly competitive firm in long-run equilibrium is earning normal profits (that is, profits equal to those obtainable elsewhere).

_____ 11. If firm X's marginal cost curve intersects its average variable cost curve at $4 per unit of output, firm X will shut down in the short-run if the price of its product falls below $4 per unit.

Multiple Choice

1. The supply curve of each firm in industry X is a vertical line. The government dictates that no firm can enter or leave industry X. The market supply curve:

   a. is upward-sloping to the right.
   b. may or may not be upward-sloping to the right.
   c. is a vertical line.
   d. does not exist.
   e. none of the above.

2. The output of industry S does not affect input prices in the industry. There are 1,000 firms in the industry, and for each firm the marginal cost of producing 5 units per month is $2, the marginal cost of producing 6 units per month is $3, and the marginal cost of producing 7 units per month is $5. If the price per unit of the industry's product is $3, the industry output will be:

   a. no more than 5,000 units per month.
   b. 5,000 units per month.
   c. 6,000 units per month.
   d. 7,000 units per month.
   e. at least 7,000 units per month.

3. In the previous question, if the price per unit of the industry's product is $6, the industry output will be:

   a. no more than 5,000 units per month.
   b. 5,000 units per month.
   c. 6,000 units per month.
   d. 7,000 units per month.
   e. at least 7,000 units per month.

4. If a firm has no fixed costs, it follows that:

   a. the firm would cease production if price were less than average total cost.
   b. average variable cost equals average total cost.
   c. average variable cost achieves a minimum at the same point that average total cost achieves a minimum.
   d. all of the above.
   e. none of the above.

5. If marginal cost exceeds average total cost at its profit-maximizing output, a competitive firm:

   a. will make positive profits.
   b. will operate at a point to the right of the minimum point on the average total cost curve.
   c. will not discontinue production.
   d. all of the above.
   e. none of the above.

6. A firm is better off in the short run to produce when the:

   a. loss from production is less than fixed costs.
   b. fixed costs are less than the loss from production.
   c. average total cost minus price is greater than average fixed cost.
   d. average total cost is greater than average fixed cost plus price.
   e. none of the above.

7. The simultaneous expansion or contraction of output by all firms is likely to alter for an individual firm:

a. input prices.   d. all of the above.
b. cost curves.   e. none of the above.
c. supply curve.

8. The shape of the short-run market supply curve may be influenced by:

a. changes in input prices.
b. number of firms in the industry.
c. size of the firm's plants.
d. the nature of technology.
e. the type of product.
f. all of the above.

9. The following graph shows the total revenue and total cost of a firm:

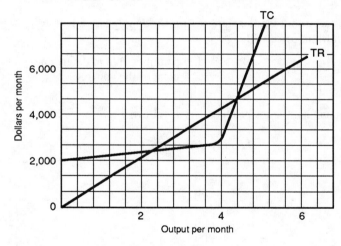

Based on this graph, it is clear that:

a. the firm is perfectly competitive.
b. the firm's fixed costs equal $2,000 per month.
c. the firm will maximize its profit if it produces about 4 units of output per month.
d. all of the above.
e. only a and b are true.

10. Based on the graph in the previous question, it is clear that:

    a. marginal cost is less than marginal revenue when output is less than 3 units per month.
    b. marginal cost is greater than marginal revenue when output is greater than 4 units per month.
    c. there is only one output rate at which average total cost equals average revenue. (Average revenue is total revenue divided by output.)
    d. all of the above.
    e. only a and b are true.

11. Oligopoly is a kind of market where there is/are _____ seller(s).

    a. one
    b. few
    c. many

    d. no
    e. too many

12. If the demand curve shifts to the right (and if the supply curve is upward-sloping), equilibrium price will:

    a. decrease.
    b. increase.
    c. stay the same.

    d. be impossible to determine.
    e. none of the above.

13. The market demand curve for product R is as follows:

Price (dollars)	Quantity demanded
30	200
20	300
10	400
5	600
3	800

    Firms in the industry can expand or contract their output without affecting input prices. Each firm has the following long-run total cost curve:

Output	Total cost (dollars)
1	10
2	12
3	15
4	30

    The total number of firms in the industry in the long run will be approximately:

    a. 100.
    b. 200.
    c. 300.

    d. 400.
    e. none of the above.

14. In the previous question the price of product R in the long run will be approximately:

   a. $10.

   b. $12.

   c. $15.

   d. $30.

   e. none of the above.

Discussion and Extension Questions

1. In the *New York Times*, Henry Ford II wrote that, "The main reason more oil hasn't been found is that, with a 34-year inventory on hand, there has been little incentive to look farther or deeper for still more. . . . As the easily recovered supply of petroleum is depleted, the cost of finding and extracting new supplies will go up and up." Based on this statement, what, according to Mr. Ford, is the shape of the long-run supply curve for oil? Do you agree? Why or why not?

2. Suppose you are currently enrolled for five courses this term. Use the principles presented in this chapter to illustrate how much time you will devote to studying for the final exam in each course. What is the cost to you of an hour's study for your economics final exam? Under what circumstances would it pay you not to study at all for a particular course, and what is the counterpart for the competitive firm?

3. Suppose the Pentagon is interested in expanding our military force by 10 percent. Describe why it is important for the Pentagon and other agencies to have some idea of the elasticity of supply of military personnel when contemplating an increase in their numbers.

4. "There is a learning curve in many industries; that is, unit costs go down as more units are produced. This is a major reason why supply curves slope downward to the right." Comment and evaluate.

5. "Higher prices don't result in greater supplies; they result in higher profits." Comment and evaluate.

6. Show why a firm will continue to produce in the short run so long as price exceeds average variable cost, even if price is smaller than average total cost.

7. Distinguish between (a) diminishing marginal returns, (b) diseconomies of scale, and (c) increasing cost industries.

8. According to Kenneth Boulding, "From the point of view of society as a whole, the inability of agriculture to reduce output in a depression is an almost unmixed blessing." Why can't agriculture reduce output? Why is this a blessing, and why is this blessing not quite unmixed? What are the effects of government farm programs on the validity of this statement?

9. "Competition is all very well in theory, but in practice it generally is a disaster, leading to low profits and eventual government intervention. Agriculture is a case in point." Comment and evaluate.

10. Explain why equilibrium in the long run under perfect competition requires that price must be equal to the lowest value of long-run average total cost.

Problems

1. Suppose that the total costs of a perfectly competitive firm are as follows:

Output rate	Total cost (dollars)
0	40
1	60
2	90
3	130
4	180
5	240

Assume that the output rate can only assume integer values.

a. If the price of the product is $50, what output rate should the firm choose?
b. Draw on the following graph the short-run supply curve of the firm.
c. Draw the firm's demand curve.
d. Draw the firm's average total cost curve.

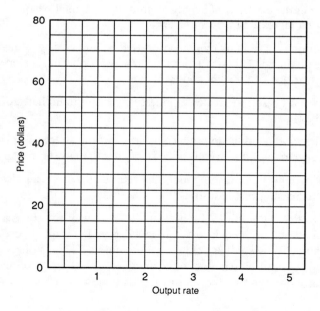

e. What will be the firm's total profit?

2. You are the owner of a firm that is currently losing $1,000 per month, with fixed costs per month of $800. A management consultant advises you to cease production. Should you accept the advice? Why or why not?

3. Suppose that the total cost curve of the Rem Sofa Company is as follows:

Output (sofas per month)	Total cost (dollars per month)
1	1,000
2	1,100
3	1,200
4	1,300
5	1,500
6	1,700
7	2,000
8	2,500

Assume that the output rate must be an integer amount per month.

a. If the price of a sofa is $300, how many sofas should Rem produce per month?

b. Suppose that Rem's fixed costs increase by $100 per month. What effect will this have on the optimal output?

c. If its fixed costs increase by $100 per month, what will be the maximum profit rate that the Rem Sofa Company can earn?

d. Does the Rem Sofa Company exhibit increasing marginal cost? What is the value of marginal cost when between 7 and 8 units of output are produced per month?

4. Data are provided below concerning the Allied Peanut Company, a firm producing peanut brittle.

a. Supposing that this firm is a member of a perfectly competitive industry, complete the table below:

Output of peanut brittle per day by Allied (tons)	Price of a ton of peanut brittle	Total cost	Total Revenue	Profit	Marginal cost
0	200	100	_____	_____	
1	_____	200	_____	_____	
2	_____	310	_____	_____	
3	_____	500	_____	_____	
4	_____	700	_____	_____	
5	_____	1,000	_____	_____	

(dollars)

Assume that the output rate must equal an integer number of tons per day.

b. If the price of a ton of peanut brittle falls to $50, will Allied continue producing it, or will it shut down?

c. What is the minimum price at which Allied will continue production (assuming that it cannot produce fractions of tons of output)?

d. If the price of a ton of peanut brittle is $200, what output rate will Allied choose? Does price equal marginal cost at this output rate?

5. The following graph shows the total cost and total revenue curves of a hypothetical competitive firm:

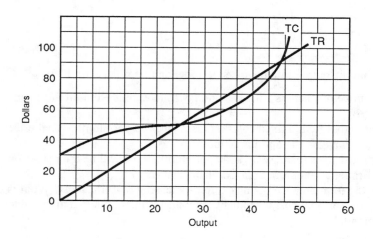

a. How much is the price of the firm's product?
b. How much is the firm's total fixed cost?
c. At what output levels will the firm's profit be zero?
d. At what output level will the firm's profit be a maximum?

6. Suppose that a perfectly competitive firm has the short-run total cost function shown below:

Output	Total cost (dollars)
0	10
1	12
2	16
3	22
4	30
5	40

a. If the firm can produce only integer amounts of output, what output level will it choose when the price of its product is (1) $3, (2) $5, (3) $7, (4) $9?

b. What will be the firm's profits when the price of its product is (1) $3, (2) $5, (3) $7, (4) $9?

c. If there are 1,000 firms in this industry, and all have the cost function shown above, the market supply curve is given below. Fill in the blanks.

Price (dollars)	Quantity supplied
3	_____
5	_____
7	_____
9	_____

d. If the market demand curve is as shown below, what will be the equilibrium price of the product?

Price (dollars)	Quantity demanded
3	3,000
5	2,000
7	1,500
9	1,000

e. What will be the output of each firm?
f. How much profit will each firm make?
g. Will firms tend to enter or leave this industry in the long run?

7. As of midnight, December 13, National Agriculture, a recently formed farmers' lobby group, is calling for a nation-wide strike by farmers. The goal is to raise the price of the crops enough to cover production costs and to provide some profit. Suppose that the current price of wheat is $1.50 per bushel, which is about one-half of the cost of growing that bushel.

a. Depict the current plight of a typical wheat farmer graphically. (Treat her as a perfect competitor.) Your diagram should correctly depict both variable and total costs relative to today's market price given the fact that the typical farmer is choosing to continue producing even while making losses.

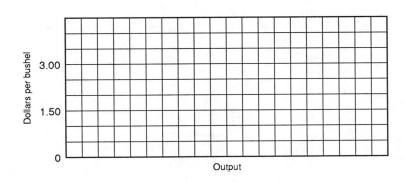

b. In perfect competition no single firm has any market power. Suppose that by such an organization as National Agriculture all farmers could coordinate the selling of their produce. What would be the effect on the price of their produce? What would be the effect on the amount they would sell?

8. Assume that perfect competition exists. Assume that marginal cost increases with increases in output. In the table below you are to fill in all spaces which do not contain a number. An asterisk in a space means that ATC or AVC is at a minimum level at that output. *Treat each horizontal row in the table as a separate problem.* Enter in the last column one of the following responses:

Number	Response
1	Firm now at correct output
2	Firm should increase price
3	Firm should decrease price
4	Firm should increase output
5	Firm should decrease output
6	Firm should shut down operations

The symbols are as follows: P = Price, Q = Quantity, TR = Total Revenue, TC = Total Cost, TFC = Total Fixed Cost, TVC = Total Variable Cost, ATC = Average Total Cost, AVC = Average Variable Cost, MC = Marginal Cost.

P	Q	TR	TC	TFC	TVC	ATC	AVC	MC	Response
10	—	800	—	500	—	10	—	—	1
—	—	400	—	100	—	2	1	5	—
—	10	30	—	20	—	—	.30	.25	—
10	100	—	—	200	—	—	10*	—	—
—	50	300	—	—	—	7*	5	—	—

ANSWERS

Completion Questions
1. perfectly competitive 2. 6, –$25, would not 3. price, marginal cost
4. supply curve 5. market supply curve 6. variable, total, nothing
7. marginal, variable, variable, price, zero 8. no 9. unlikely
10. price, elastic, large 11. lowest, minimum, profits, marginal, average, marginal, average, marginal, average, minimum 12. $10, equals, equals, does not

True-False
1. False 2. True 3. True 4. False 5. True 6. True 7. True 8. False
9. True 10. True 11. True

Multiple Choice
1. c 2. c 3. e 4. d 5. d 6. a 7. d 8. f 9. d 10. e 11. b 12. b
13. b 14. e

Problems
1. a. 3 or 4 units of output per period of time.
    b., c., d.

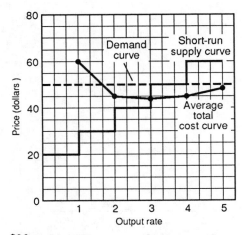

    e. $20.
2. Yes. Because you will lose less money ($800) if you cease production than at present.
3. a. 6 or 7.
    b. No effect.
    c. Zero profits.
    d. Yes. $500.

4. a.

Price of a ton of peanut brittle	Total revenue (dollars)	Profit	Marginal cost
	0	−100	
			100
200	200	0	
			110
200	400	90	
			190
200	600	100	
			200
200	800	100	
			300
200	1,000	0	

   b. It will shut down.

   c. $100.

   d. Either 3 or 4 tons per day. Yes; as shown in the answer to part a, marginal cost is $200 when output is between 3 and 4 tons per day. Price too equals $200.

5. a. $2 per unit of output.

   b. $30.

   c. 25 and 45 units of output.

   d. 35 to 40 units of output.

6. a. 1, 2, 3, 4.

   b. −$9, −$6, −$1, +$6.

   c.

Quantity supplied

1,000
2,000
3,000
4,000

   d. $5.

   e. 2.

   f. −$6.

   g. They will leave it.

7. a.

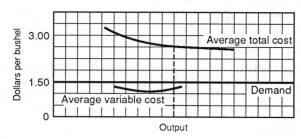

   b. Price would increase, and quantity would decrease.

8.

P	Q	TR	TC	TFC	TVC	ATC	AVC	MC	Response
10	80	800	800	500	300	10	3.75	10	1
4	100	400	200	100	100	2	1	5	5
3	10	30	23	20	3	2.3	.30	.25	4
10	100	1,000	1,200	200	1,000	12	10*	10	6
6	50	300	350	100	250	7*	5	7	5

CHAPTER 19

Monopoly and Its Regulation

Chapter Profile

A pure monopoly is a market with one, and only one, seller. Monopolies may occur because of patents, control over basic inputs, and government action, as well as decreasing average costs up to the point where the market is satisfied.

If average costs reach their minimum at an output rate large enough to satisfy the entire market, perfect competition cannot be maintained; and the public often insists that the industry (a natural monopoly) be regulated by the government.

Since the monopolist is the only seller of the product, the demand curve facing the monopolist is the market demand curve, which slopes downward (rather than being horizontal as in perfect competition). The unregulated monopolist will maximize profit by choosing the output where marginal cost equals marginal revenue, marginal revenue being defined as the addition to total revenue attributable to the addition of one unit to sales. This rule for output determination also holds under perfect competition, since price equals marginal revenue under perfect competition.

If monopolists cannot prevent losses from exceeding fixed costs, they, like perfect competitors, will discontinue production. In contrast to the case in perfect competition, the long-run equilibrium of a monopolistic industry may not be marked by the absence of economic profits.

The output of a monopoly tends to be smaller and the price tends to be higher than under perfect competition. Economists tend to believe that society would be better off if more resources were devoted to the production of the good than under monopoly, the competitive output often being regarded as best.

One way that society has attempted to reduce the harmful effects of monopoly is through public regulation. Commissions often set price at the level at which it equals average total cost, including a "fair" rate of return on the firm's investment.

There has been a great deal of controversy over the practices of the regulatory commissions. Many economists have viewed them as lax or ill-conceived. According to many studies, their decisions have resulted in substantial costs and inefficiencies.

Regulatory commissions try to prevent a monopoly from earning excessive profits; the firm is allowed only a "fair" rate of return on its investment. One difficulty with this arrangement is that since the firm is guaranteed this rate of return (regardless of how well or poorly it performs), there is no incentive for the firm to increase its efficiency.

*In defense of monopoly power, some economists, such as John Kenneth Galbraith, have asserted that the rate of technological change is likely to be greater in an imperfectly competitive industry than under perfect competition. It does seem unlikely that a perfectly competitive industry would be able—and have the

---

*The starred items pertain to material covered in the section "Exploring Further."

incentive—to carry out the research and development required to promote a rapid rate of technological change in many sectors of the economy.

*However, contrary to the allegations of Galbraith and others, there is little evidence that giant firms are needed to ensure rapid technological change in a great many sectors of the economy. The situation is much more complex than such statements indicate, and the contributions of smaller firms are much greater than is commonly recognized.

Concepts for Review

Monopoly   Public regulation
Natural monopolies   Historical cost
Total revenue   Reproduction cost
Marginal revenue

Completion Questions

1. A monopolist can sell 12 units of output when it charges $10 a unit, 11 units of output when it charges $11 a unit, and 10 units of output when it charges $12 a unit. The marginal revenue from the eleventh unit of output equals

   _____. The marginal revenue from the twelfth unit of

   output equals _____.

2. If the marginal revenue from the first unit of output is $5 and the marginal revenue from the second unit of output is $4, the total revenue from the first

   two units of output is _____. The average revenue when 1

   unit of output is produced and sold equals _____. The average revenue when 2 units of output are produced and sold equals

   _____.

3. For the monopolist, if demand is price _____, marginal

   revenue is positive; if demand is price _____, marginal revenue is negative.

4. The output of a perfectly competitive industry tends to be _____

   and the price tends to be _____ than under monopoly.

5. Commissions often set price at the level at which it equals _____ including a fair return.

6. A firm's _____ is the addition to total revenue attributable to the addition of one unit of the quantity sold.

---

*The starred items pertain to material covered in the section "Exploring Further."

7. The firm under _____ has no direct competitors at all; it is the sole _____. However, such a firm is not entirely free of rivals but is affected by certain indirect and potential forms of

   _____.

8. A firm may become a monopolist because it is awarded a(n) _____ by a government agency. The government may give a particular firm the franchise to sell a particular product in a(n) _____ or the right to provide a(n) _____, such as telephone service, to people in a particular area. In exchange for this right, the firm agrees to allow the government to _____ certain aspects of its operation.

9. A firm may become a monopolist because the average costs of producing the product reach a(n) _____ at an output rate great enough to satisfy the entire market (at a price that is _____). Under such circumstances, the firm obviously has an incentive to _____ to the point where it produces all the market will buy of the good, because its costs (increase, decrease) _____ as it continues to expand. Competition cannot be maintained in such a case.

10. A company's assets can be valued by _____ cost or _____ cost, *i.e.*, at what the company paid for them or at what it would cost to replace them. If the _____ does not change much, these two approaches are interchangeable. But if prices are rising, _____ cost will be greater than _____ cost.

11. If a monopolist's demand curve is of unitary elasticity, marginal revenue equals _____. In such a case it would be (possible, impossible) _____ for the monopolist to set marginal cost equal to marginal revenue. The monopolist would try to make its output as _____ as possible, since _____ in output reduce its total cost but not its total revenue.

12. If a monopolist's demand curve is price elastic, its marginal revenue is (positive, negative, zero) _____. If a monopolist's demand curve is price inelastic, its marginal revenue is (positive, negative, zero) _____. A monopolist will not operate at a point on its demand curve where demand is price (elastic, inelastic) _____.

True-False

_____ 1. A profit-maximizing monopolist that does not shut down will always set average revenue greater than marginal cost, if the demand curve for its product slopes downward to the right.

_____ 2. A profit-maximizing monopolist will always set average revenue greater than average total cost in the short run.

_____ 3. If a monopolist is not maximizing its profit per unit of output, it is not setting marginal cost equal to marginal revenue.

_____ 4. Cost-plus-fixed-fee contracts provide less incentive for efficiency than fixed-price contracts, but where the risk to the contractor is very great they may be the only type of contract that is feasible.

_____ 5. The monopolist's demand curve must always be horizontal.

_____ 6. A monopolist will discontinue production if its losses have to exceed its fixed costs.

_____ 7. Because price levels have been rising in the past 40 years, most regulatory commissions use replacement cost to value a firm's assets.

_____ 8. A monopolist seeks to maximize its profit per unit of output.

_____ 9. Monopoly, like perfect competition, seldom corresponds more than approximately to conditions in real industries, but it is a very useful model.

_____ 10. A monopolist has to take into account the possibility that new firms might arise to challenge its monopoly if it attempted to extract conspicuously high profits. Thus even the monopolist is subject to some restraint imposed by competitive forces.

_____ 11. Many firms with monopoly power achieved it in considerable part through patents.

_____ 12. When an industry is a natural monopoly, the public often insists that its behavior be regulated by the government.

_____ 13. For both the monopolist and the perfectly competitive firm, profits are maximized by setting the output rate at the point where price equals marginal cost.

Multiple Choice

1. If a firm's marginal cost curve always lies below its average total cost curve, it is likely to be:

    a.   a perfectly competitive firm.   c.   a monopoly.
    b.   a monopolistically competitive   d.   any of the above.
        firm.   e.   none of the above.

2. An industry that formerly was perfectly competitive is monopolized. The monopoly's demand curve is:

    a.   the same as the demand curve for an individual firm when the industry was competitive.

    b.   the same as the demand curve for the industry's product when the industry was competitive.

    c.   more price elastic than either of the above demand curves.

    d.   less price elastic than either of the above demand curves.

    e.   none of the above.

3. To maximize profit a monopoly should:

    a.   set marginal cost equal to price.

    b.   set marginal cost equal to input costs.

    c.   set marginal revenue equal to marginal cost.

    d.   set marginal revenue equal to input costs.

    e.   set average cost equal to price.

4. Economists often regard the socially optimal output of an industry as being the output:

    a.   where marginal cost equals price.

    b.   that a perfectly competitive industry would produce.

    c.   where the social value of an extra unit of the good is equal to the social cost of an extra unit of the good.

    d.   all of the above.

    e.   none of the above.

5. If the marginal cost to society of producing an extra unit of good X is $5, and if the extra value to society of an extra unit of good X is $15 when less than 10 units are produced and $4 when more than 10 units are produced, the socially optimal output of good X is:

    a.   less than 10 units.   d.   unobtainable from the information

    b.   10 units.   given.

    c.   more than 10 units.

6. Under monopoly, marginal cost ordinarily is less than price because:

    a.   price is less than marginal revenue.

    b.   price is greater than marginal revenue.

    c.   marginal cost is less than average cost.

    d.   marginal cost is greater than average cost.

    e.   none of the above.

7. A country's economy consists of two industries, one perfectly competitive and one monopolized. To improve the allocation of resources, it is likely that:

   a. the output of the competitive industry should be reduced.
   b. the output of the monopolistic industry should be increased.
   c. both a and b should occur.
   d. neither a nor b should occur.
   e. a tax should be imposed on the output of the monopolistic industry.

8. A monopolist's total cost equals $100 + 3Q$, where Q is the number of units of output it produces per month. Its demand curve is $P = 200 - Q$, where P is the price of the product. If it produces 20 units of output per month, its total revenue equals:

   a. $4,000.   d. $180.
   b. $3,600.   e. none of the above.
   c. $400.

9. In the previous question the marginal revenue from the twentieth unit of output per month equals:

   a. $3,600.   d. $400.
   b. $3,439.   e. none of the above.
   c. $180.

10. In question 8 if the monopolist is producing 19 units of output per month:

   a. its profit will increase by $158 if it increases output by 1 unit per month.
   b. its profit will increase by $3 if it increases output by 1 unit per month.
   c. its profit will decrease by $3 if it increases output by 1 unit per month.
   d. its profit will decrease by $158 if it increases output by 1 unit per month.
   e. none of the above.

Discussion and Extension Questions

1. "Monopoly prices do not reflect true opportunity costs to society." Explain.

2. "Even if a monopolist earns no economic profits whatsoever, he or she may harm society." Do you agree? If so, how does the harm come about? Be specific.

3. Is the trucking industry a natural monopoly? Why has the trucking industry been regulated by the Interstate Commerce Commission? What advantages have accrued from deregulation of the trucking industry? Why might some trucking companies be opposed to such deregulation?

4. "Whether or not one considers a firm a monopolist all depends on how the relevant market is defined. If the market is very narrow, many firms would be classified as monopolists; using a very broad definition, there may be no such thing as a monopolist." Explain.

5. Define what is meant by monopoly. Is a monopolist free of all indirect and potential forms of rivalry? What are the most important reasons for monopoly?

6. Prove that a monopolist, to maximize profit, should choose an output rate such that marginal revenue equals marginal cost.

7. How do the price and output set by a monopolist compare with those that prevail if the industry were perfectly competitive? Why do many economists argue that the allocation of resources under perfect competition is likely to be more socially desirable than under monopoly? Use diagrams to illustrate your arguments.

8. What are some of the criticisms directed at the regulatory commissions and the principles they use? Why did Congress say in 1962 that the Food and Drug Administration has to be shown that a new drug is effective as well as safe?

Problems

1. The Uneek Corporation is the only producer of battery-powered soup ladles. Suppose that the demand curve facing the firm is as follows:

Quantity of soup ladles produced per day	Price (dollars per soup ladle)
1	30
2	20
3	10
4	6
5	1

a. Using these data fill in the following table for the Uneek Corporation:

Quantity	Total revenue (dollars)	Marginal revenue (dollars)
1	_____	
2	_____	_____
3	_____	_____
4	_____	_____
5	_____	_____

b. Suppose that the Uneek Corporation has a horizontal marginal cost curve, its marginal cost being $9 per soup ladle (see following graph). Its fixed costs are zero.

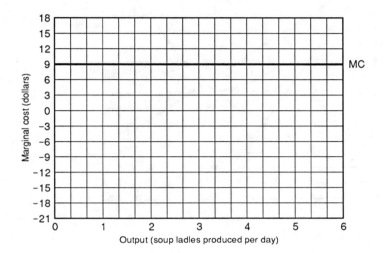

If the Uneek Corporation's costs are as described above, and if it is producing 1 unit of output, how much will a second unit of output (that is, a second ladle) add to its costs? How much will it add to its revenue? Is it profitable to produce a second unit?

c. Based on the data given above what price should the Uneek Corporation charge?

d. What output should it choose?

e. What is the Uneek Corporation's profit if it produces at the optimal output rate?

f. Suppose that its fixed costs are $10, rather than zero. Will this affect the optimal output rate? Will this affect the firm's profit? If so, how?

2. In a particular industry the minimum value of average cost is reached when a firm produces 1,000 units of output per month. At this output rate, average cost is $1 per unit of output. The demand curve for this product is as follows:

Price (dollars per unit of output)	Quantity (produced per month)
3.00	1,000
2.00	8,000
1.00	12,000
0.50	20,000

a. Is this industry a natural monopoly? Why or why not?

b. If the price is $2, how many firms, each of which is producing an output such that average cost is a minimum, can the market support?

3. The graph below pertains to a monopolist. One of the curves is its demand curve, one is its marginal revenue curve, and one is its marginal cost curve.

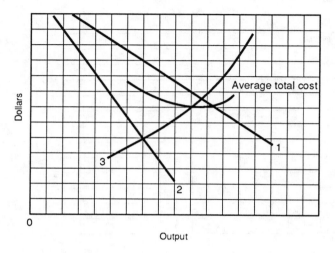

a. What is curve 1?
b. What is curve 2?
c. What is curve 3?
d. Show the output rate that the monopolist will choose and the price it will set.
e. Does the monopolist choose the output rate at which average total cost is a minimum? Do perfectly competitive firms choose such an output rate in the long run?
f. In the graph above show the total profit earned by the monopolist.
g. If the monopolist set price equal to marginal cost, what would be its output rate?

4. Suppose that a hypothetical monopoly has the following demand curve and total costs:

Output sold (per month)	Price	Total revenue	Total cost (per month)	Average total cost	Marginal cost	Marginal revenue	Profit
				(dollars)			
0	50	_____	40	_____			_____
1	45	_____	50	_____ >	_____	_____	_____
2	40	_____	70	_____ >	_____	_____	_____
3	35	_____	95	_____ >	_____	_____	_____
4	30	_____	125	_____ >	_____	_____	_____
5	25	_____	165	_____ >	_____	_____	_____
6	20	_____	225	_____ >	_____	_____	_____

a. Fill in the blanks above.
b. What output (or outputs) will maximize the monopolist's profits?
c. What price will the monopolist choose?

5. Suppose that a monopolist has 5 units of output on hand. It can sell this output in one of two markets. The demand curve for the product in each market is shown below:

Market A		Market B	
Price (dollars)	Quantity demanded	Price (dollars)	Quantity demanded
70	1	50	1
65	2	45	2
60	3	40	3
50	4	30	4
40	5	20	5

There is no way that a unit of the good sold in one market can be resold in the other market.

a. Suppose that the monopolist is selling 4 units in market A and none in market B. Should it sell the fifth unit in market A or market B? Why?
b. Suppose that the monopolist is selling 4 units in market B and none in market A. Should it sell the fifth unit in market A or market B? Why?
c. Prove that the monopolist should allocate the goods between markets so that the marginal revenues in the two markets are equal.

6. A monopolist's demand curve is as follows:

Price (dollars)	Quantity demanded
20	0
15	1
10	2
5	3

The monopolist's total cost (in dollars) equals $3 + 20Q$, where Q is its output rate. What output rate will maximize the monopolist's profit?

7. In industry X, a firm's long-run average cost (in dollars) equals $5 + 3/Q$, where Q is the firm's output per year.

a. Is this industry a natural monopoly? Why or why not?
b. If this industry is monopolized, and if the monopoly maximizes profit, what is the value of marginal revenue in the long run?
c. In the long run, under the circumstances described in part b, we can be sure that price exceeds a certain amount. What is this amount, and why must price exceed it?

8. A labor union can be viewed as a monopoly for supplying labor services. Use diagrammatic analysis together with the concept of price elasticity of demand to apply what you have learned about monopoly to the way in which a union sets the wage. Your analysis should respond to two specific questions: (a) How do the union-set wage and the wage which would be set by competition differ? (b) Even though wages for each working union member might rise when the union sets the wage, show that it is possible that total wages to all members taken together might, in fact, fall when wages are raised to the union level.

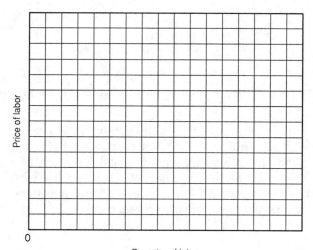

Price of labor

Quantity of labor

9. Suppose a firm is producing Quarks, and that it has a complete monopoly over Quarks. The following information is given:

> Marginal revenue = $1,000 - 20(Q)$
> Total revenue = $1,000(Q) - 10(Q^2)$
> Marginal cost = $100 + 10(Q)$
> where Q = Output of Quarks and P = Price of a Quark

How many Quarks would be sold and at what price if:

a. The firm sets price as a monopoly?
b. The industry (firm) behaves perfectly competitively?

ANSWERS

Completion Questions
1. +$1, -$1   2. $9, $5, $4.50   3. elastic, inelastic   4. greater, lower
5. average total cost   6. marginal revenue   7. monopoly, supplier, competition
8. market franchise, public facility, service, regulate   9. minimum, profitable, expand, decrease   10. historical, reproduction, price level, replacement, historical   11. zero, impossible, small, decreases   12. positive, negative, inelastic

True-False
1. True   2. False   3. False   4. True   5. False   6. True   7. False
8. False   9. True   10. True   11. True   12. True   13. False

Multiple Choice
1. c   2. b   3. c   4. d   5. b   6. b   7. c   8. b   9. e   10. a

Problems
1. a.

Total revenue (dollars)		Marginal revenue (dollars)
30		
	>	10
40		
	>	-10
30		
	>	-6
24		
	>	-19
5		

b. The second ladle will add $9 to its costs and $10 to its revenue. Yes.
c. $20.
d. 2 soup ladles per day.

    e. $22.
    f. No. Yes. It will decrease its profit by $10.
2. a. No. If price is $1, 12 firms of optimal size can exist in the market.
    b. Eight.
3. a. Demand curve.
    b. Marginal revenue curve.
    c. Marginal cost curve.
    d. It will choose a price of OP and an output of OQ.

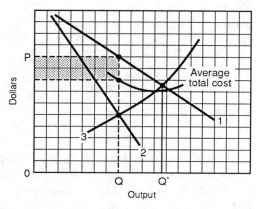

    e. No. Yes.
    f. The shaded area in the graph in the answer to part d equals this profit.
    g. OQ' in the graph in the answer to part d.
4. a.

Total revenue	Average total cost		Marginal cost	Marginal revenue	Profit
		(dollars)			
0	—				−40
		>	10	45	
45	50				−5
		>	20	35	
80	35				10
		>	25	25	
105	31 2/3				10
		>	30	15	
120	31 1/4				−5
		>	40	5	
125	33				−40
		>	60	−5	
120	37 1/2				−105

    b. 2 or 3 units per month.
    c. $40 or $35.
5. a. The marginal revenue from the fifth unit in market A is zero. The marginal revenue from the first unit in market B is $50. Thus it should be sold in market B.

    b.   The marginal revenue from the fifth unit in market B is –\$20. The marginal revenue from the first unit in market A is \$70. Thus it should be sold in market A.

    c.   If the marginal revenue in one market is less than in the other, it will pay the monopolist to allocate one more unit to the latter market and one less to the former market. Thus the monopolist will be maximizing profit only when the marginal revenue in each market is equal.

6. Marginal cost equals \$20. The marginal revenue from the first unit of output is \$15, from the second unit \$5, and from the third unit –\$5. Thus, the monopolist should produce nothing.

7. a.   Yes, because long-run average cost falls continually as output increases.

    b.   The firm's long-run total cost equals $Q(5 + 3/Q) = 3 + 5Q$. Thus, its long-run marginal cost equals \$5. Since marginal revenue equals marginal cost if the monopolist maximizes profit, long-run marginal revenue equals \$5.

    c.   Price exceeds \$5, because price exceeds marginal revenue so long as the product's demand curve is downward-sloping to the right.

8. a.   The demand and supply curves of labor are shown below. The marginal revenue curve corresponding to the demand curve is also given.

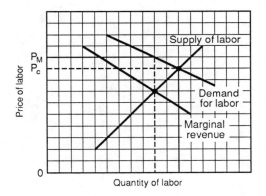

If the union behaves as a monopolist, it will set a wage of P_M. Under competition, the wage would be P_c.

    b.   If the demand curve for labor is price elastic, an increase in the wage will reduce the total wages. That is, it will reduce the quantity of labor demanded times the wage.

9. a.   Since marginal revenue = marginal cost,

$$1,000 - 20Q = 100 + 10Q,$$

which means that $900 = 30Q$, or $Q = 30$.

Since $PQ = 1,000Q - 10Q^2$, the demand curve must be

$$P = 1,000 - 10Q.$$

And if $Q = 30$, P must equal 700.

b. Since the industry's supply curve would be the same as the monopolist's marginal cost curve, the supply curve would be

$$P = 100 + 10Q.$$

As pointed out in part a, the demand curve is

$$P = 1,000 - 10Q.$$

Thus in a competitive market,

$$100 + 10Q = 1,000 - 10Q$$
$$20Q = 900$$
$$Q = 45.$$

And $P = 1,000 - 10(45) = 550$.

CHAPTER 20

Monopolistic Competition,

Oligopoly, and Antitrust Policy

Chapter Profile

Monopolistic competition occurs where there are many sellers whose products are somewhat different. The demand curve facing each firm slopes downward to the right. The conditions for long-run equilibrium are that each firm is maximizing profits and that economic profits are zero.

The firm under monopolistic competition is likely to produce less, and charge a higher price, than under perfect competition. Relative to pure monopoly, monopolistically competitive firms are likely to have lower profits, greater output, and lower prices. Firms under monopolistic competition will offer a wider variety of styles, brands, and qualities than will firms under perfect competition.

Oligopoly is characterized by a small number of firms and a great deal of interdependence, actual and perceived, among them. Oligopoly is a common market structure in the United States.

Game theory is often used to analyze oligopoly. A game is described in terms of its players, rules, payoffs, and information conditions. The relevant features of a two-person game can be shown by the payoff matrix. A dominant strategy is a strategy that is the player's best choice regardless of what the other player does.

Conditions in oligopolistic industries tend to promote collusion. A cartel is an open formal, collusive arrangement. A profit-maximizing cartel will act like a monopolist with a number of plants or divisions, each of which is a member firm. In practice, it appears that the members of a cartel often divide markets geographically or in accord with each firm's level of sales in the past.

Price leadership is quite common in oligopolistic industries, one or a few firms apparently setting the price and the rest following their lead. Two types of price leadership are the dominant-firm model and the barometric-firm model.

Relative to perfect competition, it seems likely that both price and profits will be higher under oligopoly. Moreover, oligopolistic industries will tend to spend more on advertising, product differentiation, and style changes than perfectly competitive industries.

In 1890, the Sherman Act was passed. It outlawed any contract, combination, or conspiracy in restraint of trade and made it illegal to monopolize or attempt to monopolize. In 1914, Congress passed the Clayton Act, and the Federal Trade Commission was created. A more recent antitrust development was the Celler-Kefauver Anti-Merger Act of 1950.

The real impact of the antitrust laws depends on the interpretation placed on these laws by the courts. In its early cases, the Supreme Court put forth and used the famous rule of reason—that only unreasonable combinations in restraint of trade, not all trusts, required conviction under the Sherman Act. The situation changed greatly in the 1940s when the Court decided that Alcoa, because it controlled practically all of the nation's aluminum output, was in violation of the antitrust laws.

Many observers seem to feel that the antitrust laws have not been as effective as they might—or should—have been, largely because they do not have sufficient public support. At the same time, many feel that the evidence, although incomplete and unclear, suggests that they have had an effect on business behavior and markets. Two important cases decided in the past 20 years involved AT&T and IBM.

Concepts for Review

Monopolistic competition	Cartel
Oligopoly	Price leader
Pure oligopoly	Dominant firm
Differentiated oligopoly	Barometric firm
Product differentiation	Antitrust laws
Product group	Rule of reason
Collusion	Game theory
Payoff matrix	Dominant strategy

Completion Questions

1. The demand and cost curves of a monopolistically competitive firm are given on the next page. If the firm charges a price of $4, its profits will equal about

   _____. If the firm charges a price of $6, its profits will

   equal about _____. If it charges a price of $8, its profits

   will equal about _____. In the long run, (entry, exit)

   _____ will occur in this industry.

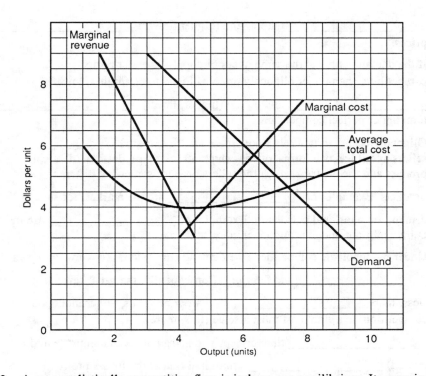

2. A monopolistically competitive firm is in long-run equilibrium. Its marginal revenue equals $5. If its marginal revenue plus its economic profit equal one-half of its price, its price equals $_____, and its marginal cost equals $_____. In game theory, a strategy is a _____ of what a player will do under each contingency.

3. All firms in an industry have marginal cost curves that are horizontal lines at $5 per unit of output. If they combine to form a cartel, the cartel's marginal cost (will, will not) _____ be $5 per unit of output. If the cartel maximizes profit, its marginal revenue will be (greater than, smaller than, equal to) _____ $5 per unit of output, and its price will be (greater than, smaller than, equal to) _____ $5 per unit of output.

4. Under monopolistic competition, the firm is likely to produce (more, less) _____ and charge a (higher, lower) _____ price than under perfect competition.

5. Relative to pure monopoly, monopolistically competitive firms are likely to have (greater, lower) _____ profits, (greater, lower)

_____ output, and (higher, lower) _____
prices.

6. If the demand curve is the same under oligopoly as under perfect competition, then under oligopoly price will tend to be (higher, lower)

_____ and output (higher, lower) _____
than under perfect competition.

7. Oligopoly occurs in markets where there are (few, many) _____
sellers and it has two forms: one in which all sellers produce an identical product and the other in which the sellers produce somewhat different

products. Examples of _____ are the markets for steel,

cement, tin cans, and petroleum. Examples of _____ are the markets for automobiles and machinery.

8. Under monopolistic competition, the demand curve slopes (downward, upward)

_____ to the right. Consequently, marginal revenue must be

(less, more) _____ than price. Thus, under monopolistic competition, marginal cost must also be (less, more)

_____ than price, since marginal revenue must (equal,

exceed) _____ marginal cost at the firm's profit-

maximizing output rate. But if marginal cost is (less, more) _____

than price, the firm's output rate must be (less, more) _____

—and the price (higher, lower) _____—than if marginal cost equals price, which is the case under perfect competition.

9. A(n) _____ is an open, formal, collusive arrangement among

firms. In many countries in Europe, _____ are common and

legally acceptable. In the United States, most _____
arrangements, whether secret or open, were declared illegal by the Sherman

Antitrust Act, which was passed in _____.

10. There is always a temptation for oligopolists to _____ on any collusive agreement. So long as the other firms stick to the agreement,

any firm that _____ its price below that agreed to under the collusive arrangement can take a lot of business away from the other

firms and (decrease, increase) _____ its profits substantially, at least in the short run.

11. In order to coordinate their behavior without outright collusion, some industries contain a(n) _____. It is quite common in oligopolistic industries for one or a few firms to _____ the price and for the rest to follow their lead. Two types of _____ leadership are the _____ model and the _____ model.

True-False

_____ 1. Under perfect competition, firms will offer a greater variety of styles, brands, and qualities than under monopolistic competition.

_____ 2. Monopolistic competition occurs in markets where there are few sellers, and oligopoly occurs where there are many sellers.

_____ 3. In an oligopoly, any change in one firm's price or output generally influences the sales and profits of its rivals.

_____ 4. In all games, every player has a dominant strategy.

_____ 5. Under monopolistic competition there must be a large number of firms in the product group.

_____ 6. The number of firms in the product group must be large enough under monopolistic competition so that each firm expects its actions to go unheeded by its rivals and is unimpeded by possible retaliatory moves on their part.

_____ 7. A firm under monopolistic competition may be somewhat inefficient because it tends to operate with excess capacity.

_____ 8. A cartel may act like a monopolist with a number of plants or divisions, each of which is a member firm.

_____ 9. In practice, it appears that cartels often divide markets geographically or in accord with a firm's level of sales in the past.

_____ 10. During the 1950s there was widespread collusion among about 30 firms selling turbine generators, switchgears, transformers, and related products with total sales of about $1.5 billion per year.

_____ 11. Collusion is often difficult to achieve and maintain because an oligopoly contains an unwieldy number of firms, or the product is quite heterogeneous, or the cost structures of the firms differ considerably.

_____ 12. Oligopolists tend to compete less aggressively through advertising and product differentiation than through direct price reduction.

_____ 13. Oligopolistic industries tend to spend more on advertising, product differentiation, and style changes than perfectly competitive industries.

_____ 14. A monopolistically competitive firm's short-run demand and cost curves are as follows:

Price (dollars)	Quantity demanded	Total cost (dollars)	Output
8	1	5	1
7	2	7	2
6	3	9	3
4	4	11	4
3	5	20	5

This firm, if it maximizes profit, will choose an output rate of 4.

_____ 15. In the previous question, the number of firms in this industry will tend to increase, if all firms in the industry are like this one.

_____ 16. In question 14, if the firm's fixed cost rises by $5, the firm's short-run output rate will be unaffected.

_____ 17. In question 14, if the firm's costs rise by $10, the number of firms in this industry will tend to decrease (because of exit), if all firms in the industry are like this one.

Multiple Choice

1. The graph below pertains to a monopolistically competitive firm:

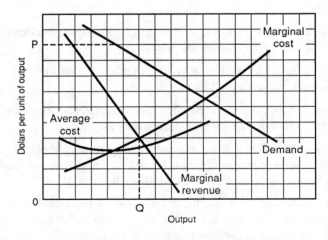

This firm would be foolish to set a price of *OP* because:

a. marginal revenue exceeds marginal cost at this price.
b. it exceeds the profit-maximizing price.

c. it results in an output that is lower than the profit-maximizing output.
d. all of the above.
e. only b and c are true.

2. In the previous question, if the firm chooses an output rate of OQ:

a. other firms will tend to enter the industry, since entry is easy.
b. the firm will make an economic profit.
c. the firm will set a price of OP.
d. all of the above.
e. only a and b are true.

3. One major assumption of Chamberlin's theory of monopolistic competition is that:

a. demand curves will be the same for each firm but cost curves will be different.
b. each firm's product is a fairly close substitute for the others in the group.
c. there are just a few firms in each group.
d. each firm expects its actions to influence those of its rivals.
e. all of the above.

4. In 1993 industry A was a perfectly competitive industry in long-run equilibrium. In 1995 it was cartelized, the result being that its economic profit was $10 million higher than in 1993. In 1995 its economic profits were:

a. zero.
b. less than $10 million.
c. $10 million.
d. more than $10 million.
e. indeterminate on the basis of the available data.

Discussion and Extension Questions

1. Suppose your economics professor states publicly that he grades on a curve (i.e., the top 10 percent of the students get an A, the next 20 percent a B, the next 40 percent a C, the next 20 percent a D, and the lowest 10 percent fail). The whole class could save itself a lot of work then by agreeing privately not to study at all (assuming the love of knowledge is negligible) for the final exam and just let the rankings thus far determine the final grades. Why might such an agreement be difficult to maintain and enforce?

2. In the middle of the 1970s there was considerable debate in Congress and elsewhere concerning the desirability of breaking up the major oil firms. Do you believe such a step would be socially desirable? Why or why not?

3. "A cartel merely redistributes income. It takes from the cartel's customers and gives to the cartel members. So long as the latter are as worthy as the former, there are no adverse social consequences." Comment and evaluate.

4. Under monopolistic competition, will the firm produce less than the minimum-cost output in the long run? Why or why not? How will the level of price under monopolistic competition compare with that under perfect competition? Under monopoly?

5. What is a cartel? How does a profit-maximizing cartel set its price? What is meant by price leadership? Does it occur frequently?

Problems

1. The cost curves and demand curve of the Jones Manufacturing Company, a monopolistically competitive firm, are shown below:

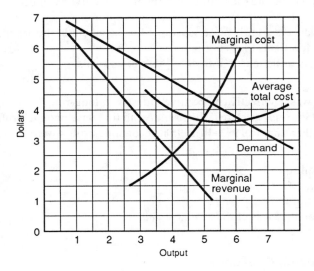

a. What output rate will this firm choose?
b. What price will it charge?
c. How great will be its profits?
d. Is this a long-run equilibrium situation?

2. The India Company and the China Company are duopolists. Each firm has two possible strategies. The payoff matrix is as follows:

Possible strategies for the China Company	Possible strategies for the India Company	
	Strategy A	Strategy B
Strategy 1	China's profit: $6 million India's profit: $5 million	China's profit: $7 million India's profit: $6 million
Strategy 2	China's profit: $5 million India's profit: $6 million	China's profit: $6 million India's profit: $7 million

a. Does the China Company have a dominant strategy?
b. Does the India Company have a dominant strategy?

c. What strategy will the China Company choose?
d. What strategy will the India Company choose?

3. Suppose that an industry is composed of 20 firms, each with a horizontal marginal cost curve. In particular, each firm can produce at a marginal cost of $2 per unit of output. Variation in industry output does not affect the cost curve of the individual firms.

   a. If the industry is cartelized, what will the marginal cost curve of the cartel look like?
   b. The marginal revenue for the cartel is $3 when it produces 100 units of output, $2 when it produces 200 units of output, and $1 when it produces 300 units of output per month. Will it produce more or less than 100 units of output per month?
   c. Will it produce more or less than 300 units per month?
   d. Can you tell what output level it will choose? If so, what is it?

4. An oligopolistic industry selling a homogeneous product is composed of two firms. The two firms set the same price and share the total market equally. The demand curve confronting each firm (assuming that the other firm sets the same price as this firm) is shown below. Each firm's total cost function is also shown below:

Price (dollars)	Quantity demanded	Output	Total cost (dollars)
10	5	5	45
9	6	6	47
8	7	7	50
7	8	8	55
6	9	9	65

   a. Assuming that each firm is right in believing that the other firm will charge the same price that it does, what is the price that each should charge?
   b. Under the assumptions in part a, what output rate should each firm set?
   c. Is there bound to be entry into this industry in the long run?
   d. Is there any incentive for each firm to cut its price to somewhat below its rival's price? If so, what is it?

5. Suppose that if industry A sets its price above $5 per unit, a swarm of new firms will enter the industry and take a very large proportion of the sales away from the established firms.

   a. What effect does this have on the shape of the demand curve confronting the established firms in the industry?
   b. What effect do you think that this will have on the industry's pricing practices?

ANSWERS

Completion Questions
1. –$6, $11, $16, entry   2. $10, $5, complete specification   3. will, equal to, greater than   4. less, higher   5. lower, greater, lower   6. higher, lower   7. few, oligopoly with an identical product, oligopoly with somewhat different products   8. downward, less, less, equal, less, less, higher   9. cartel, cartels, collusive, 1890   10. cheat, cuts, increase   11. price leader, set, price, dominant-firm, barometric-firm

True-False
1. False   2. False   3. True   4. False   5. True   6. True   7. True   8. True 9. True   10. True   11. True   12. False   13. True   14. False   15. True 16. True   17. True

Multiple Choice
1. d   2. e   3. b   4. c

Problems
1.   a. 4 units of output.
     b. $5.
     c. $4.
     d. No.
2.   a. Yes.
     b. Yes.
     c. Strategy 1.
     d. Strategy B.
3.   a. A horizontal line at $2 = MC.
     b. More.
     c. Less.
     d. Yes. 200 units of output, if it maximizes profit.
4.   a. $9.
     b. 6.
     c. Not necessarily; it depends on the extent of the barriers to entry.
     d. Yes, because its demand curve is likely to be very elastic, if the other firm does not match its price cut.
5.   a. The demand curve may have a kink at the price of $5; it may be much more price elastic above this price than below it.
     b. The established firms may avoid raising the price above $5, since this would encourage entry.

CHAPTER 21

Pollution and the Environment

Chapter Profile

One of the major social issues of the 1990s is environmental pollution. To a considerable extent, environmental pollution is an economic problem. Waste disposal and other pollution-causing activities result in external diseconomies.

Firms and individuals that pollute the water and air (and other facets of the environment) often pay less than the true social costs of disposing of their wastes in this way. Part of the true social cost is borne by other firms and individuals, who must pay to clean up the water or air, or who must live with the consequences.

Because of the divergence of private from social costs, the market system does not result in an optimal allocation of resources. Firms and individuals create too much waste and dispose of it in excessively harmful ways. Because the polluters do not pay the full cost of waste disposal, their products are artificially cheap, with the result that they produce too much of these products.

The government can intervene in several ways to help remedy the breakdown of the market system in this area. One way is to issue regulations for waste disposal and other activities influencing the environment. Another is to establish effluent fees, charges a polluter must pay to the government for discharging wastes, or transferable emissions permits. In recent decades, there has been considerable growth in government programs designed to control pollution.

It is extremely difficult to determine how clean the environment should be. The sensible goal for society is to permit the level of pollution that minimizes the sum of the costs of pollution and the costs of controlling pollution; but no one has a very clear idea of what these costs are, and to a large extent the choices must be made through the political process.

Concepts for Review

External diseconomy
Private costs
Social costs
Zero economic growth
Transferable emissions permits

Zero population growth
Direct regulation
Effluent fees
Tax credits

Completion Questions

1. When important external diseconomies are present, government can try to reduce pollution through _____, _____ and/or _____. Also, tax credits can be used.

2. A(n) _____ occurs when one person's or firm's use of a resource imposes damages on other people who cannot obtain proper compensation.

3. _____ are charges that a polluter must pay to the government for discharging waste. Faced with an effluent fee, a polluter will find it profitable to reduce waste discharge to the point where the cost of reducing an additional unit of waste is _____ the effluent fee.

4. An agency which establishes standards for air and water quality is the _____.

5. The sensible goal for our society is to minimize the sum of the costs of pollution and the _____.

6. A major contributor to air pollution is the combustion of _____ fuels, particularly _____ and _____ products.

7. If a paper mill uses water and then treats it to restore its quality, there is no divergence between _____ and _____ cost. In other words, there are no _____.

8. Some power companies (do, do not) _____ pay the full cost of disposing of wastes in the atmosphere. Thus they may set an artificially (high, low) _____ price, and the public may be induced to use (less, more) _____ electric power than is socially desirable.

True-False

_____ 1. When polluters do not pay the true cost of waste disposal, too little of their products is produced.

_____ 2. The price system is unlikely to allocate resources efficiently in the presence of significant external diseconomies.

_____ 3. As national output goes up, it is most likely that pollution levels will fall considerably.

_____ 4. If polluters are forced to pay the social costs of disposing of their wastes, the prices of many goods we buy must rise.

_____ 5. The price system is based on the supposition that the full cost of using each resource is borne by the person or firm that uses it.

_____ 6. Immediately after cans and no-deposit bottles were introduced, the consumer of beverages no longer had to pay for the cost of disposing of the cans or bottles.

_____ 7. Technological change is a potential hero in the fight against pollution, because the creation of new technology is an important way to reduce the harmful side effects of existing techniques.

_____ 8. The average American is responsible for much less pollution than the average citizen of most other countries.

_____ 9. Economists favor effluent fees or transferable emissions permits because this approach requires far less information in the hands of the relevant government agencies than does direct regulation.

_____ 10. Subsidies to promote the purchase of particular types of pollution-control equipment may result in relatively inefficient and costly reductions in pollution.

_____ 11. The sensible goal for our society is to minimize the sum of the costs of pollution and the costs of controlling pollution.

Multiple Choice

1. If a chemical firm pollutes a river and forces fishing firms downstream to install devices to clean up the water, from the point of view of society as a whole:

   a. chemical output and fish output are too high.
   b. chemical output and fish output are too low.
   c. chemical output is too low and fish output is too high.
   d. chemical output is too high and fish output is too low.
   e. none of the above.

2. At the current level of pollution suppose that the social cost of reducing pollution by one unit is less than the social benefit of reducing pollution by one unit. If so:

   a. the current level of pollution is optimal.
   b. there is too little pollution from society's point of view.
   c. there is too much pollution from society's point of view.
   d. all pollution should be eliminated.
   e. existing pollution control measures should be dropped.

3. Taylor Bingham and Allen Miedema have estimated that the cost of reducing sulfur emissions to current standards in St. Louis, Missouri, would be about $50 million per year if direct controls were used and about $29 million if effluent fees were used. The lower cost with effluent fees is due to the fact that:

   a. there are large differences in abatement costs among polluters.
   b. effluent fees induce larger reductions in sulfur emissions among steam-electric power plants (where such reductions are cheap) than among oil refineries (where such reductions are expensive).
   c. direct controls do not result in the cost of reducing emission by one unit being the same for polluters.
   d. all of the above.
   e. none of the above.

4. Bingham and Miedema estimated that an effluent fee of 13 cents per pound of sulfur discharge would induce the required curtailment of emissions in St. Louis, while in Cleveland the effluent fee would have to be 19 cents per pound. Such differences in the effluent fee may be due to:

   a. differences between cities in the amount by which the total emission of sulfur is to be reduced.
   b. differences between cities in industrial composition.
   c. differences between cities in the technology used in each industry.
   d. all of the above.
   e. none of the above.

Discussion and Extension Questions

1. The optimal amount of pollution is not zero; we're quite sure of that. However, how do we know that given some pollution is necessary for a social optimum, we currently have too much pollution? Is it possible that we do not have enough pollution yet? Is more, not less, the direction in which we should be moving?

2. Can you utilize your understanding of cost-benefit analysis, opportunity costs, and other economic principles you have absorbed to roughly analyze how one would decide whether or not a particular state should pass legislation to ban throw-away or disposable bottles and cans for soft drinks and beer? Should manufacturers also be forbidden to use throw-away containers for macaroni? Detergents? Baby food? Should consumers have to pay a deposit on egg cartons?

3. Show how too much pollution, from society's point of view, is likely to arise if the private costs of using water and air for waste disposal are less than the social costs. Is it likely that the output rate of heavy polluters is too high, from a social point of view? Why or why not? Show how, once cans and no-deposit bottles were introduced, an external diseconomy arose with regard to disposal of these items. Are there any states that now require a deposit on bottles?

4. Must economic growth necessarily result in increased pollution? Should the rate of technological change be slowed in order to reduce pollution? Explain.

5. Explain how transferable emissions permits can be used to reduce pollution. What are their advantages? Why do many economists prefer them over direct regulation? Over tax credits for pollution-control equipment?

Problems

1. a. Suppose that the cost to society of various levels of pollution is as follows:

Pollution (millions of tons per year)	Cost (billions of dollars per year)
1	3
2	6
3	10
4	15
5	22
6	30
7	40
8	60

Plot this relationship in the graph below:

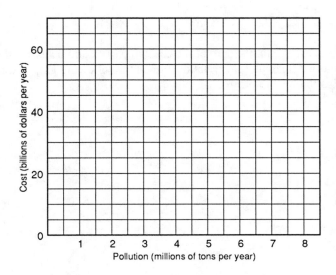

b. Suppose that the cost to society of pollution control varies as follows with the level of pollution:

Pollution (millions of tons per year)	Cost (billions of dollars per year)
1	50
2	40
3	32
4	25
5	19
6	14
7	9
8	5

Plot this relationship in the graph below:

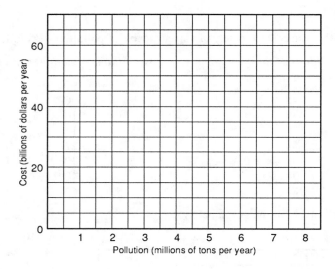

c. Does it make sense to plot the sum of the costs in parts a and b against the level of pollution? If so, plot this relationship on the following graph, and tell what this relationship means.

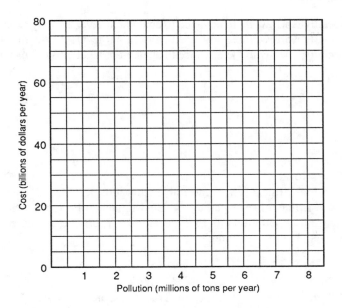

d. Given the data in parts a and b, what is the optimal level of pollution? Why isn't it sensible to aim for zero pollution?

2. Some states, such as Oregon and Vermont, have passed laws that all carbonated-beverage containers must carry a minimum refundable deposit.

   a. According to the director of communications services for American Can Company, "What *is* happening in Oregon is that consumers are paying $10 million more a year for beer and soft drinks than they did before the bottle bill became law. Retail price increases . . . have far exceeded those in neighboring states." Why do you think that this was true?

   b. According to this executive of American Can Company, "Oregon (and Vermont) consumers are denied their free choice of container. . . ." Is this true? According to William Baumol and Wallace Oates, this amounts to "a denial of . . . the freedom to pollute unpenalized." Do you agree?

3. According to one study of the Delaware River, the extra social costs involved in going from one level of pollution abatement to another are shown below. Also shown are the extra benefits to society in going from one level of pollution to another. (All figures are in millions of dollars.)

Transition	Extra cost	Extra benefit
From abatement level 1 to 2	35	200
From abatement level 2 to 3	20	20
From abatement level 3 to 4	130	10
From abatement level 4 to 5	245	25

   a. If abatement level 1 is currently being achieved, is it socially worthwhile to advance to abatement level 2? Why or why not?

b. Is it socially worthwhile to advance to abatement level 3? Why or why not?
c. Is it socially worthwhile to advance to abatement level 4? Why or why not?
d. Is it socially worthwhile to advance to abatement level 5? Why or why not?

ANSWERS

Completion Questions

1. direct regulation, effluent fees, transferable emissions permits   2. external diseconomy   3. Effluent fees, equal to   4. Environmental Protection Agency
5. costs of controlling pollution   6. fossil, coal, oil   7. private, social, external diseconomies   8. do not, low, more

True-False

1. False   2. True   3. False   4. True   5. True   6. True   7. True   8. False
9. True   10. True   11. True

Multiple Choice

1. d   2. c   3. d   4. d

Problems

1. a.

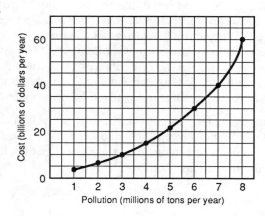

b.

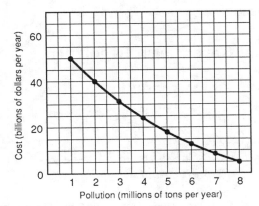

c.

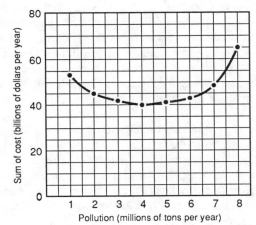

Yes. This relationship shows how the total costs—both pollution costs and pollution control costs—vary with the amount of pollution.

    d. 4 million tons. Because it costs more to reduce the pollution (below 4 million tons) than it is worth.

2. a. Because of increased costs of handling, sorting, washing, returning, and refilling bottles, according to this executive.

    b. The issue is too complex to permit a very brief answer, but many economists would agree with Baumol and Oates.

3. a. Yes, because the benefit exceeds the cost.

    b. No, because the benefit does not exceed the cost.

    c. No, because the benefit does not exceed the cost.

    d. No, because the benefit does not exceed the cost.

CASE 3

Cable Television and Government Regulation

ROBERT CRANDALL AND EDWARD MARKEY

CABLE TELEVISION: REINVENTING REGULATION
Robert Crandall

One can only hope that Vice President Albert Gore does a better job reinventing government than he did reinventing regulation. One of Gore's last big accomplishments as a senator was passing the 1992 Cable TV Consumer Protection and Competition Act, which reimposed rate regulation of cable television—just eight years after the industry was deregulated by Congress. Gore and his colleagues, tired of consumer complaints about the rapacity of the cable operators who had been freed from municipal regulation by the 1984 Cable Act, passed legislation that marked the first attempt to reverse course in the deregulation campaign that began in the mid-1970s.

Starting with the Ford presidency and continuing through every administration until that of George Bush, federal policymakers had sought to deregulate major industries—airlines, trucking, air cargo, railroads, natural gas production and pipelines, telephone equipment, banking, telephone communications, and cable television. The results had been generally favorable, with one big exception—the partial deregulation of the thrift industry that had invited unwarranted risk-taking and even fraud by banks and savings and loans.

By 1992 the deregulation of cable was threatening to go into the "failure" column too. The biggest problem was that after rates were deregulated in December 1986, monthly rates increased by nearly three times the general inflation rate. With cable operators being painted as insensitive, greedy monopolists, congressional action was inevitable and relatively quick in coming. A bill to regulate cable television was introduced in 1990, but Congress did not enact it until 1992.

The result is an extremely complex scheme of federal and municipal regulation. In the extreme, the 1992 law could even lead to cost-of-service regulation for each of the country's 11,000 systems. Given the industry's rapid pace of technical change, the widely differentiated product offered, and the difficulty of separating costs of different services, such regulation would surely be a nightmare. At the very least, the law requires that the Federal Communications Commission set regulatory "benchmarks" for basic cable rates—still no mean feat in this complicated industry.

But that is not the worst of the news. Within less than a year, cable reregulation has become almost as unpopular as deregulation. Rates may even have risen as the result of the new FCC regulations that implement the 1992 law. A recent FCC

Robert Crandall is a senior fellow at the Brookings Institution; Edward Markey is Chairman of the Subcommittee on Telecommunications and Finance of the U.S. House of Representatives. These articles appeared in the *Brookings Review* (Winter 1994, pp. 12–15 and 20–21).

survey found that 31 percent of the subscribers to systems owned by 14 national cable companies actually saw their rates rise as the result of the new FCC rules. Because the systems owned by 11 other companies so revamped their pricing strategies in response to FCC regulation, the FCC staff has not yet been able to determine whether rates have risen or fallen for these companies.

While the vice president has remained surprisingly silent about the effect of his handiwork, his erstwhile colleagues in Congress are now beginning to pass the blame to the FCC. The problem, however, is with the rate reregulation, not with those entrusted with implementing it.

A Primer on Cable Television

Cable television was not always perceived as an evil monopoly. In its early years, cable provided a competitive threat to government-franchised monopolists—the television broadcasters. The FCC, with the prodding of Congress, had so restricted television licenses to the electromagnetic spectrum that enormous monopoly rents were earned by the lucky and influential few who obtained these grants of privilege.

In many parts of the country, households had access to only two or three television stations because of the FCC's explicit decision to limit competition in this new medium. A third or fourth might be over the next hill or mountain, but inaccessible as a result. Cable television was the invention of entrepreneurs who sensed that households might pay something to get these additional stations or to improve their reception on the two or three local ones. In the 1960s cable was simply a "retransmission" medium.

Very soon cable operators discovered that they could import more signals from more distant markets, and some even mused about the possibilities of offering "pay" movies or sports channels. Clearly these discoveries were a threat to the local broadcast monopolists, who quickly used their political clout in Washington to get further protection. In the late 1960s the FCC moved aggressively to limit importing distant signals and leapfrogging over nearer signals to import better "superstations." It required that scarce channel capacity be allocated to local-origination channels that few used and no one watched, and even prohibited most forms of pay cable. And it severely limited the programming that could be offered on "pay" channels, such as HBO, Showtime, or Disney in today's market.

It took more than a decade, but these draconian regulations were eventually lifted by the FCC or invalidated by the courts. By 1980 cable was unleashed as a major competitor of broadcast television, offering pay services, superstations, and many new cable networks. The only remaining obstacle was municipal regulation—which had arguably limited cable rate increases and certainly padded the pockets of local politicians and their friends. In 1984 Congress eliminated this obstacle by banning municipal rate regulation of cable systems that faced effective competition.

Cable systems were thus free to begin to grow without much government interference. Propelled by declining electronics prices and the end of government prohibitions on signal carriage, cable operators vastly expanded their channel capacity. In 1980 the median system had fewer than 12 channels. Today all but a few subscribers have access to 30 or more, and one-third of subscribers have access to more than 54 channels.

Cable was also extended into the large cities from which it had been essentially excluded by the earlier FCC signal-carriage rules. In 1980 fewer than 25 percent of households had cable service. Today nearly two-thirds subscribe and more than 95 percent have a distribution cable passing their home. Cable is essentially ubiquitous.

It is far from clear that coaxial cable is or will be the best medium for delivering video signals to residences. Terrestrial radio systems (perhaps in a cellular format), broadcast satellites, or even fiber-optics lines might be better. The market will have to separate the winners from the losers unless government intervenes. Unfortunately, the fiber-optics alternative is already hamstrung by the 1984 Cable Act, which not only freed cable companies from rate regulation but banned local telephone companies from offering "cable television" service in their franchised areas, surely a bad combination of policies.

Fortunately, the courts and the FCC have already moved to rectify Congress's penchant for creating monopoly power and then complaining about the subsequent abuse of the public interest by its beneficiaries. In 1991 the Bush FCC decided to allow telephone companies to offer "video dial tone" over their networks. This common carrier distribution service would allow third parties—for example, television networks, film companies, sports leagues, General Motors, or Ross Perot—to distribute television programming. In the FCC's view, the service would not violate the 1984 law because telephone companies would simply be in the transmission business and would not control the programming choices as cable operators do.

The courts have made a second, more fundamental attack on the 1984 Cable Act's prohibition of telephone company entry into cable television. Bell Atlantic, a regional telephone holding company, argued in federal court that the prohibition violates the First Amendment, and a U.S. District Court has agreed. If the decision is upheld on appeal, it may start an assault on a variety of government intrusions into the regulation of the media, surely a signal victory for civil libertarians.

As the telephone companies now ponder entry into some form of video distribution, they confront an array of technological choices—and the chance to be serious competitors. Advances in digital signal compression technology may allow them to offer some video service, probably pay-per-view, through ordinary copper wires, thus relieving them of the necessity of extending fiber optics to every home at perhaps $1,500 per subscriber. Of course, variants of the new technology will also enable cable companies to expand their service to 400 or 500 channels and new satellite services to provide 100 channels or more to subscribers who purchase a small dish to receive them. Two direct broadcast satellite services are scheduled to begin service early this year.

Home video watchers, it seems, are in for some technological fireworks and for vastly increased competition despite Congress's continuing attempts to protect monopoly in the "public interest." Even video stores are in trouble.

The Dreary Mechanics of Regulation

Swimming fiercely against the tide of this exciting and brave new world of competition, the FCC has just hired hundreds of new staff to implement the 1992 cable law. As entrepreneurs and skilled engineers go about the business of inventing new distribution technologies, bureaucrats are busy reinventing government regulation. It is no mean task, for the new law requires the FCC to set rates for "basic" service at "competitive" levels. But how are they to know what competitive levels *are* if Congress keeps blocking new entry into video services?

The 1992 law requires the FCC to set benchmarks for basic rates—rates for a complement of local broadcast signals and various low-value services—in terms of rates observed in recent years in markets in which there are two or more cable companies or a thriving multichannel video competitor (such as a microwave multipoint distribution service), or in which cable service is taken by fewer than 30 percent of households. That approach would appear reasonable—better than flipping a coin, at least. But there is simply no way to know whether these rates are those that would emerge from a competitive market in equilibrium.

The problem with the law's fundamental approach to a regulatory benchmark is that cable companies may have often been *below* these benchmark rates for a variety of reasons. They might have been building a subscriber base by offering low initial prices, surely not an antisocial activity. Or they may have priced basic service low while charging high rates for set-top converters, remote controls, additional connections, or enhanced basic service. Because the new rules prohibit many of these practices, cable operators have re-tiered their basic service and often have *raised* rates to permissible levels set by the FCC.

Not surprisingly, many of the congressional promoters of cable reregulation have now cried foul. They want to force the FCC to reconsider its initial rules, suppressing rates so that voters will think that Congress has delivered them something.

The basic service rates are only part of the complex web of regulations required by the 1992 law. The FCC must also establish rules for rates charged by cable networks owned in part or in whole by cable television companies. Most such networks are indeed owned by consortia of cable companies who have struggled to get more and more programming to feed their expanding number of channels. In addition, the FCC is supposed to set rules on "horizontal" integration of cable—the number of cable systems that a single entity or set of related entities may own. Both rule requirements are supposed to reduce the "market power" of cable companies in dealing with programmers, though it is far from clear how such power actually affects programming outcomes.

The Future of Reinventing Regulation

The initial troubles of the reregulation process are little more than the comic relief sometimes inadvertently provided from Washington. The danger in cable reregulation lurks elsewhere. First, there is some small risk that Congress will pressure the FCC into so depressing the benchmark for basic services that cable operators will begin to seek refuge in the provisions of the 1992 law that allow for cost-of-service ratemaking.

If the FCC becomes enmeshed in trying to determine the "cost" of basic service, it will sink hopelessly into the regulatory quagmire. Given the technological change that has swept the industry, how will the FCC determine the appropriate value of the cable system's assets for ratemaking purposes? And how will the share of these assets devoted to "basic" programming be determined, given that the same cable and headend equipment carries *all* services? If only one-third of cable systems opt for this variant of regulation, the FCC or municipal regulatory authorities will have to conduct more than 3.500 separate evidentiary proceedings to disentangle these costs, establish allowed rates of return, and set forward-looking subscriber rates. Surely this is not the way to reinvent regulation.

Second, Congress is not going to be content to regulate just the rates of basic cable service as the number of channels explodes to several hundred. The typical cable offering is about to become very complicated, local broadcast signals will become obsolete, and federal regulation of basic service will appear irrelevant. If competition does not develop soon, Congress may be tempted to extend regulation to the pricing of new services, such as movies on demand, interactive programming, or new speciality shopping channels.

If the average cable bill continues to rise as consumers eagerly scan through 400 channels, will Congress be tempted to extend regulation to the rates on each *new* program service also? President Clinton has surely not emerged as a champion of market forces and probably would not veto such a law, as President Bush surely would have. The effect on innovation would be chilling, much as it was in the early days of pay television when regulators decided that two-year-old movies—but not twenty-year-old ones—were appropriate for pay television.

Finally, since Congress already regulates the copyright royalty payments to be made for cable importation of distant *broadcast* signals, it might reason that it could easily extend its reach to cable networks, regulating not only the rates charged by cable systems to subscribers but the payments made to cable networks for the programming.

Invention, Not Regulatory Reinvention

The best way out of the current mess is to encourage competition and wait for its effects to be felt in the marketplace. A good start would be for Congress to repeal the prohibition on telephone provision of cable television if the states implement price-cap regulation in place of rate-of-return regulation for local telephone companies. Alternatively, the Clinton administration could have supported the lower court's position in the Bell Atlantic case, declaring the 1984 telephone company prohibition unconstitutional, but it has chosen to appeal it instead.

Thirty years after deregulation began with the investigation into New York Stock Exchange cartel agreements, we now have an impressive body of evidence that shows that deregulation has served consumers well. Indeed, according to Brookings economist Clifford Winston, the benefits of deregulation have tended to be *underestimated.* Competition has proved to be the best regulator in most markets because government regulators cannot possibly get the prices right and are too often subject to political pressure. For example, it was no accident that Austin, Texas, had only two television stations in the 1950s and 1960s, one of which was owned by Lyndon Johnson. Nor was it an accident that the Reagan administration leaned over backwards to prevent the abolition of truly foolish television network program-ownership rules sought by the movie companies after the chairman of a major motion picture company paid a social visit to the former actor, President Reagan.

The media are too important to be sacrificed up as guinea pigs for experiments in reinventing regulation. Of course, one might make much the same argument about health care, but that is for others to evaluate. For the moment, Congress should not be expected to muster the courage to admit that it was wrong last year. The risk is that Congress might pile on new regulatory requirements. For the present, it should stand aside while the FCC struggles to implement a bad law.

Congress could step up and admit its error of 1984 in banning telephone companies from cable television. If not, the courts may invalidate this ban on competition anyway. Finally, Congress should avoid any further actions to limit competition in this dynamic market, such as funding a new "telecommunications infrastructure" program or mandating regulatory cross subsidies to pay for billions of dollars of fiber-optics highways and off-ramps. The competition for the video customer will be sufficient to induce a great deal of investment in infrastructure.

CABLE TELEVISION: PROMOTING COMPETITION AND THE PUBLIC INTEREST
Edward Markey

Over the past decade the telecommunications marketplace has experienced both explosive growth and intense industry pressure toward concentration. Through it all, Congress has tried to keep the market competitive to guarantee affordable and high-quality telecommunications for the American consumer.

Some observers of congressional efforts, whether to promote competition to AT&T in the long-distance market or, more recently, to promote competition in the cable industry, urge government to get out of the way of the largest companies so they can "compete" freely. This "let the marketplace decide" mentality, however, misses the point that the cable market has not and structurally cannot evolve into a competitive market without some regulatory structure to ensure that new competitors and entrants can compete freely.

The 1984 Cable Act

In 1984, when Congress deregulated the cable television industry and took the power to regulate rates out of the hands of local authorities, it expected that emerging competition in the video marketplace from wireless satellite-based technologies would result in reasonable rates for cable service, improved customer services, and diversity in programming. The ensuing years were not to bear out that expectation.

With deregulation, the cable industry saw a period of unprecedented growth. Between 1984 and 1992 cable subscribership rose from 37 million to 57 million. The percentage of homes passed by a cable wire rose from 71 percent in 1984 to 97 percent in 1992. The number of programming services grew exponentially. Cable evolved from its roots as an antenna service to a video medium in its own right. Cable's arrival as a full-fledged competitor changed the entire face of the video market and, with its second stream of income from subscriber revenues, fundamentally altered the economics of video programming distribution.

The price consumers paid for this transformation, however, was steep. In a series of studies, the General Accounting Office (GAO) documented that in the years following cable deregulation, rates for cable service and equipment increased at more than three times the rate of inflation. A 1990 Consumers' Research study found that in areas where only one cable company existed, fewer channels were provided on average (33 as against 40) and the cost per channel was a third higher than in areas with competition.

The Wireless Cable Association reported that cable rates in 110 localities where microwave distribution systems existed were an average of 30 percent lower than in areas where the cable operator had an unchallenged monopoly. In 1990 a Department of Justice estimate confirmed what many consumers had long suspected, that up to half of basic rate increases since deregulation reflected monopoly power to charge above-competitive prices.

Cable industry customer service standards also failed to keep pace with the needs of a growing subscriber base. Growing customer service complaints underscored the fact that, as local monopolies, cable operators had little incentive to provide customer service as good as that consumers had come to expect from local businesses or from regulated industries such as the telephone company and electric utilities.

Finally, cable operators who controlled both supply and distribution used their control of cable programming services to suppress the much-hoped-for competition from new wireless technologies such as satellite dishes or terrestrial relay systems. By obstructing or outright denying them access to programming, cable operators assured that no consumer would view these new technologies as viable alternatives.

The 1992 Cable Act

Passage of the 1992 Cable Act marked the realization that cable's competitors were not succeeding in their efforts to compete with the existing cable monopoly in 99 percent of the country. The primary purpose of the 1992 act, therefore, was to promote competition and, only in its absence, to regulate rates.

To encourage competition, the act required that programmers provide their product to other forms of video delivery in addition to cable, thus ensuring that satellite and wireless cable delivery systems would have access to programming, such as HBO, Showtime, and Discovery, that they had been denied in the past. Direct broadcast satellite competitors will be up and running within the next year, providing competition to cable operators across the country.

The Cable Act also abolished the exclusive franchise agreement, whereby local governments grant a single cable operator a monopoly and bar all competitors from offering cable services in the franchise area. These agreements, of course, are one big reason why almost 99 percent of Americans have only one choice of a cable operator today.

Both these provisions have successfully begun to limit anticompetitive practices in the cable industry.

Implementing the Cable Act

Over the past 10 months the FCC has issued many regulations implementing the Cable Act. Rules mandating equal access to programming by cable's competitors, reordering cable-broadcaster relations, imposing tough new customer service standards, and mandating equipment compatibility have all been enacted quickly, professionally, and without incident, largely assuring a fairer, more competitive cable marketplace in the years to come.

Unfortunately, the FCC rules implementing rate regulation have apparently allowed rate hikes to an extent that even cable operators never anticipated and that were clearly contrary to the intent of the act. However, the final chapter of the FCC's rate regulations has yet to be written. The first series of enforcement letters from the

FCC should be going out as this article goes to press and will represent the beginning of their efforts to prevent violations and evasions.

Blueprint for the Future

What is often overlooked in the debate over regulation is that regulation means far more than controlling rates. In fact, the most important purpose of most regulation, including the 1992 Cable Act, is to ensure that genuinely competitive markets exist and that the benefits of competition flow to the general public.

There have been many instances in which government regulation has opened up monopoly bottlenecks to increase competition, particularly in the field of telecommunications. Congress, the courts, and the FCC helped encourage competition in the long-distance marketplace through an antitrust case and a series of decisions designed to promote the viability of competitors to AT&T. In the mobile communications field, Congress and the FCC worked to structure a competitive market where none existed only 10 years ago. Spectrum sufficient for two competitors in each market was initially allocated to start up the cellular industry. More recently, spectrum for the new generation of mobile communications—Personal Communications Services—was allocated so that as many as seven operators will compete in a single market.

In its early days, the cable industry itself was a beneficiary of government efforts to foster competition. In 1976 Congress passed the compulsory license provision that enabled cable operators to transmit television programming easily and inexpensively. Furthermore, the FCC did not require cable operators to compensate broadcasters for retransmitting their signals, essentially allowing cable to carry broadcasters' lineups without compensation. In addition, Congress assisted the growing cable industry by forcing utility pole owners to give cable operators access to their poles—freeing cable operators from unreasonable demands by telephone companies and electric utilities.

Through considerable effort and persistence, balancing consumer protection and new competition, today we have two wires running down the street, a cable wire and a phone wire. We have, in addition, wireless delivery systems. Government regulation, not the free market, has guaranteed that these delivery systems are independent and stand ready to compete with each other to provide information and entertainment.

The blueprint for a competitive telecommunications marketplace must ensure multiple means of delivering information to the home and office. One company should not control both the phone and the cable wire running down the street. Two competing wires and the potential for a third wireless option ensure that service and technology entrepreneurs with new ideas will not be forced to pay a high toll or sell out to the owner of the wire.

The philosophy of fostering competition must also apply to the merger proposals between telephone company giants and cable operators that have grabbed headlines in recent months. Telephone companies have argued that their entry into the cable business as owners of programming would result in lower rates for consumers. That may be true, if they become competitors to existing cable monopolies. But it won't be true if they simply become a bigger cable monopoly by eliminating the competition.

Only through true competition, with the cable and telephone wires and additional wireless options serving as competing and independently-owned delivery systems, will the American public realize the promise and benefits of the Information Age.

Discussion Questions

1. Does the available evidence indicate that rates for cable service were higher in areas with only one cable operator? Would you expect this to be true? If so, why?

2. What was the purpose of the 1992 Cable Act? Do you agree with this purpose? Why or why not?

3. What are Robert Crandall's criticisms of the 1992 Cable Act?

4. According to Crandall, "The best way out of the current mess is to encourage competition and wait for its effects to be felt in the marketplace." Do you agree? Why or why not?

5. According to Markey, "the cable market has not and structurally cannot evolve into a competitive market without some regulatory structure to ensure that new competitors and entrants can compete freely." Do you agree? Why or why not?

CHAPTER 22

The Supply and Demand for Labor

Chapter Profile

Assuming perfect competition, a firm will employ each type of labor in an amount such that its marginal product times the product's price equals its wage. In other words, the firm will employ enough labor so that the value of the marginal product of labor equals labor's price.

The firm's demand curve for labor—which shows, for each price of labor, the amount of labor the firm will use—is the firm's value-of-marginal-product curve (if labor is the only variable input). The market demand curve for labor shows the relationship between its price and the total amount of labor demanded in the market.

Labor's price depends on its market supply curve as well as on its market demand curve. Labor's market supply curve is the relationship between the price of labor and the total amount of labor supplied in the market. (Labor's market supply curve may be backward bending.)

An input's price is determined under perfect competition in essentially the same way that a product's price is determined—by supply and demand. The price of labor will tend in equilibrium to the level at which the quantity of labor demanded equals the quantity of labor supplied. By the same token, the equilibrium amount of labor utilized is also given by the intersection of the market supply and demand curves.

There are about 200 national unions in the United States, the biggest being the National Education Association. Each national union is composed of local unions, which operate within the context of the constitution of the national union.

The AFL-CIO is a federation of national unions created by the merger in 1955 of the American Federation of Labor and the Congress of Industrial Organizations. The AFL-CIO is a very important spokesman for the American labor movement, but because the national unions in the AFL-CIO have given up relatively little of their power to the federation, its authority is limited.

There are several ways that unions can increase wages—by shifting the supply curve of labor to the left, by shifting the demand curve for labor to the right, and by influencing the wage directly. Collective bargaining is the process of negotiation between union and management over wages and working conditions.

Concepts for Review

Firm's demand curve for labor	American Federation of Labor
Value of the marginal product of labor	Yellow-dog contracts
Market demand curve for labor	Congress of Industrial Organizations
Derived demand	Checkoff
Market supply curve for labor	Featherbedding
Backward-bending supply curve	Collective bargaining
Noncompeting groups	Closed shop
National unions	Union shop
Local unions	Open shop

Completion Questions

1. A perfectly competitive firm's demand curve for labor slopes downward and to the right because of the law of _____. This is because the firm's demand curve for labor is the same as its _____ curve, and the _____ is equal to the price of the product times the marginal product of labor.

2. In competitive firm X, the marginal product of the first unit of labor is 3 units of output, the marginal product of the second unit of labor is 2 units of output, and the marginal product of the third unit of labor is 1 unit of output.

   If the price of a unit of output is $15, the firm will demand _____ unit(s) of labor when the price of a unit of labor is $40, _____ unit(s) of labor when the price of a unit of labor is $25, and _____ unit(s) of labor when the price of a unit of labor is $20.

3. The profit-maximizing competitive firm uses each input in an amount such that the input's _____ multiplied by the _____ equals the input's _____.

4. Since inputs are demanded to produce other things, the demand for labor and other inputs is called a(n) _____ demand.

5. Labor's _____ is the relationship between the price of labor and the total amount of labor supplied in the market.

6. The supreme governing body of the national union is the _____.

7. An agreement whereby a worker agrees with his or her employer not to join a union is called a(n) _____.

8. The Wagner Act established the _____ and made it an unfair labor practice for employers to _____ to bargain collectively with a union representing a(n) _____ of their workers, or to interfere with their workers' _____ to organize.

9. In 1947, despite bitter labor opposition, the _____ Act was passed. Its aim was to redress the balance between labor and employers. The act established standards of conduct for _____ as well as _____, defined unfair union practices, and stated that unions can be _____ for acts of their agents.

10. In a(n) _____ shop a worker must be a union member before he or she can be hired. This gives the union more power than a(n) _____shop, in which the employer can hire nonunion workers who must then become union members in a certain length of time after being hired. In a(n) _____ shop, the employer can hire both union and nonunion workers, and the latter need not join a union once employed.

True-False

_____ 1. If a union shifts the supply curve of labor to the left, and if the price elasticity of demand for labor is infinite, the price of labor will rise.

_____ 2. If a technological change occurs which increases the marginal productivity of labor, and if at the same time the supply curve of labor shifts to the right, the price of labor must fall.

_____ 3. The Norris-LaGuardia Act permitted state legislatures to pass right-to-work laws.

_____ 4. If the value of the marginal product is greater than the input's price, the perfectly competitive firm can increase its profit by decreasing its utilization of the input.

_____ 5. An example of a backward-bending supply curve might be that for labor.

_____ 6. Union growth was most rapid during the 1920s.

_____ 7. A firm's demand curve for an input shows the relationship between the input's price and the amount of the input utilized by the firm. That is, it shows, for each price, the amount of the input that the firm will use.

_____ 8. Beyond some point, increases in wages may result in smaller amounts of labor being supplied.

_____ 9. The reason for a backward-bending supply curve for labor is that, as the price of labor increases, the individual supplying the labor becomes richer and wants to increase his or her amount of leisure time.

_____ 10. The wage for surgeons is higher than for unskilled labor because the demand curve for surgeons is farther to the right and the supply curve for surgeons is farther to the left than the corresponding curves for unskilled labor.

_____ 11. The Taft-Hartley Act said that, unless workers agree in writing, the employer may not deduct union dues from each worker's paycheck and give them to the union.

Multiple Choice

1. Suppose that the production function of a hypothetical competitive firm is as follows:

Number of workers employed per day	Output per day
1	0
2	5
3	20
4	35
5	38

If the value of the marginal product of a worker is $150 when between 2 and 3 workers are employed per day, the price of a unit of output must be:

a. $1,000. d. $10.
b. $100. e. none of the above.
c. $20.

2. The price elasticity of demand for a particular input will be greater:

a. the more easily other inputs can be substituted for it.
b. the smaller the price elasticity of demand for the product the input helps to produce.
c. in the short run than in the long run.
d. all of the above.
e. none of the above.

3. If the supply curve is backward bending, increases in price (beyond some point) may result in _____ of the input being supplied.

a. amounts increasing quickly to zero c. smaller amounts
b. an imaginary quantity d. a negative amount
   e. none of the above

4. The president of the United States tells the attorney general to obtain an injunction forbidding a strike for 80 days. He is acting on the basis of the:

   a. Norris-LaGuardia Act.   d. Landrum-Griffin Act.
   b. Taft-Hartley Act.   e. none of the above.
   c. Wagner Act.

5. It makes perfectly good sense for a labor union to want to:

   a. maximize the wage rate.   d. all of the above.
   b. maximize its marginal revenue. e. none of the above.
   c. keep its members fully employed.

6. If a union tries to force firms to hire only workers who are already union workers, this is illegal based on:

   a. the Wagner Act.   d. the Norris-LaGuardia Act.
   b. the Landrum-Griffin Act.   e. none of the above.
   c. the Taft-Hartley Act.

7. If firm X refuses to bargain collectively with a union that represents a majority of its workers, this is an unfair labor practice based on:

   a. the Wagner Act.   d. the Norris-LaGuardia Act.
   b. the Landrum-Griffin Act.   e. none of the above.
   c. the Taft-Hartley Act.

8. Which of the following is *not* a provision of the Taft-Hartley Act?

   a. standards of conduct for unions established
   b. unions can be sued for acts of their agents
   c. Federal Mediation Service established
   d. the closed shop outlawed
   e. union elections held by secret ballot

Discussion and Extension Questions

1. Pro football salaries are about half of those in pro baseball and basketball. What factors help to account for this difference?

2. One study suggests that union workers have over the last several decades earned wages that are 10 to 20 percent higher than the wages paid to nonunion labor. Does that imply that wages in the United States would, on average, be lower if there were no unions?

3. How might a consumer boycott of grapes or lettuce work to the detriment of Mexican-American farm laborers in California?

4. "Keynes regarded wages as fixed; Milton Friedman regards them as flexible. Neither is really correct, and it is important that unions, with their immense power, be willing to settle for limited wage increases to prevent ruinous inflation. Unfortunately, there is no evidence they will do so." Discuss and evaluate.

5. "Unions of state and local workers have far too much power. They can shut down entire regions." Comment and evaluate.

6. Why is the Wagner Act often called American labor's Magna Charta?

7. Describe three ways that unions can increase wages. Give examples where each has occurred.

8. If you were an employer, would you prefer a closed shop, an open shop, or a union shop? Why? Which would you prefer if you were president of the union? Why?

Problems

1. Suppose that the demand curve for lawyers is as follows:

Annual wage (thousands of dollars)	Quantity of labor demanded (thousands of person-years)
40	200
60	180
80	160
100	140
120	120
140	100
160	80

a. Draw the demand curve for lawyers.

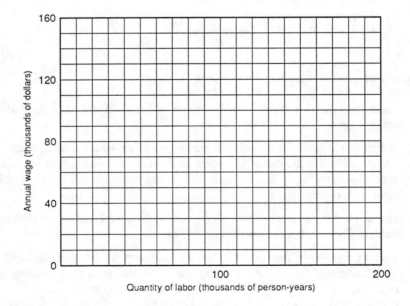

b. Suppose that the supply curve for lawyers is as follows:

Annual wage (thousands of dollars)	Quantity of labor supplied (thousands of person-years)
40	80
60	100
80	120
100	140
120	160
140	180
160	200

Draw the supply curve for lawyers on the graph for part a.

c. What is the equilibrium wage for lawyers if the market is perfectly competitive?

d. Suppose that lawyers form a union, and that the union forces the wage up to $140,000 a year. How many person-years of labor will be supplied but will be unable to find work?

2. Suppose that the relationship between the number of laborers employed per day in a car wash and the number of cars washed per day is as follows:

Number of laborers	Cars washed
1	15
2	40
3	50
4	55

a. Suppose that the owner of the car wash receives $2 for each car wash, and that the price of labor is $20 per day. How many laborers will the owner hire per day?

b. What is the value of the marginal product of labor when between 1 and 2 laborers per day are used? When between 2 and 3 laborers per day are used? When between 3 and 4 laborers per day are used?

c. If the owner of the car wash hires 3 laborers per day, does the value of the marginal product of labor equal the wage?

3. Suppose that the Ace Manufacturing Company is a member of a perfectly competitive industry. Suppose that the relationship between various amounts of labor input and output is as shown below.

Product price	Units of labor	Units of output	Marginal product of labor	Value of marginal product (dollars)
10	0	0	_____	_____
10	1	2 1/2	_____	_____
10	2	5	_____	_____
10	3	7	_____	_____
10	4	8		

a. Fill in the blanks.

b. If you are told that the Ace Manufacturing Company is hiring 3 units of labor, you can establish a range for the value of the wage rate prevailing in the labor market (assuming that the firm maximizes profit). What is this range? Specifically, what is the maximum value that the wage (for a unit of labor) may be? What is the minimum value? Why?

c. Suppose that the Ace Manufacturing Company must pay $20 for a unit of labor. How many units of labor will it hire? Why?

d. In the graph below, draw the Ace Manufacturing Company's demand curve for labor.

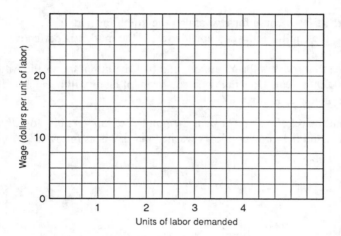

4. The demand and supply curves for musicians in a particular area in 1994 are as shown below.

a. If a union makes the users of musicians demand 50 percent more hours per week of musicians' time than in 1994 at each wage rate, draw the new demand curve in the graph.

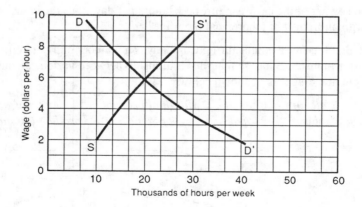

b. After the union shifts the demand curve, perhaps due to featherbedding, what will be the new equilibrium wage? What will be the new equilibrium quantity employed?

5. A perfectly competitive firm has the following value-of-marginal-product curve:

Number of units of labor per day	Value of marginal product (dollars)

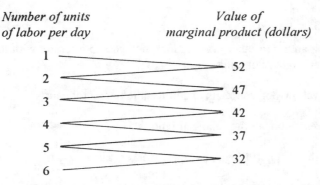

a. If there are 1,000 firms, all of which have the same value-of-marginal-product curve, the market demand curve for labor is as follows:

Price of a unit of labor per day (dollars)	Number of units of labor demanded per day
50	_____
45	_____
40	_____
35	_____

Fill in the blanks above. (Assume that only integer numbers of units of labor can be used.)

b. The supply curve for labor is as follows:

Price of a unit of labor per day (dollars)	Number of units of labor supplied per day
35	3,000
40	4,000
45	5,000
50	6,000

What is the equilibrium price of a unit of labor per day?

c. What will be the total amount of labor demanded in the market? What will be the amount demanded by each firm?

d. What will be the extra cost that a firm would incur if it added an extra unit of labor per day?

e. What will be the value of the marginal product of labor for this firm?

f. If a minimum wage of $45 per day for a unit of labor were established, what would be the total amount of labor demanded in the market?

6. Four very important labor laws are listed below, after which are listed various provisions of these laws. In the space before each provision, put the letter (A to D) corresponding to the relevant labor law.

A. Landrum-Griffin Act
B. Taft-Hartley Act
C. Wagner Act
D. Norris-LaGuardia Act

_____ a. Made it an unfair labor practice for employers to interfere with their workers' right to organize.

_____ b. Made yellow-dog contracts unenforceable in federal courts.

_____ c. Requires unions to file financial reports.

_____ d. Made the checkoff illegal, except if workers agree in writing.

_____ e. Established the National Labor Relations Board.

_____ f. Established the Federal Mediation Service.

_____ g. Contained a "bill of rights" for labor.

_____ h. Outlawed the closed shop.

ANSWERS

Completion Questions

1. diminishing marginal returns, value-of-marginal-product, value of the marginal product   2. 1, 2, 2   3. marginal product, product's price, price
4. derived   5. market supply curve   6. convention   7. yellow-dog contract
8. National Labor Relations Board, refuse, majority, right   9. Taft-Hartley, unions, employers, sued   10. closed, union, open

True-False

1. False   2. False   3. False   4. False   5. True   6. False   7. True   8. True
9. True   10. True   11. True

Multiple Choice

1. d   2. a   3. c   4. b   5. c   6. c   7. a   8. e

Problems

1. a.

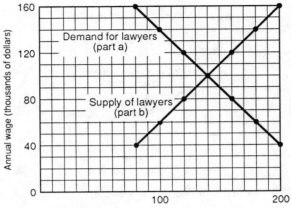

Quantity of labor (thousands of person-years)

b. See answer on the graph for part a.
c. $100,000.
d. 80,000.

2. a. 2 or 3.
b. $50, $20, $10.
c. Yes.

3. a.

Marginal product of labor	Value of marginal product (dollars)
2 1/2	25
2 1/2	25
2	20
1	10

b. The wage must be between $10 and $20, because if it were more than $20, the firm would hire only 2 units of labor, and because if it were less than $10, the firm would hire 4 units of labor.

c. 3 units of labor or 2 units of labor. Because this will maximize its profit.

d.

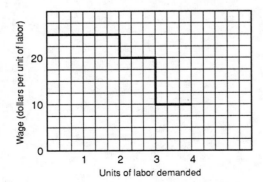

Units of labor demanded

4. a.

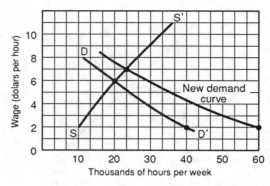

b. About $7. About 23,000 hours per week.

5. a.

Number of units of labor
demanded per day

2,000
3,000
4,000
5,000

b. $40.
c. 4,000 units, 4 units.
d. $40.
e. $42.
f. 3,000 units.

6. a. C
   b. D
   c. A
   d. B
   e. C
   f. B
   g. A
   h. B

CHAPTER 23

Interest, Rent, and Profits

Chapter Profile

Interest is a payment for the use of money. Interest rates vary a great deal, depending on the nature of the borrower and the type and riskiness of the loan. One very important function of interest rates is to allocate the supply of loanable funds.

The pure interest rate—the interest rate on riskless loans—is, like any price, determined by the interaction of supply and demand. However, because of the influence of the government on both the demand and supply sides of the market, it is clear that the pure interest rate is to a considerable extent a matter of public policy.

In a capitalist system, each asset has a market value that can be determined by capitalizing its earnings. Holding constant an asset's annual return, the asset's worth is higher the lower the rate of return available on other investments.

Any asset has a rate of return, which indicates its net productivity. An asset's rate of return is the interest rate earned on the investment in the asset. If firms maximize profits, they must carry out all projects where the rate of return exceeds the interest rate at which they can borrow.

Rent is the return derived by inputs that are fixed in supply. Since the supply of the input is fixed, its price can be lowered without influencing the amount supplied. Thus if the government imposes taxes on rents, there will be no effect on the supply of resources to the economy.

Another important type of property income is profits. Available statistics on profits are based on the accountant's concept, not the economist's, with the result that they include the opportunity costs of the labor, capital, and land contributed by the owners of the firm. Profits play a very important and legitimate role in a free enterprise system.

Two of the important factors responsible for the existence of profits are innovation and uncertainty. Profits are the rewards earned by innovators and a payment for risk-bearing. Still another reason for the existence of profits is monopoly power; because of contrived scarcity, profits are made by firms in imperfectly competitive markets.

Concepts for Review

Interest	Capitalization
Rate of interest	Land
Pure rate of interest	Rent
Demand curve for loanable funds	Innovators
Rate of return	Risk
Supply curve for loanable funds	Profit

Completion Questions

1. Mr. Smith buys a bond for $1,000. If the bond pays interest of $50 per year indefinitely, the interest rate is _____ percent. If the price of the bond increases to $1,500, the interest rate is _____ percent. If the price of the bond falls to $500, the interest rate is

   _____ percent.

2. A bond yields $100 per year in interest indefinitely. If the rate of interest is 8 percent, the bond is worth _____. The price of the bond will (rise, fall, be unaffected) _____ if the interest rate rises. For example, if the interest rate rises to 10 percent, the price of the bond will be _____.

3. If the interest rate is 10 percent, a dollar received a year from now is currently worth _____, and a dollar received 2 years from now is currently worth _____. Thus, a business venture that will pay you both a dollar a year from now and a dollar 2 years from now is currently worth _____.

4. If the present value of a dollar received 2 years from now is 85.7 cents, the interest rate must be _____ percent. If the present value of $2 received 3 years from now is $1.78, the interest rate must be

   _____ percent. If the interest rate is more than

   _____ percent, one dollar received 20 years from now is worth less than 15 cents now.

5. Interest rates vary as a function of the loan's _____, its _____, and the cost of _____.

6. The equilibrium pure interest rate is given by the intersection of the _____ and _____ curves for loanable funds.

7. Holding an asset's annual returns constant, the asset's worth is higher, the (lower, higher) _____ the rate of return available on other investments.

8. _____ is a process of computing an asset's worth.

9. The _____ for loanable funds is the relationship between the quantity of loanable funds supplied and the pure interest rate.

10. The price of an input which has a fixed supply is _____.

    A(n) _____ is a payment above the minimum necessary to attract this amount of the input.

11. Were the government to impose a tax on rents, there would be (some, no) _____ effect on the supply of resources to the economy.

    Because he felt rent was _____ and the supply of land (would, would not) _____ be affected by such a tax, Henry George felt that it was justifiable to _____ rent.

12. Critics of George's position argued that land can be improved; thus the supply (is, is not) _____ completely price inelastic. They further argued that if land rents are _____, many other kinds of income are likewise.

13. In the accountant's definition, the money the owner of a firm has left after paying wages, interest, and rent, and after providing proper allowance for the depreciation of buildings and equipment, is _____. The economist's definition differs in that he or she would also deduct the _____ costs of the labor, capital, and land contributed by the owner.

True-False

_____ 1. If Pennsylvania has a usury law that puts a limit of 10 percent on interest rates, and if a bond yielding $100 per year indefinitely is selling for $800 on Wall Street, the quantity of loanable funds supplied is likely to be less than the quantity of loanable funds demanded in Pennsylvania.

_____ 2. If people become more willing to postpone consumption to future time periods, and if very profitable new investment opportunities are opened up, the interest rate must rise.

_____ 3. If the Federal Reserve pursues a policy of easy money, and at the same time profitable new investment opportunities open up, the equilibrium quantity of loanable funds will increase.

_____ 4. The pure rate of interest is the rate on a riskless loan.

_____ 5. If the firm maximizes profit, it will accept investments where the interest rate exceeds the rate of return.

_____ 6. Interest rates serve to allocate the supply of loanable funds.

_____ 7. If a firm borrows money to buy equipment at an interest cost that is less than the rate of return from the equipment, it will lose money.

_____ 8. Capital budgeting refers to decisions concerning a firm's choice of investment projects.

_____ 9. One reason for the existence of profits is "contrived scarcity" due to monopoly power.

_____ 10. Before taxes, corporation profits average about 50 percent of gross national income.

_____ 11. A very large demand for loanable funds stems from firms that want to borrow money to invest in capital goods like machine tools, buildings, and so forth.

_____ 12. An asset's rate of return is the interest rate earned on the investment in the asset.

_____ 13. The lower the interest rate, the smaller the amount firms will be willing to borrow.

_____ 14. The government is an important factor on the demand side of the market for loanable funds, because it is a big borrower, particularly during wartime and during recent years.

Multiple Choice

1. Mrs. X can either pay $50 now (for the coming year) and $50 a year from now (for the next year) for a service that protects against termites. Alternatively, she can pay $100 now (for the coming two years) for this service. Mrs. X should be indifferent between these two alternatives if the rate of interest is:

   a. zero.
   b. 2 percent.
   c. 5 percent.

   d. 10 percent.
   e. none of the above.

2. In the previous question, if the rate of interest is 10 percent, the cost of the second alternative exceeds that of the first alternative by:

   a. zero.
   b. $4.55.
   c. −$5.00.

   d. $5.00.
   e. none of the above.

3. In question 1, if the rate of interest is 8 percent, Mrs. X should be indifferent

   between the first alternative and paying _____ now (for the coming two years) for this service.

   a. $96.00
   b. $96.30
   c. $100.00

   d. $104.00
   e. none of the above

4. The proportion of national income going to proprietors has:

   a. decreased slightly.   d. increased markedly.
   b. decreased markedly.   e. stayed the same.
   c. increased slightly.

5. The largest of the following five income categories in the United States is:

   a. proprietor's income.   d. wages and salaries.
   b. corporate profits.   e. rent.
   c. interest.

6. Suppose that the rate of return on alternative investments is 6 percent, and that a particular asset will yield $1,500 per year indefinitely. The asset is worth:

   a. $9,000.   d. $250,000.
   b. $25,000.   e. $100,000.
   c. $90,000.

7. If a firm maximizes profit, the rate of return of the least productive project that is accepted by the firm must be _____ the interest rate at which the firm can borrow.

   a. less than   d. twice
   b. 1/2   e. less than or equal to
   c. greater than or equal to

8. Profits are:

   a. a reward for efficiency.
   b. an incentive for innovation.
   c. an indicator of where resources are needed.
   d. all of the above.
   e. none of the above.

Discussion and Extension Questions

1. "Interest rates are set largely by New York financiers and Washington politicians, not by the market. To a considerable extent, they are set to maximize the profits of the big banks, who control much of the American economy." Discuss and evaluate.

2. "Money really doesn't produce anything. You can stick a dollar bill in the earth, and it won't grow. You can't wear it or eat it. Why should it receive any return? Interest is merely a trick to obtain unearned income for the moneyed classes." Discuss and evaluate.

3. Suppose your paternalistic (and rich) uncle promises you a gift of $10,000 when you "grow up," which he defines as ten years from right now. If the interest rate is currently 6 percent, and it is expected to remain at that level,

how much could he give you now instead of $10,000 ten years from now, so that the two gifts would have equal value?

4. What is the relationship between the concept of rent and the concept of opportunity cost?

5. According to Richard Freeman's calculations, the present value of lifetime income (in the 1960s) was about $230,000 for a Ph.D. in electrical engineering, but about $208,000 for a B.A. (or B.S.) in electrical engineering. Discuss the relevance of this finding for the decision of whether or not to do graduate work in electrical engineering.

6. Define what is meant by the rate of interest. What difference, if any, is there between interest and usury?

7. What is the relationship between the riskiness of a loan and the rate of interest?

8. What are the social functions of the interest rate?

9. If the government imposes a tax on economic rent, will this affect the supply of resources to the economy? Why or why not?

Problems

1. Suppose that the demand curve for loanable funds in the United States is as follows:

Interest rate (percent)	Quantity of loanable funds (billions of dollars)
4	60
6	50
8	40
10	30
12	20

a.   Draw the demand curve in the graph on the following page:

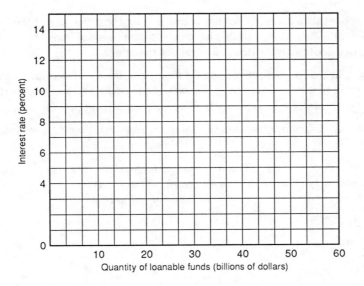

Quantity of loanable funds (billions of dollars)

b. Suppose that the existing supply of loanable funds in the United States is $40 billion. What is the equilibrium interest rate, given the data presented above?

c. If the interest rate is the one indicated in part b, what is the worth of an asset that yields $1,000 a year permanently?

d. If the interest rate is the one indicated in part b, and if you are considering investing your money in an investment with a rate of return of 7 percent, should you accept the investment? Why or why not?

2. Suppose that the supply curve for a particular type of mineral is as shown below:

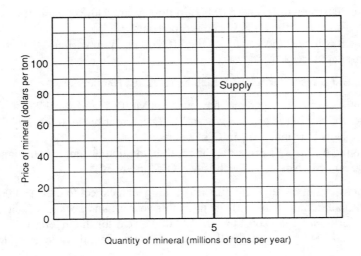

Quantity of mineral (millions of tons per year)

a. Is the price of this mineral a rent?

    b.   Suppose that a tax of $2 per ton is imposed on the producers of this mineral. What effect will this have on the quantity supplied? Does the answer depend on the demand curve for the mineral?

3. Suppose that the Jones Construction Company can borrow money at 15 percent per year and that it is willing to accept only those (riskless) investments that yield 20 percent per year or more. Is this firm maximizing profit?

4. Suppose that the Jones Construction Company has the following investment opportunities:

Rate of return (percent)	Amount of money the firm can invest at the given rate of return (millions of dollars)
35	5
30	10
25	8
20	9
17	4

    a.   If it has to pay 15 percent interest, which investment opportunities should it accept?

    b.   How much less should it invest in these projects if it has to pay 18 percent interest?

5. Mr. Smith buys a very long-term bond that pays annual interest of $50 per year. It is a 5 percent bond that has a face value of $1,000. Mr. Smith bought it in 1955 when the prevailing interest rate was 5 percent, and he paid $1,000 for it. In 1985, the prevailing interest rate was about 10 percent. Approximately how much was the bond worth then?

6. a.   Suppose that you will receive $10,000 in three years. How much is it worth now? (Assume that the interest rate is 6 percent.)

    b.   How much is it worth to you to get the $10,000 one year earlier—that is, in two years, not three?

7. Mr. Q owns 100 acres of farm land which he rents at $100 per acre.

    a.   If the interest rate is 10 percent, how much is Mr. Q's land worth?

    b.   Because of a fall in the price of wheat, Mr. Q can rent his land for only $75 per acre. Now how much is Mr. Q's land worth?

    c.   Oil is found on Mr. Q's property, the result being that he can rent his land for $400 an acre. Now how much is Mr. Q's land worth?

8. Ms. Q, if she does not undergo any further training, can expect to earn $30,000 per year for the indefinite future. If she takes this year off and goes to school rather than works, she can expect to earn $32,000 a year for the indefinite future. The school is free, but she will not be able to work at all while going to school.

a. If Ms. Q expects to live and work forever, what rate of return will she earn from this investment in her own education?
b. Suppose that Ms. Q can obtain 10 percent on alternative investment opportunities. Is this investment worthwhile?
c. To make this investment worthwhile, how much must she be able to earn per year after the year in school?

9. Firm X must choose between investing in machine A or machine B. The machines do exactly the same work, but their purchase prices and maintenance costs differ. The purchase price of machine A is $10,000, while the purchase price of machine B is $5,000. The maintenance cost each year with machine A is $1,000, while the maintenance cost each year with machine B is $1,600. Both machines last so long that it is reasonable to assume (for simplicity) that they last forever.

a. If the interest rate is 5 percent, which machine should firm X buy? Why?
b. If the interest rate is 10 percent, which machine should firm X buy? Why?
c. If the interest rate is 15 percent, which machine should firm X buy? Why?
d. At what interest rate would firm X be indifferent between the two machines? Why?

ANSWERS

Completion Questions
1. 5, 3 1/3, 10 2. $1,250, fall, $1,000 3. 90.9 cents, 82.6 cents, 173.5 cents
4. 8, 4, 10 5. riskiness, term, bookkeeping and collection 6. demand, supply
7. lower 8. Capitalization 9. supply curve 10. rent, rent 11. no, unearned
income, would not, tax away 12. is not, "unearned" 13. profit, opportunity

True-False
1. True 2. False 3. True 4. True 5. False 6. True 7. False 8. True
9. True 10. False 11. True 12. True 13. False 14. True

Multiple Choice
1. a 2. b 3. b 4. b 5. d 6. b 7. c 8. d

Problems

1. a.

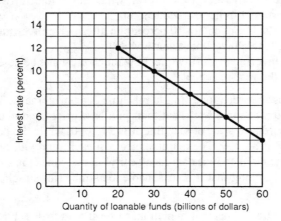

   b. 8 percent.
   c. $12,500.
   d. No. Because you can get 8 percent if you lend your money elsewhere.
2. a. Yes.
   b. None. No.
3. No.
4. a. All shown in the table.
   b. $4 million less.
5. About $500.
6. a. Using Table 23.1 in the text, we see that it is worth .839 × $10,000, or $8,390.
   b. Using Table 23.1, we see that it is worth .89 × $10,000, or $8,900 to get it in two years. Thus it is worth $510 more than if you got the money in three years.
7. a. $100,000.
   b. $75,000.
   c. $400,000.
8. a. 2,000 ÷ 30,000 = 6.7 percent.
   b. No.
   c. $33,000.
9. a. If firm X buys machine A rather than machine B, it is investing an additional $5,000 now in order to reduce annual maintenance costs by $600. Thus, the rate of return on the extra $5,000 investment is $600/$5,000, or 12 percent. Since the interest rate is 5 percent, firm X should make this extra investment; it should buy machine A.
   b. Machine A. See part a.
   c. Machine B. See part a.
   d. 12 percent. See part a.

CHAPTER 24

Poverty, Income Inequality, and Discrimination

Chapter Profile

Many factors are responsible for existing income differentials. Some people are abler, better educated, or luckier than others. Some people have more property, or more monopoly power, than others.

Critics of income inequality argue that it lessens total consumer satisfaction because an extra dollar given to the poor provides them with more extra satisfaction than the loss of a dollar taken away from the rich. Also, they argue that income inequality leads to social and political inequality.

Defenders of income inequality point out that it is scientifically impossible to make interpersonal comparisons of utility, and argue that income inequality is needed to provide incentives for people to work and create, and that it permits greater capital formation.

There is no well-defined income level that can be used in all times and all places to determine poverty. Perhaps the most widely accepted definition of poverty in the United States today is the one developed by the Social Security Administration, according to which about 14 percent of the population in the United States—over 36 million people—fell below the poverty line in 1992. Over the long run, the incidence of poverty has been declining in the United States.

Nonwhite families, families headed by a female, and very large families are more likely than others to be poor. To a considerable extent, the reasons for their poverty lie beyond the control of the poor people. About one-third of poor adults have suffered a disability of some sort, or the premature death of the family breadwinner, or family dissolution. Most heads of poor families do not have jobs.

Because private charity is judged to be inadequate, the nation has authorized its government to carry out various public programs to aid the poor. There are programs to provide them with goods and services—food-stamp programs, for instance. Other programs, like aid to families with dependent children, give them cash. When these programs are taken into account, the percentage of the population falling below the poverty line is reduced considerably.

There is widespread dissatisfaction with existing antipoverty—or welfare—programs. They are judged to be inefficient; their costs have increased at an alarming rate; and they provide little incentive for people to get off welfare. One suggestion to remedy these problems is a negative income tax. In most of the forms put forth it involves a transfer of income that may be beyond the realm of political feasibility.

Despite recent improvements, the sad fact is that racial discrimination occurs in many walks of life in many areas of the United States. Nonwhites often are cut off from educational and job opportunities; and even when nonwhites do essentially the same kind of work as whites, there is sometimes a tendency to pay them less. The effects of discrimination are to reduce the wages of nonwhites relative to whites and to lower the nation's total output.

There is also much discrimination against women, making them less likely than men to enter the better-paying occupations. Even after adjusting for factors such as education and work experience, women earn about 20 percent less than men.

Concepts for Review

Progressive tax	Food programs
Regressive tax	Welfare
Poverty	Aid to families with dependent children
Social Security Act	Negative income tax
Old-age insurance	Break-even income
Medicare	Discrimination
Unemployment insurance	

Completion Questions

1. The most important single program to aid the poor gives aid to

   _____.

2. Suppose that families earning $4,000 or less per year pay no taxes and receive a welfare payment equal to the difference between their earned income and $4,000. If such a family earns $3,000, its total income is _____.
   If such a family earns $4,000, its total income is _____.
   There is (considerable, little, no) _____ incentive to earn more income up to $4,000.

3. The proposal calling for poor families to receive a payment, while families with incomes above a certain minimum would pay a graduated tax, is called a(n) _____.

4. The federal income tax is (progressive, regressive) _____, whereas the sales tax is (progressive, regressive) _____.

5. The _____ Act, passed in 1935, established a government-sponsored _____ system providing compulsory old-age insurance for both workers and self-employed people, as well as _____ insurance. By 1990 about _____ million Americans were receiving old-age and survivors' insurance benefits.

6. Under discrimination, the demand curve for white labor is (different from, the same as) _____ that for black labor, and the supply curve of white labor is (different from, the same as) _____ that of black labor.

7. Assume that a negative income tax exists whereby the government pays each family (of four people) an amount equal to $3,000 – I/3, where I is the family's earned income. Families earning less than _____ per year will receive some payment from the government. The maximum amount that any family can receive from the government is _____ per year. If the poverty line is $5,000, a family must earn _____ to reach this line.

8. The amount that a family pays for a given tax is shown below, at each of a number of income levels of the family. This tax is progressive when a family's income is between _____ and _____, and regressive when a family's income exceeds _____.

Income (dollars)	Tax (dollars)
$1,000	$10
$5,000	$100
$10,000	$300
$20,000	$600
$30,000	$900
$50,000	$1,200
$100,000	$2,000

True-False

_____ 1. The demand curve for unskilled labor is $P = 5 - 2Q$, and the supply curve for unskilled labor is $P = 3Q$, where P is the wage rate (in dollars per hour) and Q is the quantity of labor (in millions of hours). If a minimum wage of $5 an hour is established, all unskilled labor will be unemployed.

_____ 2. Under a negative income tax, a family which earns more income would not necessarily receive more money (both in earned income and payments from the government) than if it did not earn more income.

_____ 3. In question 1, if a minimum wage of $4.50 an hour is established, the quantity supplied of unskilled labor will exceed the quantity demanded by 1.50 million hours.

_____ 4. One effect of discrimination against blacks is to lower the nation's total output.

_____ 5. There has been little reduction in the past 20 years in the amount of racial discrimination in businesses.

_____ 6. There has been little reduction in income inequality in the United States in the past 25 years.

_____ 7. Every industrialized country has greater income inequality than every less developed country.

_____ 8. In the United States, inequality of after-tax income is more than inequality of before-tax income.

_____ 9. To finance old-age insurance, payroll taxes must be paid by each worker and his or her employer.

_____ 10. If the government gives all families of four persons $4,000 per year and imposes a tax of 25 percent on earned income, a family's disposable income would be greater than its earned income if its earned income is less than $16,000 per year.

Multiple Choice

1. If a negative income tax is established whereby the government pays each family (of four people) an amount equal to $3,000 - 0.6I$, where I is earned income (in dollars), and families who receive no such payment must pay taxes, the break-even income is:

   a. $9,000.
   b. $6,000.
   c. $5,000.
   d. $3,000.
   e. none of the above.

2. If the negative income tax in the previous question were adopted, a family below the break-even income that increased its earned income by $1 would net:

   a. nothing.
   b. 40 cents.
   c. 60 cents.
   d. $1.
   e. none of the above.

3. The Social Security system is:

   a. an ordinary insurance system.
   b. mandatory, not voluntary.
   c. financed by a regressive tax on earnings.
   d. all of the above.
   e. only b and c are true.

4. In 1993 it was estimated by the Social Security Administration that an urban family of four to be just above the poverty line needed an annual income of:

a. less than $2,000.
b. between $2,000 and $3,000.
c. between $6,000 and $8,500.
d. between $4,500 and $6,000.
e. over $13,000.

5. Which of the following kinds of families is most likely to be poor?

a. white family with 6 members
b. nonwhite family with 2 members
c. nonwhite family with 6 members
d. white family with 2 members
e. all of the above are equally likely to be poor

6. Which of the following is not a progressive tax?

a. inheritance tax
b. federal income tax
c. estate tax
d. payroll tax
e. all of the above

7. Suppose that each family must pay each year either $500 or 5 percent of its income (whichever is greater) to support local schools. This tax is:

a. regressive for families with incomes under $10,000.
b. proportional to income for families with incomes over $10,000.
c. both a and b.
d. more progressive than the federal income tax.
e. none of the above.

8. Suppose that each family in nation A receives $1,000 in benefits from federal highways, and that each family pays $500 plus 10 percent of its income in taxes to pay for the maintenance of these highways.

a. This government program provides more benefits to families with incomes under $4,000 than they pay for.
b. Families with incomes over $6,000 pay more for this program than the benefits are worth to them.
c. Families with incomes under $555 have negative disposable incomes.
d. both a and b.
e. all of the above.

Discussion and Extension Questions

1. In finding solutions for poverty would you like to distinguish between individuals who are temporarily (or voluntarily) poor—like students—and those who are more likely to remain poor over a longer period of time?

2. Suppose that over the next generation or so, we have more older people and fewer younger people. How will this alter the Social Security program, both from the cost and benefit sides?

3. Should the prize money at professional tennis tournaments be distributed equally between men and women players? Why might the men be paid more? When should the women be paid more?

4. Generation-skipping trusts are one device the wealthy have used to avoid estate taxes. As put by one expert, "You provide income to your child for life, then to your grandchildren who are living today, with principal to their children at age 21." What are the gains and costs to society of allowing the use of such trusts? Are you for or against permitting their use?

5. "Since one cannot make interpersonal comparisons of utility (or satisfaction) there is no way to tell whether progressive taxes are really to be preferred over regressive ones." Comment and evaluate.

6. Is a sales tax progressive or regressive? Why? Is the personal income tax progressive or regressive? Why?

7. Suppose that the amount paid for a particular tax is related to the income of the taxpayer in the following way:

Income (dollars)	Tax (dollars)
1,000	50
10,000	600
100,000	7,000

Is this tax progressive or regressive?

8. What are some of the salient characteristics of poor families in the United States? What is meant by a negative income tax? Do you favor or oppose such a scheme?

Problems

1. Suppose that the break-even income under a negative income tax is $8,000. This is the income at which a family of four neither pays nor receives taxes. Suppose that such a family receives 50 percent of the difference between its income and the break-even income, if its income is below the break-even income, and that it pays 25 percent of the difference between its income and the break-even income, if its income exceeds the break-even income.

a. In the table below, indicate how much a family at each income level would receive or pay in taxes.

Family income (dollars)	Payment received (dollars)	Taxes paid (dollars)
4,000	_____	_____
6,000	_____	_____
8,000	_____	_____
10,000	_____	_____
12,000	_____	_____
14,000	_____	_____
16,000	_____	_____
20,000	_____	_____
40,000	_____	_____

b. What incentive is there for an unemployed person heading a family with an income of $4,000 to get a job?

2. Suppose that the demand and supply curves for unskilled labor in a perfectly competitive labor market in the land of Canam are as shown below:

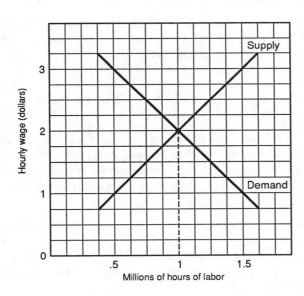

a. If a minimum wage of $2.50 per hour is established, what will be the effect on the total employment of unskilled labor?
b. What will be the effect on the total income received by unskilled labor?
c. Will the minimum wage solve the poverty problem in Canam?

291

3. a. Suppose that the amount of tax paid by a person with income equal to X is given by the formula

$$T = .3X$$

where T is the amount of the tax. Is this tax progressive or regressive? Why?

   b. Suppose that the formula is

$$T = .2X + .1X^2.$$

Is the tax now progressive or regressive? Why?

4. Nation X's tax system exempts the first $5,000 of a person's income and taxes away 50 percent of the rest.

   a. Suppose that Mr. Poor's before-tax income is $10,000 and Mr. Smith's before-tax income is $50,000. Mr. Smith's before-tax income is five times Mr. Poor's. What is the ratio of Mr. Smith's after-tax income to Mr. Poor's?
   b. Is it true that, if any person has 5 times as much before-tax income as another person, the former person's after-tax income will be less than 5 times as much as the latter person's? Why or why not?
   c. Does nation X's tax system tend to reduce the inequality of income? Is the tax system progressive or regressive? Why?

5. Nation Y is considering three alternative tax systems. The first would exempt the first $5,000 of a person's income and tax away 50 percent of the rest. The second would exempt the first $8,000 of a person's income and tax away 70 percent of the rest. The third would exempt the first $10,000 of a person's income and tax away the rest. Nation Y's government assumes that the nation's total output will be the same regardless of which tax system is adopted. Do you agree? Why or why not?

6. Nation Z changes its tax system. After the change, the first $5,000 of a person's income is exempted and 50 percent of the rest is taxed away. Before the change, the first $2,500 of a person's income was exempted, and 1/3 of the rest was taxed away. John Jameson worked 2,000 hours at a wage rate of $5 per hour before the change.

   a. If he continues to work as much as before the tax change, will his after-tax income change?
   b. Assuming that he could vary the number of hours he worked, was an extra hour of leisure worth more or less than $3.33 to him before the change in the tax system? Why or why not?
   c. Was an extra hour of leisure worth more than $2.50 to him after the change in the tax system? Why or why not?

7. The table below shows how much, according to the Family Assistance Plan proposed by President Nixon in 1969, a family would receive in welfare payments, given that its earned income was a particular amount.

Earned income (dollars)	Welfare payment (dollars)
500	1,600
1,000	1,460
2,000	960
3,000	460

a. Assuming no taxes have to be paid on earned income under $3,000, what percentage of an extra dollar of earned income would a person keep if his or her income were $600?

b. What percentage of an extra dollar of earned income would a person keep if his or her income were $1,500?

c. What percentage of an extra dollar of earned income would a person keep if his or her income were $2,500?

d. In evaluating the Family Assistance Plan, why would the answers to previous parts of this question be relevant?

ANSWERS

Completion Questions

1. families with dependent children   2. $4,000, $4,000, no   3. negative income tax   4. progressive, regressive   5. Social Security, social insurance, unemployment, 40   6. different from, different from   7. $9,000, $3,000, $3,000   8. $1,000, $10,000, $30,000

True-False

1. True   2. False   3. False   4. True   5. False   6. True   7. False   8. False   9. True   10. True

Multiple Choice

1. c   2. b   3. e   4. e   5. c   6. d   7. c   8. e

Problems

1. a.

Payment received (dollars)	Taxes paid (dollars)
2,000	—
1,000	—
0	—
—	500
—	1,000
—	1,500
—	2,000
—	3,000
—	8,000

   b. He or she will keep 50 cents of every extra dollar earned, since the payments he or she receives decline by 50 cents for every extra dollar earned.

2. a. Employment will decline from 1 million to .75 million hours of labor.
   b. Income will decline from $2 million to $1.875 million.
   c. No.

3. a. It is neither regressive nor progressive, since the amount of the tax is proportional to income.
   b. Progressive, because $\frac{T}{X} = .2 + .1X$, which means that $\frac{T}{X}$ increases as X increases.

4. a. 3.67 to 1.
   b. No. If one person has a before-tax income of $5,000, and another has a before-tax income of $1,000, the former person's after-tax income will not be less than 5 times as much as the latter person's.
   c. Yes. Progressive because the proportion of income going for taxes rises with income.

5. No. In the third tax system, there would be no incentive to earn more than $10,000. In the second tax system, the incentive to earn more than $8,000 would not be very strong.

6. a. No.
   b. More, because if this were not the case, he would work an extra hour before the change in the tax system. After taxes, he would receive $3.33 for each extra hour he worked.
   c. More, because if this were not the case, he would work an extra hour after the change in the tax system. After taxes, he would receive $2.50 for each extra hour he worked.

7. a. 72 percent.
   b. 50 percent.
   c. 50 percent.
   d. Because it is generally believed that a welfare program should contain incentives for welfare recipients to increase their income and get off welfare.

CASE 4

The Well-Paid Receptionist

ROLAND B. COUSINS

Harvey Finley did a quick double take when he caught a glimpse of the figure representing Ms. Brannen's salary on the year-end printout. A hurried call to payroll confirmed it. Yes, his receptionist had been paid $127,614.21 for her services last year. As he sat in stunned silence, he had the sudden realization that, since his firm was doing so well this year, she would earn at least 10 to 15 percent more money during the current fiscal year. This was a shock, indeed.

With a second call to payroll, Harvey found out that Ms. Brannen's salary had been approximately $112,000 the year before last and $100,000 the year before that. She had been well paid for some time, he concluded.

Background

Harvey began his career as a service technician for a major manufacturer of copy machines. He received rather extensive technical training, but his duties were limited to performing routine, on-site maintenance and service for customers. After a year's experience as a service technician, he asked for and received a promotion to sales representative. In this capacity, he established many favorable contacts in the business community of Troupville and the surrounding towns. He began to think seriously about capitalizing on his success by opening his own business.

Then, seven years ago, he decided to take the plunge and start his own firm. He was tired of selling for someone else. When he mentioned his plan to his friends, they all expressed serious doubts; Troupville, a city of approximately 35,000 people located in the deep South, had just begun to recover from a severe recession. The painful memories of the layoffs, bankruptcies, and plummeting real estate values were too recent and vivid to be forgotten.

Undeterred by the skeptics, Harvey was optimistic that Troupville's slow recovery would soon become a boom. Even though his firm would certainly have to be started on a shoestring, Harvey thought his sales experience and technical competence would enable him to survive what was sure to be a difficult beginning. He was nervous but excited when he signed the lease on the first little building. A lifelong dream was either about to be realized or dashed forever. Troupville Business Systems was born.

Roland B. Cousins is Professor of Business Administration and Economics at La Grange College. This case appeared in the spring 1992 issue of the *Case Research Journal*. Management cooperated in the field research for this case, which was written solely for the purpose of stimulating student discussion. All individuals and incidents are real, but names and data have been disguised at the request of the organization.

While he had managed to borrow, rent, lease, or subcontract for almost everything that was absolutely necessary, he did need one employee immediately. Of course, he hoped the business would expand rapidly and that he would soon have a complete and competent staff. But until he could be sure that some revenue would be generated, he thought he could get by with one person who would be a combination receptionist/secretary and general assistant.

The typical salary for such a position in the area was about $14,000 per year; for Harvey, this was a major expense. Nevertheless, he placed what he thought was a well-worded ad in the "Help Wanted" section of the local newspaper. There were five applicants, four of whom just did not seem quite right for the position he envisioned. The fifth applicant, Ms. Cathy Brannen, was absolutely captivating.

Ms. Brannen was a twenty-seven-year-old divorcée with one small child. Her resume showed that she had graduated from a two-year office administration program at a state university. She had worked for only two employers following graduation, one for five years and the most recent for two years. Since returning to her hometown of Troupville two months ago, following her divorce, she had not been able to find suitable employment.

From the moment she sat down for the interview, Harvey and Ms. Brannen seemed to be on exactly the same wavelength. She was very articulate, obviously quite bright, and, most important, very enthusiastic about assisting with the start-up of the new venture. She seemed to be exactly the sort of person Harvey had envisioned when he first began to think seriously about taking the big plunge. He resisted the temptation to offer her the job on the spot, but ended the hour-long interview by telling her that he would check her references and contact her again very soon.

Telephone calls to her two former employers convinced Harvey that he had actually underestimated Ms. Brannen's suitability for the position. Each one said without equivocation that she was the best employee he had ever had in any position. Both former employers concluded the conversation by saying they would rehire her in a minute if she were still available. The only bit of disturbing information gleaned from these two calls was the fact that her annual salary had risen to $15,900 in her last job. Although Harvey thought that the cost of living was probably a bit higher in Houston, where she had last worked, he wasn't sure she would react favorably to the $14,000 offer he was planning to make. However, he was determined that, somehow, Cathy Brannen would be his first employee.

Ms. Brannen seemed quite pleased when Harvey telephoned her at home that same evening. She said she would be delighted to meet him at the office the next morning to discuss the position more fully.

Cathy Brannen was obviously very enthusiastic about the job as outlined in the meeting. She asked all of the right questions, responded quickly and articulately to every query posed to her, and seemed ready to accept the position even before the offer was extended. When Harvey finally got around to mentioning the salary, there was a slight change in Cathy's eager expression. She stiffened. Since Harvey realized that salary might be a problem, he decided to offer Cathy an incentive of sorts in addition to the $14,000 annual salary. He told her that he realized his salary offer was lower than the amount she had earned on her last job. And, he told her, he understood that a definite disadvantage of working for a new firm was the complete absence of financial security. Although he was extremely reluctant to guarantee a larger salary because of his own uncertainty regarding the future, he offered her a sales override in the amount of two percent of sales. He explained that she would largely determine the success or failure of the firm. She needed to represent the firm in the finest possible manner to potential customers who telephoned and to those who walked in the front door. For this reason, the sales override seemed to be an appropriate addition to her straight salary. It would provide her with incentive to take an active interest in the firm.

Cathy accepted the offer immediately. Even though she was expecting a salary offer of $16,000, she hoped the sales override might make up the difference. "Who knows," she thought, "two percent of sales may amount to big money someday." It did not, however, seem very likely at the time.

Troupville Business Systems began as a very small distributor of copy machines. The original business plan was just to sell copy machines and provide routine, on-site service. More extensive on-site service and repairs requiring that a machine be removed from a customer's premises were to be provided by a regional distributor located in a major city approximately 100 miles from Troupville.

Troupville Business Systems did well from the start. Several important changes were made in the services the firm offered during the first year. Harvey soon found that there was a greater demand for the leasing of copy machines, particularly the large expensive models which he originally planned to sell. He also soon discovered that his customers wanted to be able to contract directly with his firm for all of their service needs. Merely guaranteeing that he could get the machines serviced was not sufficient in the eyes of potential customers. In attempting to accommodate the market, he developed a complete service facility and began to offer leasing options on all models. These changes in the business all occurred during the first year. Growth during that year was steady but not spectacular. While sales continued to grow steadily the second year, it was early in the third year that Harvey made what turned out to be his best decision. He entered the computer business.

Harvey had purchased a personal computer soon after Troupville Business Systems was founded. The machine and its capabilities fascinated him, although he knew virtually nothing about computers. He was soon a member of a local users club, was subscribing to all the magazines, and was taking evening computer courses at the local university—in short, he became a computer buff. Harvey recognized the business potential of the rapidly growing personal computer market, but he did not believe that his original business was sufficiently stable to introduce a new product line just yet.

During his third year of operations, he decided the time was right to enter the computer business. He added to his product line a number of personal computers popular with small businesses in the area. This key decision caused a virtual explosion in the growth of his firm. Several key positions were added, including that of comptroller. By the fourth year of operations, computers produced by several other manufacturers had been added to Harvey's product line, and he had developed the capability of providing complete service for all products carried. His computer enterprise was not limited to business customers, because he quickly developed a significant walk-in retail trade. Rapid growth continued unabated.

During the first seven years of the company's existence, Cathy Brannen had proven truly indispensable. Her performance exceeded Harvey's highest expectations. Although her official position remained that of secretary/receptionist, she took it upon herself to learn about each new product or service. During the early years, Harvey often thought that she did a better job than he did whenever a potential customer called in his absence. Even after he acquired a qualified sales staff, Harvey had no concerns when Cathy had to field questions from a potential customer because a regular salesperson was not available. The customer never realized that the professional young lady capably handling all inquiries was "only" the receptionist.

Cathy began performing fewer sales functions because of the increased number of professional salespersons, but her secretarial duties expanded tremendously. She was still Harvey's secretary, and she continued to answer virtually every telephone call coming into the business. Since her office was in an open area, she still was the first to greet many visitors.

Cathy took a word processing course at a local business school shortly after joining the firm. As she began working with Harvey's first personal computer, she, too, developed into a computer aficionado and became the best computer operator in the firm.

The Current Situation

Harvey was shaken by the realization that Cathy Brannen had been paid over $127,000 last year. As he wondered what, if anything, should be done about her earnings, he began to reflect on the previous seven years.

Success had come almost overnight. It seemed as thought Troupville Business Systems could do no wrong. The work force had grown at a rate of approximately 15 percent per year since the third year of operations. Seventeen people were now employed by the firm. While Harvey did acknowledge that some of this success was due to being in the right place at the right time, he also had reason to be proud of the choices he had made. Time had proven that all of his major decisions had been correct. He also could not overestimate Cathy's contribution to the success of the firm. Yes, certainly, one of the most important days in the life of the firm was the day when Cathy responded to his ad in the newspaper.

Success had brought with it ever-increasing demands on his time. He had never worked so hard, but the rewards were certainly forthcoming. First there was the new Jaguar, then the new home on Country Club Drive, the vacation home on the coast, the European trips. . . . Yes, success was wonderful.

During these years Cathy, too, had prospered. Harvey had not thought much about it, but he did remember making a joking comment the first day she drove her new Mercedes to work. He also remembered commenting on her mink coat at the company banquet last December. Cathy had been dazzling.

Now that Harvey realized what he was paying Cathy, he was greatly disturbed. She was making over twice as much money as anyone else in the firm with the exception of himself. The best salesman had earned an amount in the low sixties last year. His top managers were paid salaries ranging from the high forties to the mid-fifties. The average salary in the area for executive secretaries was now probably between $22,000 and $25,000 per year. A good receptionist could be hired for under $20,000, and yet Cathy had been paid $127,614.21 last year. The sales override had certainly enabled Cathy to share in the firm's success. Yes, indeed.

As Harvey thought more and more about the situation, he kept returning to the same conclusion. He felt something had to be done about her compensation. It was just too far out of line with other salaries in the firm. Although Harvey was drawing over $200,000 per year in salary and had built an equity in the business of more than $1 million, these facts did not seem relevant as he pondered what to do. It seemed likely that a number of other employees did know about Cathy's compensation level. Harvey wondered why no one ever mentioned it. Even the comptroller never mentioned Cathy's compensation. This did seem quite odd to Harvey, as the comptroller, Frank Bain, knew that Harvey did not even attempt to keep up with the financial details. He relied on Frank to bring important matters to his attention.

With no idea of how to approach this problem, Harvey decided to begin by making a list of alternatives. He got out a piece of paper and, as he stared at the blank lines, overheard Cathy's cheerful exchange with a customer in the next room.

Discussion Questions

1. Was Cathy Brannen a typical receptionist or secretary? Why or why not?

2. Were her services an input to Troupville Business Systems? If so, what was the marginal product of her services?

3. Was she being paid the value of the marginal product of her services? Can you tell? Why or why not?

4. If she could make no more than $40,000 in another job, was her pay equal to the opportunity cost of her services? Why or why not?

5. Is it always sensible for a firm to give an employee a bonus of a certain percentage of sales? Why or why not?

CHAPTER 25

Economic Growth

Chapter Profile

Economic growth is measured by the increase of per capita real gross domestic product, an index that does not measure accurately the growth of economic welfare, but is often used as a first approximation.

One factor that may influence a nation's rate of economic growth is the rate at which its population grows. In Malthus's view, population growth, unless checked in some way, ultimately meant economic decline, since output could not grow in proportion to the growth in population. The law of diminishing marginal returns ensured that beyond some point, increases in labor, holding the quantity of land constant, would result in smaller and smaller increments of output. However, Malthus underestimated the extent and importance of technological change, which offset the law of diminishing marginal returns.

Another factor that determines whether per capita output grows rapidly or slowly is the rate of expenditure on new plant and equipment. Without technological change, more and more of this sort of investment would result in decreases in the profitability of investment in plant and equipment, as Ricardo pointed out. But because of technological change, this has not occurred. According to the available evidence, a nation's rate of economic growth seems directly related to its rate of investment in plant and equipment.

To a considerable extent, economic growth here and abroad has resulted from technological change. A change in technology, when applied for the first time, is called an innovation, and the firm that first applies it is called an innovator. Innovation is a key stage in the process leading to the full evaluation and utilization of a new process or product. Unless knowledge is used, it has little effect on the rate of economic growth.

Another factor with an important effect on a nation's rate of economic growth is the rate at which it invests in human capital. The United States invests in human capital on a massive scale, and these enormous and rapidly growing investments have unquestionably increased the productivity, versatility, and adaptability of our labor force.

Still another set of basic factors influencing the rate of economic growth is the economic, social, and political climate of the nation. Some societies despise material welfare, are subject to violent political upheavals, and are governed by corrupt groups. Such societies are unlikely to have a high rate of economic growth.

Finally, the rate of economic growth is also affected by the extent and behavior of the gap between actual and potential GDP. However, once a nation gets to full employment, it cannot grow further by reducing this gap.

Concepts for Review

Economic growth	Technological change	Innovator
Capital formation	Innovation	Diffusion process
Capital-output ratio		

Completion Questions

1. Ricardo and Malthus thought that the marginal product of labor would (increase, decrease) _____ as the labor force increased.

2. _____ occurs when an economy adds to its plant, equipment, structures, and inventories.

3. A(n) _____ is a change in technology when applied for the first time.

4. The _____ process, in which the use of an innovation spreads, begins once a change in technology has been applied for the first time.

5. The technological lead of the United States over other nations was due partly to superior _____.

6. The additional output resulting from the addition of an extra person-year of labor is called the _____.

7. A nation's output under full employment is its _____.

8. The two most common measures of the rate of _____ growth are: (1) the rate of growth of a nation's _____, which tells us how rapidly the economy's total real output of goods and services is increasing; and (2) the rate of growth of _____ _____, which is a better measure of the rate of increase of a nation's standard of living.

9. To achieve a more rapid rate of growth, consumers must frequently be willing to give up some _____ now so that they can have (more, less) _____ goods and services in the future. A nation's potential output increases when its production possibilities curve shifts (inward, outward) _____.

10. Although the U.S. economy has spent a great deal of money on new plant and equipment, the productivity of new investment opportunities (has, has not) _____ been exhausted or even reduced. The

_____ on investment in new plant and equipment has not fallen.

11. If the capital-output ratio is 2, full-employment GDP will increase by $50 billion as a consequence of _____ billion of investment.

True-False

_____ 1. In the United States, the total investment in the education of the population has grown much more rapidly in this century than total investment in plant and equipment.

_____ 2. The rate of investment in plant and equipment is directly related to a nation's rate of economic growth.

_____ 3. National governments under peacetime conditions have few opportunities to push actual output close to potential output.

_____ 4. The bulk of the long-term increase in per capita output in the United States has been due to increases in the capital-labor ratio.

_____ 5. A nation's rate of economic growth is influenced by its social and religious climate, as well as by technological change and changes in its educational level.

_____ 6. The greater the percent of GDP that the society devotes to investment, the greater will be the increase in its full-employment GDP.

_____ 7. The law of diminishing marginal returns does not apply to cases where there is a proportional increase in all inputs.

_____ 8. Malthus believed that the population tends to grow at a geometric rate.

_____ 9. Technological change has shifted the marginal-product-of-labor curve to the right.

_____ 10. There has been a tendency for growing populations to push hard against food supplies in some of the countries of Africa, Latin America, and Asia; and the Malthusian model can explain important elements of the situation.

_____ 11. A nation's rate of economic growth is not influenced by the rate at which it invests in human capital.

_____ 12. How rapidly an innovation spreads depends heavily on its economic advantage over older methods or products. The more profitable the use of the innovation is, the more rapidly it will spread.

_____ 13. Joseph Schumpeter, Harvard's distinguished economist and social theorist, stressed the important role played by the innovator in the process of economic growth.

_____ 14. Until the twentieth century, it was seldom true that technology was built on science. Even today, many technological advances rely on little in the way of science.

Multiple Choice

1. Country X, which has an average propensity to consume that is the same for all levels of disposable income (and no government or net exports), wants to establish a constant rate of growth of GDP. To do so, investment expenditure must:

   a. increase at a faster rate than GDP.
   b. increase at a slower rate than GDP.
   c. increase at the same rate as GDP.
   d. be the same each year.
   e. none of the above.

2. In 1985 suppose that $MP_K = 300 - 100K$, where MP_K is the marginal productivity of capital and K is the amount of capital (in billions of dollars). In 1995 suppose that $MP_K = 400 - 100K$. If the marginal product of capital is the same in 1995 as in 1985, the amount of capital increased between 1985 and 1995 by:

   a. nothing.   d. $100 billion.
   b. $1 billion.   e. none of the above.
   c. $5 billion.

3. In country X the capital-output ratio is 3, whereas in country Y it is 2. If the proportion of GDP that is saved (and invested) is the same in the two countries, country X's rate of growth of GDP is:

   a. 50 percent greater than country Y's.
   b. 1/2 of country Y's.
   c. 2/3 of country Y's.
   d. 33 1/3 percent greater than country Y's.
   e. none of the above.

4. In country A the proportion of GDP that is saved (and invested) is .15, whereas in country B it is .10. If the capital-output ratio is the same in the two countries, country A's rate of growth of GDP is:

   a. 50 percent greater than country B's.
   b. 5 percentage points greater than country B's.
   c. 33 1/3 percent greater than country B's.
   d. the same as country B's.
   e. none of the above.

5. When between 3 and 4 million hours of labor are used, the marginal product of labor is 2 bushels per hour. If the average product of labor is 3 bushels per hour when 3 million hours are used, what is the average product of labor when 4 million hours are used?

a. 3 bushels per hour
b. 2 bushels per hour
c. 2 1/4 bushels per hour
d. 2 1/2 bushels per hour
e. 2 3/4 bushels per hour

6. Which of the following is *not* an advance in technology?

a. a new industrial process
b. a new type of hybrid corn
c. a new surgical procedure
d. a new educational technique
e. a new house of old design

7. The law of diminishing marginal returns:

a. applies to cases where there is a proportional increase in all resources.
b. is an empirical generalization that holds in the real world.
c. assumes that technology is variable.
d. all of the above.
e. none of the above.

8. A nation's rate of economic growth depends on:

a. its rate of technological change.
b. the extent of the changes in the amounts of various inputs used.
c. the rate at which it invests in human capital.
d. all of the above.
e. none of the above.

9. Malthus's most important mistake was to:

a. underestimate population growth in industrialized countries.
b. underestimate the extent and importance of technological change.
c. be too optimistic concerning the relationship between the rate of population increase and the rate of economic growth.
d. assume that population increase was unimportant.
e. feel that capital formation would solve the problem of poverty.

Discussion and Extension Questions

1. Some studies seem to indicate that what matters most to people is their income relative to others around them rather than the absolute level of their income. Would this fact tend to reduce the importance of growth as a means of helping the poor?

2. "Growth is merely an illusion, since no generation can experience the difference between its own living standard and that of previous times. We may be better off than the ancient Greeks, but we cannot really appreciate that fact since we cannot trade places with them. What really counts is how a person's lot compares with that of his or her contemporaries." Discuss and evaluate.

3. "Anyone who prefers more to less should be in favor of economic growth, and should vote for government measures to encourage economic growth." Comment and evaluate.

4. What are the defects in the rate of economic growth as a measure of the rate of increase of economic welfare?

5. State the law of diminishing marginal returns. Is this law applicable if technology changes? Why or why not?

6. To what extent have Malthus's views concerning the effects of population increase on economic growth been confirmed by history? To what extent have Ricardo's views concerning the effects of capital formation on economic growth been confirmed by history? What factor did both Malthus and Ricardo underestimate?

7. What factors determine the rate of technological change and the rate at which changes in technology are applied and spread?

8. Can economic growth be stimulated by reducing unemployment? Explain.

Problems

1. In a highly industrialized economy, suppose that the relationship between hours of labor and production of steel is as follows:

Hours (millions)	Tons of steel (millions)
1	2
2	4
3	7
4	9
5	10
6	9

   a. At what point does the marginal product of labor decline? At what point does the average product of labor decline?
   b. Suppose that an advance in technology allows this economy to obtain twice as many tons of steel (as shown above) for each number of hours of labor. Under these conditions, what is the marginal product of labor when between 4 and 5 million hours of labor are used? What is the average product of labor when 6 million hours are used?
   c. If the economy produced 4 million tons of steel before the technological advance and 8 million tons after the technological advance, by what percentage did labor productivity—output per hour of labor—increase?
   d. Plot the average product curve for labor, before the technological change in the graph on the next page:

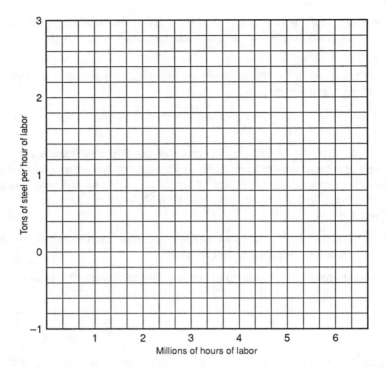

Millions of hours of labor

2. Suppose that the relationship between output per worker and the quantity of labor in Bangladesh is as shown below:

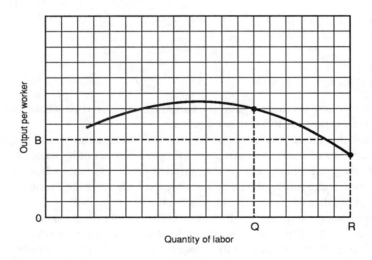

Quantity of labor

a. Suppose the current labor force is such that the quantity of labor is *OQ*. If the subsistence level of output per worker is *OB*, what would the Malthusian theory predict about the change in population in Bangladesh?

b.   Suppose that Bangladesh's labor force is *OR* rather than *OQ*. What would the Malthusian theory predict about the change in population in Bangladesh?

3. a.   If the capital-output ratio is 3 in Bangladesh, what effect will $10 million in investment have on Bangladesh's full-employment GDP?

b.   If Bangladesh saves 5 percent of GDP, and if the capital-output ratio is 3, what will be the rate of growth of full-employment GDP?

c.   Under the circumstances described in part b, what will be the effect on the rate of growth of full-employment GDP if Bangladesh saves 10 percent (rather than 5 percent) of GDP?

d.   If Bangladesh's population increases by 4 percent per year, what is the rate of increase of per capita full-employment GDP under the circumstances described in part b? Under the circumstances described in part c?

4. Assume that the capital-output ratio is 2 in a certain less developed country, and that its full-employment GDP is $20 billion. For simplicity, assume that there is no government nor foreign trade. The consumption function, *CC'*, is plotted in the graph below.

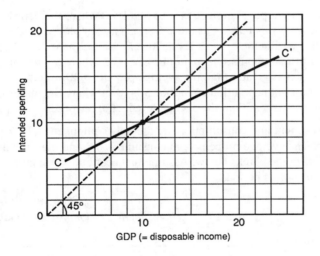

a.   How much investment must there be this year, if there is full employment?

b.   If there is full employment this year, what will be the full-employment value of GDP next year?

c.   Next year, how much investment must there be to maintain full employment? (Hint: the marginal propensity to consume is 1/2.)

5. The following table shows the output of an economy where various amounts of capital are employed. The amounts of all other resources used are held constant. Fill in the blanks.

Amount of capital (billions of dollars)	Total output	Average product of capital	Marginal product of capital
0	0	_____	
1	100	_____	_____
2	210	_____	_____
3	310	_____	_____
4	400	_____	_____
5	480	_____	_____
6	540	_____	_____

6. Some economists regard the optimal population as being the population where output per worker is a maximum.

   a. Prove that the optimal population *cannot* be at a level where the marginal product of a worker is increasing as more workers are employed (and where this is true at all employment levels lower than this as well).
   b. Prove that the optimal population *cannot* be at a level where the marginal product of a worker is greater than the average product of a worker.
   c. Prove that the optimal population *cannot* be at a level where the marginal product of a worker is less than the average product of a worker.

7. In economy R, investment and consumption are the only components of aggregate demand. The average propensity to consume is 0.8 and the capital-output ratio is 2. Fill in the blanks below. Assume that economy R remains at full employment during this period.

Year	GDP	Saving	Investment	Change in full-employment GDP
1992	$1 billion	_____	_____	_____
1993	_____	_____	_____	_____
1994	_____	_____	_____	_____
1995	_____	_____	_____	_____

ANSWERS

Completion Questions
1. decrease   2. Capital formation   3. innovation   4. diffusion
5. management   6. marginal product of labor   7. potential output
8. economic, real gross domestic product, per capita real gross domestic product
9. consumption, more, outward   10. has not, rate of return   11. $100

True-False
1. True   2. True   3. False   4. False   5. True   6. True   7. True   8. True
9. True   10. True   11. False   12. True   13. True   14. True

Multiple Choice
1. c   2. b   3. c   4. a   5. e   6. e   7. b   8. d   9. b

Problems
1. a. Beyond 3 million hours of labor, the marginal product falls. The average product of labor increases up to 3 million hours of labor, then falls.
   b. 2 tons of steel per hour of labor. 3 tons of steel per hour of labor.
   c. It doubled; i.e., there was a 100 percent increase.
   d.

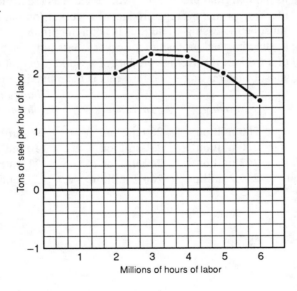

2. a. Population will increase until output per worker tends toward the subsistence level, *OB*.
   b. Population will decrease until output per worker tends toward the subsistence level, *OB*.

3. a. It will increase full-employment GDP by $3 1/3 million.
   b. 1 2/3 percent per year.
   c. The growth rate will be 3 1/3 percent per year.
   d. Minus 2 1/3 percent per year. Minus 2/3 percent per year.
4. a. $5 billion.
   b. $22 1/2 billion.
   c. If GDP is $22 1/2 billion, consumption expenditure will be $16 1/4 billion. Thus investment must be $6 1/4 billion.

5.

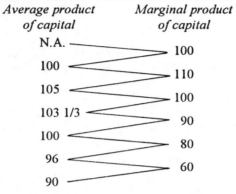

Average product of capital	Marginal product of capital
N.A.	100
100	110
105	100
103 1/3	90
100	80
96	60
90	

6. a. If the marginal product of a worker is increasing as more workers are hired, output per worker must be increasing—and thus is not a maximum.
   b. So long as the marginal product of a worker exceeds the average product of a worker, the average product of a worker (output per worker) must be increasing—and thus is not a maximum.
   c. So long as the marginal product of a worker is less than the average product of a worker, the average product of a worker (output per worker) must be decreasing—and thus this is not a maximum.

7.

GDP	Saving	Investment	Change in full-employment GDP
1 billion	200 million	200 million	100 million
1.1 billion	220 million	220 million	110 million
1.21 billion	242 million	242 million	121 million
1.331 billion	266.2 million	266.2 million	133.1 million

CHAPTER 26

Public Goods and the Role of the

Government

Chapter Profile

To a considerable extent, the government's role in the economy has developed in response to the limitations of the price system. There is considerable agreement that the government should redistribute income in favor of the poor, provide public goods, and offset the effects of external economies and diseconomies. Also, it is generally felt that the government should establish a proper legal, social, and competitive framework for the price system.

Beyond this, however, there are wide differences of opinion on the proper role of government in economic affairs. Conservatives tend to be suspicious of "big government" while liberals are inclined to believe that the government should do more.

Basically, the amount that the government spends on various activities and services must be decided through the nation's political processes. Voting by ballots must be substituted for dollar voting.

Just as the price system suffers from limitations, so does the government. Special-interest groups sometimes gain at the expense of society as a whole. Government agencies sometimes have little incentive to increase efficiency. Citizens find it difficult to be selective in their choice of goods and services in the public sector. In recent years, economists seem to have put more emphasis on these (and other) limitations of the public sector.

It is generally agreed that people who receive more in benefits from a certain government service should pay more in taxes to support it. It is also generally agreed that people should be taxed so that the result is a socially desirable redistribution of income, and that equals should be treated equally. But these general principles, although useful, cannot throw light on many of the detailed questions a real-life tax code must answer.

The personal income tax is a very important source of federal revenues, the sales tax is an important source of state revenues, and the property tax is an important source of local revenues.

Concepts for Review

Public good	Property tax
Personal income tax	Sales tax
Marginal tax rate	

Completion Questions

1. The government often tries by establishing _____ to control the activities of firms in markets where competition cannot be expected to prevail.

2. _____ are those that the government must provide, since there is no way that the market mechanism will provide them in the proper amounts.

3. Public goods are generally paid for by _____.

4. At the federal level the biggest money raiser is the _____ tax.

5. Some _____ cannot be provided through the price system because there is no way to _____ a citizen from consuming the good. For example, there is no way to _____ a citizen from benefiting from national expenditures on defense, whether he or she _____ money toward defense or not. Consequently, the _____ cannot be used to provide such goods.

6. A(n) _____ is said to occur when consumption or production by one person or firm results in uncompensated benefits to another person or firm. A good example of a(n) _____ exists where fundamental research carried out by one firm is used by another firm.

7. Where external economies exist, it is generally agreed that the price system will produce too (little, much) _____ of the good in question and that the government should _____ the amount produced by private enterprise. This is the basic rationale for much of the government's huge _____ in basic science.

8. A(n) _____ is said to occur when consumption or production by one person or firm results in uncompensated costs to another person or firm. A good example of a(n) _____ occurs when a firm dumps pollutants into a stream and makes the water unfit for use by firms and people downstream.

True-False

_____ 1. The research activities of industrial firms often result in external economies.

_____ 2. Tickets to a concert by the Chicago Symphony Orchestra are an example of a public good.

_____ 3. The government should impose taxes on goods that result in external economies in order to promote an optimal allocation of resources.

_____ 4. Public goods frequently are sold in the private market.

_____ 5. The government relies on the legitimate and systematic use of force.

_____ 6. Prices determined in noncompetitive markets provide incorrect signals regarding what consumers want and how scarce resources and commodities are.

_____ 7. The price system cannot be used to handle the production and distribution of public goods.

_____ 8. The government should discourage the production of goods and services that entail external economies.

_____ 9. Government expenditures in the United States have grown much more rapidly than total output in this century.

_____ 10. At the federal level the personal income tax brings in almost half of the tax revenue collected by the federal government. The next most important taxes at the federal level are the social security, payroll, and employment taxes, and the corporation income tax.

Multiple Choice

1. A public good:

   a. cannot be provided to one person without making it available to others as well.
   b. costs nothing (or essentially nothing) to produce and thus is provided by the government at a zero price.
   c. can never be provided by a nongovernmental organization.
   d. generally results in substantial external diseconomies.
   e. all of the above.

2. The functions of taxes are:

   a. to reduce the amount of resources at the disposal of firms and individuals.
   b. to increase the amount of resources at the disposal of the government.
   c. to raise money needed to finance government expenditures.
   d. to redistribute income.
   e. all of the above.

3. An economic activity that would be unlikely to be financed or subsidized by the government is:

   a. basic scientific research.
   b. development of new weapons systems.
   c. development of new smog-control devices.

    d.   development of improved varieties of corn.

    e.   none of the above.

4. Which of the following is *not* a public good?

    a.   national defense   d.   blood donated to the Red Cross

    b.   the services of the U.S. Army   e.   the Apollo space program

    c.   a smog-free environment

5. If government activities could be made more efficient, this would permit:

    a.   an increase in the output of public goods.

    b.   an increase in the output of private (nonpublic) goods.

    c.   an increase in either the output of private goods or the output of public goods or both.

    d.   no increase in output since the added efficiency would be offset by higher wages for government workers.

    e.   none of the above.

6. If a tax of 10 cents per gallon is imposed on gasoline, all of the tax is paid by consumers if:

    a.   the supply curve for gasoline is vertical.

    b.   the supply curve is upward sloping.

    c.   the demand curve for gasoline is vertical.

    d.   the demand curve is downward sloping.

    e.   the demand curve is horizontal.

7. The property tax:

    a.   tends to discriminate against the poorer property owners.

    b.   is not very flexible.

    c.   typically is based on an assessed value, which is markedly different from actual value.

    d.   all of the above.

    e.   none of the above.

8. An example of a tax which relies very heavily on the benefit principle of taxation is the:

    a.   personal income tax.   d.   inheritance tax.

    b.   gasoline tax.   e.   sales tax.

    c.   estate tax.

9. If a tax of $1 per gallon is imposed on gasoline in the United States:

    a.   the equilibrium price of gasoline will increase by $1.

    b.   there will be a shortage of gasoline if the price of gasoline is frozen at its pretax equilibrium level.

    c.   there will be more gasoline supplied.

    d.   none of the above.

    e.   all of the above.

10. The supply curve of good Y is a horizontal line. A tax of $1 per unit is imposed on good Y. The increase in the price of good Y due to the tax will be:

    a. greater if the demand curve is vertical than if it is downward sloping.
    b. less if the demand curve is vertical than if it is downward sloping.
    c. the same if the demand curve is vertical as if it is downward sloping.
    d. zero.
    e. infinite.

11. In the circumstances described in the previous question, the reduction in the output of good Y due to the tax will be:

    a. greater if the demand curve is vertical than if it is downward sloping.
    b. less if the demand curve is vertical than if it is downward sloping.
    c. the same if the demand curve is vertical as if it is downward sloping.
    d. zero.
    e. infinite.

Discussion and Extension Questions

1. Former president Gerald Ford has been quoted as saying that, "A government big enough to give you everything you want is a government big enough to take from you everything you have." Do you agree? Why or why not? How relevant do you think this statement is for the determination of public policy?

2. What are the principal limitations of the price system? It is generally agreed that government must establish the "rules of the game." What does this mean? It is also agreed that the government must see to it that markets remain reasonably competitive. Why?

3. Describe the rationale for the government's efforts to redistribute income. Do all government programs transfer income from rich to poor? Explain.

4. It is generally agreed that the government should discourage the production of goods and services that entail external diseconomies. What are external diseconomies? Give some examples.

5. Why are government expenditures so much bigger now than forty years ago?

Problems

1. The paper industry has the demand and supply curves shown below:

Price of paper (dollars per ton)	Quantity demanded	Quantity supplied
	(millions of tons)	
2	80	40
3	70	50
4	60	60
5	50	70

315

a. Suppose that this industry results in substantial external diseconomies. What can be said about its optimal output rate?

b. In the graph below, draw the supply and demand curves for paper. Does the supply curve reflect the true social costs of producing the product? If not, will a supply curve reflecting the true social costs lie above or below the supply curve you have drawn?

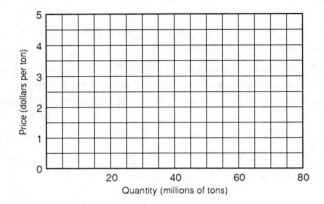

c. What is the equilibrium price of paper? From the point of view of reflecting the true social costs, is this price the correct one, or too low or too high?

2. The town of Lucretia is faced with a serious smog problem. The smog can be dispelled if an air treatment plant is installed at an annual cost of $1 million. There is no way to clean up the air for some but not all of the town's population. Each of the town's families acts independently, and no single family can afford to carry out the project by itself. Why doesn't a private firm build the air treatment plant and sell its services to the town's families (acting individually)?

3. Indicate the economic rationale for the government's carrying out the following functions.

a. regulating the sale and development of drugs
b. maintaining an army
c. granting aid to families with dependent children
d. supporting agricultural experiment stations
e. establishing the Antitrust Division of the Department of Justice
f. imposing an income tax
g. establishing unemployment insurance

4. In the United States, what processes are used to reallocate resources from the private sector (firms and individuals) to the government?

5. Besides its smog problem, the town of Lucretia has a transportation problem which it hopes can be solved by building a new road through the center of town.

There are three types of roads that can be built, their annual costs and benefits to the townspeople being as follows:

Road	Total cost (dollars)	Total benefit (dollars)
No road	0	0
Road 10 miles long	5 million	8 million
Road 20 miles long	12 million	16 million
Road 30 miles long	20 million	20 million

a. What is the extra annual cost of building a 20-mile road rather than a 10-mile road? What is the extra annual cost of building a 30-mile road rather than a 20-mile road?

b. What is the extra annual benefit from building a 20-mile road rather than a 10-mile road? What is the extra annual benefit from building a 30-mile road rather than building a 20-mile road?

c. Should the town build one of these roads? If so, which one?

6. Suppose that the demand and supply curves for good X are as follows:

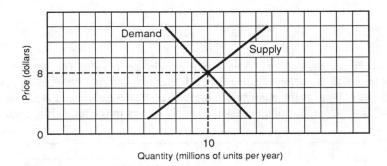

a. If the market for good X is in equilibrium, how much would consumers be willing to pay for an additional unit of good X?

b. The supply curve shows the extra cost of producing an extra unit of good X. If the market for good X is in equilibrium, how much would it cost to produce an extra unit of good X?

c. If the social costs of producing good X *exceed* the private costs, will the social cost of producing an extra unit of good X be equal to the amount consumers would be willing to pay for this extra unit? If not, will the social cost of the extra unit be greater or less than the amount consumers would pay for it? Why?

d. Under the circumstances described in part c, indicate why the socially optimal output of good X is less than 10 million units per year.

e. If the social costs of producing good X were *less* than the private costs, indicate why the optimal output of good X would be more than 10 million units per year.

7. Suppose that a tax of 20 cents per pack is imposed on cigarettes. The tax is collected from the sellers. The before-tax supply curve for cigarettes was:

Price (cents per pack)	Quantity supplied (millions of packs)
50	90
60	100
70	120
80	140

a. After the tax, how much will be supplied when the price is 80 cents per pack? 90 cents per pack?

b. If the demand curve for cigarettes is shown below, what is the equilibrium price of cigarettes before and after the tax?

Price (cents per pack)	Quantity supplied (millions of packs)
50	110
60	100
70	100
80	100
90	90

c. Suppose that the demand curve in part b no longer is valid. Instead, suppose that the demand curve for cigarettes is a horizontal line at 70 cents per pack. What is the equilibrium price of cigarettes before and after the tax? Draw the relevant demand and supply curves in the following graph:

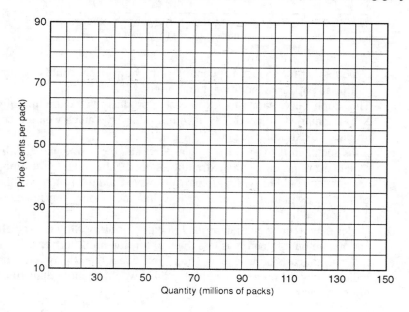

ANSWERS

Completion Questions
1. regulatory commissions   2. Public goods   3. taxes   4. personal income
5. goods and services, exclude, prevent, pays, price system   6. external
economy, external economy   7. little, supplement, investment   8. external
diseconomy, external diseconomy

True-False
1. True   2. False   3. False   4. False   5. True   6. True   7. True   8. False
9. True   10. True

Multiple Choice
1. a   2. e   3. e   4. d   5. c   6. c   7. d   8. b   9. b   10. c   11. b

Problems
1. a. It is less than 60 million tons.
    b. The supply curve does not reflect the true social costs. A supply curve
        reflecting these costs would be above and to the left of the one shown
        below.

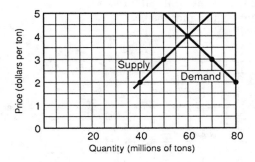

    c. $4. Too low.
2. If any family buys smog-free air, it automatically buys it for others too,
   regardless of whether the latter pay for it or not. And since no family can
   afford the cost, so long as families act independently, it will be unprofitable
   for a private firm to carry out this project.
3. a. The government must make sure that goods like drugs are properly
        labeled and reasonably safe.
    b. National defense is a public good.
    c. Redistribution of income is an accepted concern of government.
    d. There are external economies from such research.
    e. The government must try to maintain reasonably competitive markets.

    f. Redistribution of income is an accepted concern of government.

    g. Redistribution of income and economic stabilization are accepted concerns of government.

4. Taxes and borrowing are used for this purpose.

5. a. $7 million. $8 million.

    b. $8 million. $4 million.

    c. Yes. The 20-mile road, because the extra benefit from the 30-mile road is less than the extra cost.

6. a. $8.

    b. $8.

    c. No. It will be greater than the amount that consumers would be willing to pay for it, since consumers would be willing to pay only $8 for it, but its social cost exceeds $8.

    d. The optimal output of good X is less than 10 million units per year because the optimal output is at the intersection of the demand curve with the supply curve reflecting social costs. Because this supply curve lies to the left of the industry's supply curve (in the diagram), the optimal output must be less than 10 million units per year.

    e. If the social costs of producing good X were less than the private costs, the supply curve reflecting social costs would lie to the right of the industry's supply curve. Thus, the intersection of the supply curve reflecting social costs with the demand curve would be at an output exceeding 10 million units per year.

7. a. 100 million packs. 120 million packs.

    b. 60 cents before the tax, 80 cents after the tax.

    c. 70 cents both before and after the tax.

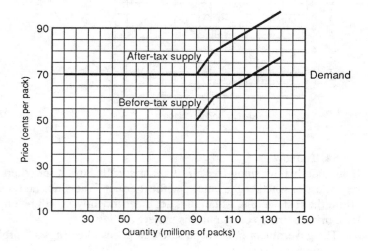

CHAPTER 27

International Trade

Chapter Profile

International trade permits specialization, and specialization increases output. This is the advantage of trade, both for individuals and for nations.

Country A has an absolute advantage over country B in the production of a good when country A can produce a unit of the good with fewer resources than can country B. Trade can be mutually beneficial even if one country has an absolute advantage in the production of all goods.

Specialization and trade depend on comparative, not absolute, advantage. A nation is said to have a comparative advantage in those products where its efficiency relative to other nations is highest. Trade can be mutually beneficial if a country specializes in the products where it has a comparative advantage and imports the products where it has a comparative disadvantage.

If markets are relatively free and competitive, producers will automatically be led to produce in accord with comparative advantage. If a country has a comparative advantage in the production of a certain good, it will turn out—after the price of the good in various countries is equalized and total world output of the good equals total world demand—that this country is an exporter of the good under free trade.

A tariff is a tax imposed by the government on imports, the purpose being to cut down on imports in order to protect domestic industry at the expense of the general public, and, in general, a tariff costs the general public more than the protected industry (and its workers and suppliers) gains.

Quotas are another barrier to free trade. They too reduce trade, raise prices, protect domestic industry from foreign competition, and reduce the standard of living of the nation as a whole.

Tariffs, quotas, and other barriers to free trade can sometimes be justified on the basis of national security and other noneconomic considerations. Moreover, tariffs and other forms of protection can sometimes be justified to protect infant industries, to prevent a country from being too dependent on only a few industries, and to carry out other national objectives. But many arguments for tariffs are fallacious.

Concepts for Review

Exports
Imports
Absolute advantage
Comparative advantage
Export subsidies

Terms of trade
Tariff
Prohibitive tariff
Quotas

Completion Questions

1. If the United States exports corn to France, this results in a(n) (increase, decrease) _____ in the price of corn in the United States and a(n) (increase, decrease) _____ in the price of corn in France. If France exports wine to the United States, this results in a(n) (increase, decrease) _____ in the price of wine in the United States and a(n) (increase, decrease) _____ in the price of wine in France.

2. In the absence of trade, suppose that wheat would sell for $3 per bushel in the United States and for £2 in England and that cloth would sell for $2 per yard in the United States and for £0.5 in England. If 1£ = $2.25, the United States will (export, import) _____ wheat because American wheat can be bought for £_____ by the English. England will (export, import) _____ cloth because English cloth can be bought for $_____ by Americans.

3. Trade permits specialization, and specialization increases _____.

4. Specialization and trade depend on _____ advantage between countries.

5. Assuming for simplicity that only two countries exist, the price of a good tends to settle at the level where the amount of the good that one country exports (equals, is unequal to) _____ the amount that the other country imports.

6. Both a(n) _____ and a(n) _____ generally increase the price of an imported good. Two ways in which governments try to help protect their domestic industries are by _____ and_____.

7. One country has a(n) _____ advantage over another when it can produce one unit of a good with fewer resources than can the other country.

8. Suppose that one country has a comparative advantage in producing one good and another country has a comparative advantage in producing another good. Then if each country specializes in producing the good in which it (has, has not) _____ the comparative advantage, each (can, can not) _____ benefit from trade.

9. _____ will indicate whether a country has a comparative advantage or disadvantage in producing a commodity. If there is a comparative advantage, after the price of a good in various countries is equalized and total world output of the good equals total world demand for

   it, a country will (export, import) _____ the good under free trade and competition.

10. Specialization can reduce production costs to a lower level than would be possible if each nation tried to be _____.

11. Country A can produce a bushel of wheat or a ton of steel with 1 unit of resources. Country B can produce 3 bushels of wheat or 1 1/2 tons of steel

    with 1 unit of resources. Country A (has, does not have) _____ a comparative advantage in the production of wheat, and it (has, does not

    have) _____ a comparative advantage in the production of

    steel. Country B (has, does not have) _____ a comparative advantage in the production of wheat, and it (has, does not have)

    _____ a comparative advantage in the production of steel.

    Country A has an absolute advantage in the production of _____.

    Country B has an absolute advantage in the production of _____.

True-False

_____ 1. If Brazil could produce each and every good and service with 80 percent as much of each and every input as Argentina, Brazil would have a comparative advantage over Argentina in all goods and services.

_____ 2. If country A has an absolute advantage over country B in the production of every good, then trade would be beneficial for country A, but not for country B.

_____ 3. If the United States has relatively bountiful supplies of land relative to Japan, and Japan has relatively bountiful supplies of labor relative to the United States, and if the production of electronic goods requires relatively little land and large amounts of labor, while the production of grain requires relatively little labor and large amounts of land, Japan is likely to export electronic goods.

_____ 4. Even though one country may be more efficient than another at producing two commodities, both countries may benefit if each specializes and trades.

_____ 5. Under free trade a nation's economic welfare is always lower than under a tariff.

_____ 6. Quotas can be even more effective than tariffs in keeping foreign goods out of a country.

_____ 7. International differences in resource endowments and in the relative quantity of various types of human and nonhuman resources are important bases for specialization.

_____ 8. The purpose of a tariff is to cut down on imports in order to protect domestic industry and workers from foreign competition.

_____ 9. Tariffs or other forms of protection are sometimes justified to foster the growth and development of young industries.

_____ 10. If country A uses 20 percent less of all inputs to produce every good and service than does country B, there may be no advantage in two-way trade between these two countries.

Multiple Choice

1. If a nation wishes to protect an industry that is young or necessary to its security:

   a. a subsidy is likely to be preferable to a tariff.
   b. a subsidy is likely to be preferable to a quota.
   c. both a and b.
   d. a quota is likely to be preferable to a subsidy.
   e. none of the above.

   $1F = 4C$
   $2F = 5C$
   $1F = 2.5C$

2. Country C can produce a ton of food or 4 tons of coal with 1 unit of resources. Country D can produce 2 tons of food or 5 tons of coal with 1 unit of resources.

   a. Country C will export food and import coal.
   b. Country D will export food and import coal.
   c. Country C will neither import nor export food.
   d. Country D will neither import nor export coal.
   e. none of the above.

3. If France exports wine to England and England exports textiles to France, an increase in the price of wine (relative to the price of textiles) means:

   a. an improvement for France in the terms of trade.
   b. an improvement for England in the terms of trade.
   c. no change in the terms of trade.
   d. all of the above.
   e. only a and b are true.

4. The purpose of a tariff is to:

   a. reduce imports to protect domestic industry and workers from foreign competition.
   b. produce revenue to pay for shipping costs.
   c. reduce costs.
   d. all of the above.
   e. none of the above.

5. One difference between tariffs and quotas is that only tariffs:

   a. reduce trade.
   b. raise prices.
   c. provide the government with revenue.
   d. reduce the standard of living of the nation as a whole.
   e. none of the above.

6. In addition to national defense, tariffs and other forms of protection are sometimes defended on the grounds that they:

   a. promote growth and development of young industries.
   b. protect domestic jobs and reduce unemployment.
   c. prevent overdependence of a country on only a few industries.
   d. improve a country's terms of trade.
   e. all of the above.

Discussion and Extension Questions

1. According to *Business Week*, "Brazil's government has extracted commitments from foreign-owned auto and truck makers to export nearly $21 billion worth of vehicles and other products through 1989, in return for the right to import duty-free parts for their Brazilian plants." *Business Week* regards this as a "threat of open, mutilated world trade." Do you agree? Why or why not?

2. "It is a foolish and dangerous thing for U.S. firms to export their technology since this will result in foreign firms' imitating our products and beating us in foreign markets." Discuss and evaluate.

3. In an emergency people frequently are called upon to carry out tasks that are far removed from their normal occupations. Suppose that four people escape from a ship wreck and are marooned on a desert island. One member of the group, a college graduate, is given the job of sweeping the floor. He complains that this is a poor use of his talents. Using the theory of comparative advantage, explain why he may be wrong.

4. Why do the less developed countries tend to trade with the industrialized countries, not with one another?

5. Is it better to "buy American" because we then have both the goods and the money? Explain.

6. If the free flow of goods will lead to an increase in world output, should we also press for a free flow of people across countries (i.e., no immigration restrictions)?

Problems

1. Suppose that the demand and supply curves for transistor radios in the United States are as follows:

Price (dollars)	Quantity demanded (millions)	Quantity supplied (millions)
5	5	2
10	4	3
15	3	4
20	2	5

Further suppose that the demand and supply curves for transistor radios in Japan are:

Price (expressed in dollar equivalent of Japanese price)	Quantity demanded (millions)	Quantity supplied (millions)
5	2.5	1
10	2.0	3
15	1.5	5
20	1.0	7

   a. Suppose that there is free trade in transistor radios. What will be the equilibrium price?
   b. Which country will export transistor radios to the other country?
   c. How large will be the exports?
   d. Suppose that the United States imposes a tariff of $10 per transistor radio. What will happen to exports and imports?

2. Suppose that the United States can produce 3 computers or 3,000 cases of wine with 1 unit of resources, while France can produce 1 computer or 5,000 cases of wine with 1 unit of resources.

   a. Will specialization increase world output?
   b. Is this an example of absolute or comparative advantage?

3. Suppose that labor is the only input and that two countries, Argentina and Brazil, can produce the following amounts of two commodities, bananas and nuts, with a day of labor:

	Bananas (lbs.)	Nuts (lbs.)
Argentina	10	3
Brazil	5	4

a. In order for both countries to gain from trade, between what limits must the ratio of the prices lie?

b. Suppose that there is free trade and the price of bananas increases relative to the price of nuts. Is this change in the terms of trade to the advantage of Argentina or Brazil?

4. Countries A and B are neighbors and produce only food and machines. Both countries' production possibilities curves are straight lines. Country A has 500 units of resources, while country B has 200 units of resources. In country A, a unit of resources can produce 22 units of food or 11 units of machinery. In country B, a unit of resources can produce 15 units of food or 10 units of machinery. Before there was any international trade, output in the two countries was:

	Output	
	Food	Machinery
Country A	836 units	1,320 units
Country B	2,250 units	500 units

a. What is the price of a unit of machinery (in terms of food) in each of the countries when they do not trade with each other? Explain.

b. Can the two countries benefit from international trade? If so, explain why.

c. Between what limits will the ratio of the price of machinery to the price of food be once international trade begins?

5. Countries D and E have not traded with each other because of political differences. Suddenly, they reconcile their political differences and begin to trade. Cigars are relatively cheap, but beef is relatively expensive in country D. Beef is relatively cheap, but cigars are relatively expensive in country E.

a. When these countries begin to trade, will the demand for cigars produced in country D increase or decrease? Will the price of cigars increase or decrease in country D?

b. Will the demand for cigars produced in country E increase or decrease? Will the price of cigars increase or decrease in country E?

c. Will the demand for beef produced in country D increase or decrease? Will the price of beef increase or decrease in country D?

d. Will the demand for beef produced in country E increase or decrease? Will the price of beef increase or decrease in country E?

e. Will the demand for resources used in country D to produce cigars increase or decrease? Will the demand for resources used in country E to produce beef increase or decrease?

f. Will the demand for resources used in country E to produce cigars increase or decrease? Will the demand for resources used in country D to produce beef increase or decrease?

ANSWERS

Completion Questions

1. increase, decrease, decrease, increase   2. export, 1 1/3, export, 1 1/8
3. output   4. comparative   5. equals   6. tariff, quota, tariffs, quotas
7. absolute   8. has, can   9. Market forces, export   10. self-sufficient
11. does not have, has, has, does not have, neither, both

True-False

1. False   2. False   3. True   4. True   5. False   6. True   7. True   8. True
9. True   10. True

Multiple Choice

1. c   2. b   3. a   4. a   5. c   6. e

Problems

1. a. $10.
   b, c. Japan will export 1 million transistor radios to the U.S.
   d. Exports and imports will drop.
2. a. Yes.
   b. The United States has an absolute advantage in computers; France has the same in wine.
3. a. The price of a pound of bananas must be between 3/10 and 8/10 of the price of a pound of nuts.
   b. Argentina.
4. a. The price of machinery is double that of food in country A and is 1 1/2 times that of food in country B, because of the relative costs of machinery and food in each country.
   b. Yes, because country A has a comparative advantage in food and country B has a comparative advantage in machinery.
   c. The ratio will be between 1.5 and 2.0.
5. a. Increase. Increase.
   b. Decrease. Decrease.
   c. Decrease. Decrease.
   d. Increase. Increase.
   e. Increase. Increase.
   f. Decrease. Decrease.

CHAPTER 28

Exchange Rates and the Balance

of Payments

Chapter Profile

An important difference between international business transactions and business transactions within a country is that international business transactions involve more than one currency. The exchange rate is the number of units of one currency that exchanges for a unit of another currency.

Under a system of flexible exchange rates, the market for foreign exchange functions like any other free market, the exchange rate being determined by supply and demand. Under such a system, exchange rates tend to move in a way that removes imbalances among countries in exports and imports. The price of a country's currency tends to fall (rise) if its inflation rate and growth rate are relatively high (low) or if its interest rate is relatively low (high).

Until 1973, when exchange rates became more flexible, most exchange rates were fixed by government action and international agreement. They were allowed to vary slightly, but only slightly, about the official rate.

If exchange rates are fixed, the amount of a foreign currency demanded may not equal the amount supplied. To maintain exchange rates at the official levels, governments enter the market and buy and sell their currencies as needed. They also intervene by curbing imports, limiting foreign travel, and other measures.

Under a system of fixed exchange rates, a country will have a balance-of-payments deficit if its currency is overvalued and a balance-of-payments surplus if its currency is undervalued. A balance-of-payments deficit is the difference between the quantity demanded and quantity supplied of the currency.

The United States experienced a chronic balance-of-payments deficit during the 1950s, 1960s, and 1970s. This deficit was the result of the growing productivity of other economies, our large investments abroad, and our military and foreign aid expenditures abroad. In 1973, the system of fixed exchange rates was abandoned.

Concepts for Review

Exchange rate
Gold standard
Appreciation
Depreciation
Devaluation of currency

Balance-of-payments deficit
Balance-of-payments surplus
International Monetary Fund
Gold exchange standard

Completion Questions

1. If the American economy is growing more rapidly than other economies, U.S. (exports, imports) _____ are likely to grow more rapidly than its (exports, imports) _____. Thus U.S. demand for foreign currency will grow (more, less) _____ rapidly than the amount of foreign currency supplied. Consequently the dollar is likely to _____.

2. According to the _____ theory of exchange rate determination, the exchange rate between any two currencies reflects differences in the _____ in the two countries. If the rate of inflation in the United States is higher than in Germany, the mark will _____ relative to the dollar, and the dollar will _____ relative to the mark.

3. If the rate of interest is higher in Japan than in Germany, investors will sell _____ and buy _____ in order to switch from the lower-yielding German securities to the higher-yielding Japanese securities. Consequently the mark will tend to _____ relative to the yen.

4. When exchange rates are allowed to fluctuate freely, they are determined by _____.

5. Under the gold standard, when a country increases the price of gold, this is called a(n) _____.

6. When country A's currency becomes more valuable relative to country B's currency, country A's currency is said to _____ relative to that of country B, and country B's currency is said to _____ relative to that of country A.

7. Representatives of the Allied governments met in Bretton Woods, New Hampshire, in _____ to work out a more effective monetary system for the postwar era. It was generally agreed that competitive _____, such as occurred in the 1930s, should be avoided. The _____ was set up to maintain a stable system of _____ exchange rates and to insure that, when exchange rates had to be changed because of significant trade _____, disruption would be minimized.

8. Suppose that Spain's currency is overvalued. If so, the quantity of its currency supplied will (exceed, be less than) _____ the quantity demanded. The difference is called Spain's _____. To make up the difference, Spain's central bank must give up some of its

_____.

True-False

_____ 1. Under the gold standard exports and imports tended toward balance, because as a country's gold stock declined, its price level fell, and as its gold stock increased its price level rose.

_____ 2. If there is a "run" on the dollar, speculators sell the dollar because they are convinced its price will fall and they do not want to experience losses by holding it, the result being that the price of the dollar does indeed fall.

_____ 3. The gold standard was abandoned because wages and prices fluctuated too much.

_____ 4. From 1950 to 1970 the United States showed a chronic deficit in its balance of payments.

_____ 5. During the latter part of the nineteenth century, the gold standard seemed to work very well, but serious trouble developed after World War I.

_____ 6. Throughout the 1960s our gold stock increased substantially.

_____ 7. A country might change its general price level in order to restore equilibrium in its balance of payments.

_____ 8. A country might adopt various types of controls to interfere with market forces in order to restore equilibrium in the balance of payments.

_____ 9. In February, 1973, the dollar was depreciated.

_____ 10. One way for a country to combat a persistent deficit in its balance of payments is to keep a close rein on inflation.

Multiple Choice

1. If the German mark depreciates from 50 cents to 45 cents, the dollar price of a Dual hi-fi turntable selling in Germany for 150 marks:

   a. falls by $10.   d. increases by $7.50.
   b. falls by $7.50.   e. none of the above.
   c. falls by $5.00.

2. In order to support its currency, a government would be least likely to:

   a. enter the market and buy its own currency.
   b. increase defense expenditures abroad.
   c. limit the travel abroad of its citizens.
   d. curb imports.

3. Exchange rates during the 1950s and 1960s usually were:

   a. on a crawling peg basis.   b. determined by the gold standard.
   b. fluctuating.   e. none of the above.
   c. fixed.

4. The only factor listed below which did *not* contribute to the chronic deficit in our balance of payments in the 1960s and 1970s was:

   a. recovery of European and Japanese economies.
   b. the amount we spent abroad for military uses and foreign aid.
   c. American firms' investment abroad.
   d. increased foreign demand for some of our major exports.
   e. none of the above.

5. A shift to the right in the demand for French francs will occur if:

   a. French interest rates are relatively high and French inflation is relatively low.
   b. French interest rates are relatively low and French inflation is relatively high.
   c. both French interest rates and French inflation are relatively low.
   d. both French interest rates and French inflation are relatively high.
   e. none of the above.

6. A country's balance of payments surplus will tend to become greater if it:

   a. reduces its interest rates.
   b. allows its inflation rate to increase.
   c. increases its economic growth rate.
   d. all of the above.
   e. none of the above.

7. Spain decides to use controls over trade to reduce its balance of payments deficit, one result being:

   a. a decrease in the rate of inflation.
   b. a decrease in the growth rate.

c. a decrease in Spain's exports.
d. a decrease in Spain's imports.
e. a decrease in the balance of merchandise trade.

8. Under a regime of fixed exchange rates, if the rate of inflation is higher in Japan than elsewhere:

a. Japan's exports and imports will fall.
b. Japan's exports and imports will rise.
c. Japan's exports will rise and Japan's imports will fall.
d. Japan's exports will fall and Japan's imports will rise.
e. Japan's balance of payments surplus will become larger or its deficit will become smaller.

Discussion and Extension Questions

1. "France raised its discount rate to 9 1/2 percent from 8 percent in a move to bolster the franc." Explain what this statement means, and why this action would have that effect.

2. "Under floating exchange rates, a deficit in our balance of payments is not a measure of pressure on the dollar, as it was under fixed exchange rates." Comment and evaluate.

3. The Bretton Woods agreements established a system of fixed exchange rates. What happened if the amount demanded of a currency did not equal the amount supplied?

4. What does a country's balance-of-payments deficit or surplus measure? What factors were responsible for the chronic deficit in the U.S. balance of payments?

5. What are some of the ways that a country with a deficit can try to restore equilibrium in its balance of payments?

6. During the late 1960s was the dollar "overvalued"? Explain.

Problems

1. The supply curve for Japanese radios to the American market is shown on the next page for two periods of time.

a. One curve is before a depreciation of the dollar relative to the yen; one curve is after it. Which curve is which? Why?

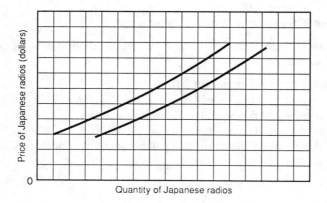

Quantity of Japanese radios

b. What will be the effect of the depreciation on the dollar price of Japanese radios?

c. What will be the effect on American expenditures (in dollars) for Japanese radios, if the demand for them in the United States is price elastic?

d. What will be the effect on American expenditures (in dollars) for Japanese radios, if the demand for them in the United States is price inelastic?

2. Suppose that the demand curve in Japan for American computers is as shown below.

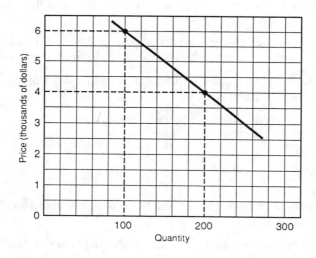

a. If the Japanese yen depreciates relative to the U.S. dollar, will the quantity of computers sold in Japan at a dollar price of $4,000 rise or fall?

b. Under these circumstances, will the demand curve rise or fall?

c. Under these circumstances, will the dollar expenditures on American computers in Japan rise or fall?

3. a. Suppose that people in Germany want to import a product from the United States. If the product costs $5 in the United States, how much will it cost in Germany if the exchange rate is 3 marks = 1 dollar? If the exchange rate is 4 marks = 1 dollar? If the exchange rate is 2 marks = 1 dollar?

   b. Suppose that the quantity of the product (in part a) demanded in Germany is related to its price (in marks) in the way indicated below. The table below shows the desired expenditure by Germans on this product at various levels of the exchange rate. Fill in the blanks:

Exchange rate	Dollar price of good	German price of good (marks)	Quantity demanded	Total desired expenditure (in dollars)
4 marks = 1 dollar	5	_____	500	_____
3 marks = 1 dollar	5	_____	1,000	_____
2 marks = 1 dollar	5	_____	1,200	_____

   c. Plot the relationship between the price of a dollar (in marks) and the quantity of dollars demanded by the Germans to buy the product in parts a and b.

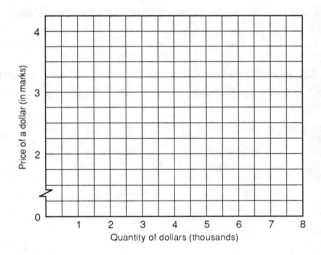

4. a. Suppose that people in the United States want to import a product from Germany. The following table relates to the demand for this good in the United States. It shows the desired expenditure on this product by Americans at various levels of the exchange rate. Fill in the blanks.

Exchange rate	German price of good (marks)	Dollar price of good	Quantity demanded	Total desired expenditure (in dollars)
4 marks = 1 dollar	12	_____	2,000	_____
3 marks = 1 dollar	12	_____	1,250	_____
2 marks = 1 dollar	12	_____	500	_____

   b. Plot in the graph in Problem 3c the relationship between the price of a dollar (in marks) and the quantity of dollars supplied by Americans to buy the product in part a.

   c. If the only international trade between Germany and the U.S. is that described above, what will be the equilibrium exchange rate?

   d. In the situation described in part c, would there be a shortage or surplus of marks if exchange rates were fixed, and the exchange rate for the mark was $0.30?

5. Assume that countries X and Y are both on the gold standard and that a unit of country X's currency is worth 1/40 of an ounce of gold, and a unit of country Y's currency is worth 1/8 of an ounce of gold.

   a. How much is a unit of country X's currency worth in terms of country Y's currency?

   b. How much is a unit of country Y's currency worth in terms of country X's currency?

   c. If a unit of country Y's currency suddenly begins to sell for 3 units of country X's currency, what forces will push the exchange rate back toward equilibrium?

6. The demand and supply curves for the Swiss franc are as follows:

Price of franc (dollars)	Millions of francs demanded	Millions of francs supplied
.80	300	400
.70	320	370
.60	340	340
.50	360	310
.40	380	280

   a. What is the equilibrium rate of exchange for the dollar?

   b. What is the equilibrium rate of exchange for the Swiss franc?

   c. How many dollars will be bought in the market?

   d. How many Swiss francs will be bought in the market?

7. The demand curve for British pounds is as follows:

Price of British pound (dollars)	Millions of pounds demanded
2.00	200
2.10	190
2.20	180
2.30	170
2.40	160
2.50	150

a. Suppose that the British government sets the exchange rate at $2.40, and that the quantity of pounds supplied at this exchange rate is 180 million pounds. Will the British government have to buy or sell pounds? If so, how many?

b. If the British government has to buy pounds with dollars, where will it get the dollars?

ANSWERS

Completion Questions
1. imports, exports, more, depreciate   2. purchasing-power parity, rates of inflation, appreciate, depreciate   3. German marks, Japanese yen, depreciate
4. supply and demand   5. devaluation of its currency   6. appreciate, depreciate
7. 1944, devaluations, International Monetary Fund, fixed, imbalances
8. exceed, balance-of-payments deficit, reserves

True-False
1. True   2. True   3. False   4. True   5. True   6. False   7. True   8. True
9. True   10. True

Multiple Choice
1. b   2. b   3. c   4. d   5. a   6. e   7. d   8. d

Problems
1. a. The higher curve is the one following the depreciation. Because of the depreciation, it takes more dollars to elicit the same supply as before.
   b. It will increase the price.
   c. It will reduce expenditures.
   d. It will increase expenditures.
2. a. It will fall.
   b. It will fall.
   c. They will fall.
3. a. 15 marks. 20 marks. 10 marks.

b.

German price of good (marks)	Total desired expenditure (in dollars)
20	2,500
15	5,000
10	6,000

c.

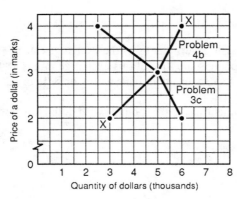

4. a.

Dollar price of good	Total desired expenditure (in dollars)
3	6,000
4	5,000
6	3,000

b. See answer to Problem 3c.

c. 3 marks = 1 dollar.

d. More marks would be demanded than supplied. There would be a shortage of marks.

5. a. A unit of country X's currency is worth 1/5 as much as a unit of country Y's currency.

b. A unit of country Y's currency is worth 5 times as much as a unit of country X's currency.

c. People in country Y can exchange a unit of their currency for 1/8 ounce of gold and ship it to country X, where it can be exchanged for 5 units of country X's currency. Thus people in country Y will not accept only 3 units of country X's currency for 1 unit of country Y's currency.

6. a. A dollar will sell for 1 2/3 Swiss francs.

b. 60 cents.

c. 340 million francs x 60 cents = 204 million dollars.

d. 340 million francs.

7. a. Buy. 20 million pounds.

b. From its reserves.

CASE 5

Ownership and Pricing of Natural Resources

COUNCIL OF ECONOMIC ADVISERS

In the United States, the government owns a substantial share of the Nation's resources. The Federal Government owns about one-third of the total land in the United States, including 29 percent of forestlands and 43 percent of rangeland. State and local governments and American Indian Nations own another 8 percent of U.S. lands. Over 10 percent of the U.S. population receives water from Federal projects. The land and water bring with them other important natural resources, including wildlife and minerals.

The principles of regulatory reform—allowing markets to work where possible, and harnessing the power of market incentives to accomplish regulatory objectives—should also be applied to issues of government ownership and pricing of resources. Some resources such as Federal rangelands and industrial timber stands are indistinguishable from adjacent privately owned lands and have no special features warranting public stewardship. In addition, the U.S. Government often sets the price for using resources below the market price, sometimes even below the direct cost of providing them. These low prices can lead to overconsumption, distorted economic priorities, damage to the environment, and lost revenue.

Why Does the Government Own and Manage Resources?

Most goods and services in our economy are private property, traded in markets that determine prices and quantities. As has been noted, markets efficiently allocate commodities to serve the best interests of all. Government ownership of land and other natural resources in the United States is, in large part, a residual effect of policies adopted in the last century to encourage settlement of sparsely populated western territory. In many cases, there is no economic reason for the government to own these resources.

However, for some resources, there may be a market failure that does provide an underlying reason for government activity. There are two interrelated ways in which private markets for natural resources and the right to use them may fail:

First, a private market may fail to produce the right amount of a public good. Public goods are goods that can be used or enjoyed by one person without detracting from the use or enjoyment of others. For example, suppose Farmer Jones paves the road into town. The neighbors can use the road without affecting its usefulness to Jones, and, therefore, the road meets the definition of a public good. While roads are not a natural resource, this example illustrates how a private market may fail: The

---

This article comes from the *Economic Report of the President* (Washington, D.C.: Government Printing Office, 1993, pp. 203–212).

339

neighboring farmers have an incentive to wait, hoping someone else will incur the costs of paving the road that all of them can use. Some natural resources have the character of public goods; one person can enjoy the beauty of a forest without detracting from another person's use of it. On the other hand, grazing land and timberland are not public goods: Timber harvested by one person is then not available to anyone else. In fact, it is not uncommon for grazing land and timberland to be privately owned.

Second, in many cases, markets fail to reflect external costs or benefits of using a resource. External costs and benefits, or externalities, affect individuals who are not parties to the economic transaction. For example, logging on a hillside may cause soil erosion, imposing a cost on the people living at the bottom of the hill. The cost to these people is not taken into account in the private market for trees and lumber. Often, people are excluded from an economic transaction affecting them because of the high costs of negotiating and enforcing a settlement.

External costs and benefits are often a consequence of the failure to establish property rights for natural resources. An example is a communal grazing field. Anyone can bring cows to graze, but no single farmer owns the field. Because every farmer can use the field for free, farmers tend to bring more and more cows until the field becomes congested. Each farmer using the field is creating an external cost to the other farmers. Unless property rights have been assigned stating which parties "own" the rights to the land or the rights to graze on the land, the private market will not allocate the pasture in a way that maximizes the joint benefits of all users.

Establishing Markets for the Right to Use Resources

Establishing private markets for the right to use a resource often requires government action. The establishment and enforcement of property rights is quintessentially in the realm of government. During the 18th and 19th centuries, the U.S. Government established property rights for lands on the western frontier and then sold or gave away those rights to homesteaders.

The most direct way for the government to address certain failures in markets for natural resources is to sanction legally valid private property rights and allow owners to limit or sell access to resources. For example, the common grazing field could be given or sold into private hands and access limited by a fence. Private property rights give owners the incentive to stop the resource from being overused and to manage it in a way that maintains or increases its value. Private timber companies in the United States replant their lands to maintain forested areas. On the other hand, timber companies in some developing countries hold only short-term logging concessions or government-owned land and have little incentive to replant or otherwise sustain forest resources.

Not all natural resources lend themselves to ordinary boundaries and fences. It is difficult to assign ownership of the atmosphere as a storage space for waste products. One way to address this problem is to have the government create a special kind of property right—the right to use the resource—and then to allow holders of the right to sell it like any other property.

A familiar example of a government-issued right to use a resource is a deer hunting license that permits the licenseholder to hunt and kill a specified number of deer. However, hunting licenses cannot be traded or transferred. If a hunter wishes to kill more deer than the license allows, he or she cannot legally buy the licenses from other hunters and in that way gain the right to kill more deer.

Making permits tradable (allowing them to be bought and sold) is critical to ensure that the resource is used in an economically efficient way. People who attach a low value to using the resource will sell their right to use it to those who attach a relatively high value to use of the resource. The 1990 Clean Air Act Amendments, for example, use tradable permits in order to lower the cost of reducing pollution. The law sets yearly caps on sulfur dioxide emissions from electric utilities. Over time, the caps will be lowered, so that by the year 2000 these emissions will be about one-half of their 1990 levels. Plants receive permits each year for the amount of sulfur dioxide that may legally be released. Since the cost of limiting emissions may be much higher at some facilities than at others, it is not economical to force each plant to reduce emissions by the same amount. To deal with this, the law allows the permits to be bought and sold. Plants that would find it expensive to reduce emissions may be willing to pay a high price for the permits. Plants that can reduce emissions relatively cheaply may be willing to sell their permits. In this way, the market for permits reallocates them so that those plants able to reduce pollution inexpensively will reduce pollution the most. This system of tradable permits is expected to save the economy an estimated $1 billion per year, or about 15 to 25 percent of the cost of reducing pollution without tradable permits. Box 1 describes another example.

Pricing of Government-Owned Natural Resources

Where privatizing a resource is not feasible, another solution to the problem of market failure is for the government itself to hold the resource on behalf of the public. Government ownership of a resource is most appropriate when the resource has the character of a public good (Box 2). Goods and services typically provided by the government include armed forces and public fire departments. The U.S. Government has purchased or created national parks such as the Grand Canyon. These are public goods that can be used and enjoyed by many people at the same time. As noted earlier, the private market may fail to provide the optimal quantity of public goods as potential users wait for others to make the investment. To an increasing extent, the government has adopted this prescription. Under this Administration, funds for State land and water conservation were tripled, and 20 new national park units and 57 new national wildlife refuges have been added or proposed.

The fact that the government owns certain resources does not automatically guarantee that they will be allocated and used in the best possible way. Prices charged for use of a resource significantly affect the economic efficiency of that use. The appropriate price is one where marginal social cost is equal to marginal social benefit. Marginal costs are the expenses involved in providing an incremental unit of a resource, marginal benefits are the gains associated with that additional unit. Social costs and benefits reflect the economic impact on all members of society and include externalities as well as direct economic effects. Box 3 discusses some difficulties in measuring social costs and benefits.

Box 1. Government Creates a Market for Fishing Rights

There is no practical way to establish ownership rights of ocean fish stocks. Traditionally, fish have been free for the taking—a common pool resource. Theory teaches that such underpricing leads to overconsumption. In the halibut fisheries off Alaska, fishing fleets caught so many halibut that the survival of the stock was threatened. No single fishing boat had an incentive to harvest fewer fish since the impact on its own future catch would be minimal and others would only increase their take. This is an example of what is known as "the tragedy of the commons."

Officials tried limiting the length of the fishing season. But this effort only encouraged new capital investment such as larger and faster boats with more effective (and expensive) fishing equipment. In order to control the number of fish caught, the season was shortened in some areas from 4 months to 2 days by the early 1990s. Most of the halibut caught had to be frozen rather than marketed fresh, and halibut caught out of season had to be discarded.

In late 1992, the Federal Government proposed a new approach: assigning each fisherman a permit to catch a certain number of fish. The total number of fish for which permits are issued will reflect scientific estimates of the number of fish that can be caught without endangering the survival of the species. Also, the permits will be transferable—they can be bought and sold. By making the permits transferable, the system in effect creates a market where one did not exist previously. The proposed system will encourage the most profitable and efficient boats to operate at full capacity by buying permits from less successful boats, ensuring a fishing fleet that uses labor and equipment efficiently. Moreover, the transferable permits system establishes a market price for the opportunity to fish—a price that better reflects the true social costs of using this common resource.

Box 2. Forests as a Public Good

Government ownership of natural resources is sometimes intended to help produce the public goods that private ownership has failed to provide. A prime example is the recent reform of government stewardship of forests. Many private forests are harvested by logging companies through clearcutting, which involves removing every tree on a plot of land and then replanting the land with seedlings. While clearcutting can be the least costly way to produce timber for industrial uses, it does detract from the scenic value of forestlands.

In 1992 the Administration adopted a new "ecosystem approach" for managing these federally owned forests which phases out clearcutting as a standard timber harvest practice. Instead, trees in Federal forests will be selectively harvested in order to preserve the scenic value of the forests. The Forest Service expects that the new policy will reduce clearcutting on Federal lands by as much as 70 percent from 1988 levels while reducing the volume of logs cut by only 10 percent or less. This policy exemplifies the appropriate role of government, not as an owner of commercial timberland, but as a protector for forests as a public good.

Box 3. Measuring the Value of Nonmarket Goods

Since a public good is not traded on a competitive market, the market cannot assign it a price based on its value. Measuring the benefits public goods provide is problematic. One method is to infer the value of public goods from actual markets or observable economic behavior. For example, to estimate the value people put on scenic beauty, economists may measure the effect of scenic beauty on actual real estate prices. The value that people put on a park may be reflected in the amount of time and money that they spend to visit and use it.

The contingent valuation method (CVM) uses public opinion surveys. A polltaker asks people to estimate the amount they would be willing to pay to maintain or create a certain public good or the amount they would require to compensate for its loss. Advocates of the CVM argue that it can generate reliable estimates of value in cases where it is impossible to make inferences from actual markets or behavior, and in principle, it takes into account the fact that some people value a good more highly than others do.

However, the CVM also has generated considerable criticism. For example, those surveyed do not actually have to pay the amount they report, a factor that can lead to overstatements. Responses are sensitive to the way questions are posed. (In one case, the estimated value of protection from oil spills changed by a factor of 300 when polltakers asked additional questions before eliciting this value.) CVM results can be inconsistent. (For example, one CVM study showed that people were willing to pay more money to clean up small oil spills than to clean up both small and large spills.) In many cases CVM results cannot be verified except by another CVM study.

These problems are exacerbated when the CVM is used to estimate the value of goods that are abstract, symbolic, or difficult to comprehend. One study showed that if the CVM were used to estimate the value of saving whooping cranes from extinction, resulting estimates might be as high as $37 billion per year (more than the Federal Government spends each year on education and Head Start programs). Finally, even if all the problems of the CVM could be resolved, care must be taken to ensure that it is not used to analyze policy in a one-sided way. For example, a proposed program to protect whooping cranes might put people out of work. The $37 billion figure could be cited by those who claim that the benefits of the program exceed its costs. But opponents of that view could undertake a CVM study of their own asking people how much they would be willing to pay to protect these jobs.

Chronic Underpricing

The rights to use government-owned natural resources are often sold at prices that fail to incorporate the full costs to society and sometimes at prices that do not even cover management expenses (Box 4). Nineteenth-century government policies set prices low to encourage settlement and development of the West. Powerful local constituencies have helped keep them low.

Timber from Federal forests has been sold at prices even lower than the government's cost of providing the timber—and without incorporating possible externalities such as environmental damage. Likewise, rights to graze on Federal lands are sold at prices that fail to cover administrative costs.

Box 4. Reform of California Water

One highly publicized example of government underpricing of natural resources has been California water. Forty-year contracts signed in the 1940s and 1950s guaranteed California farmers water from Federal projects at prices of about $3 per acre-foot, even though the government's current cost to supply that water is often about ten times that amount. Cities and industries that need water cannot obtain it from farmers because archaic legal restrictions block the development of water markets.

The Reclamation Projects Authorization and Adjustment Act of 1992 was signed by the President, despite his concern over certain aspects of the bill, in large part because it encouraged more market-oriented pricing of Federal water in California. The act allows those receiving water from Federal Central Valley Project to pay low subsidized prices for the first 90 percent but increases the price for the last 10 percent, so that the price for the final units used will more closely reflect the full costs of providing the water.

The act also allows recipients of Federal water to sell their water rights. In this way, water can be shifted from relatively low-value agricultural use to relatively high-value municipal or industrial use. The high value of water to urban users is indicated by the fact that, in 1991, the California State Water Bank sold nearly 400,000 acre-feet of State water to cities and industrial users at a price of $175 per acre-foot.

Drawbacks of Underpricing

Whether or not it was warranted in the past, underpricing the right to use natural resources today can create budgetary, economic, and environmental problems. On the first point, the budgetary consequences are readily apparent: When the government sells natural resources below their market value, the taxpayer is subsidizing those uses. Under the 1872 Mining Law, mining companies are able to buy land from the Federal Government for $2.50–$5.00 per acre and then resell the land at market prices. in one extreme example, the government sold 17,000 acres of land for $42,500. Weeks later, these lands were resold to major oil companies for $37 million.

Second, underpricing diverts resources from uses that would benefit society the most to less valuable tasks. In California, cities and industries are often willing to pay substantially more than farmers for water, demonstrating the high value water can have. But low-priced Federal water is often used to grow crops such as alfalfa—a crop fed to dairy cattle—in effect subsidizing the production of milk which has been in oversupply and is already subsidized by Federal support programs. Letting farmers transfer water from low-value agricultural uses to high-value uses could generate substantial economic gains for farmers and nonfarmers alike.

Third, when underpricing leads to overuse, the environment may suffer. For example, if the government underprices grazing rights on federally owned land, overgrazing may lead to soil erosion. *Pricing the right to use government-owned natural resources to reflect actual social costs and benefits could help the environment as well as improve economic performance.*

Reforming Public Resource Policy

Given the chronic problems of government ownership of natural resources, what practical steps can be taken toward developing a better system? As mentioned above, in some cases, government-owned natural resources can be "privatized"—given or sold to private individuals. Once in private hands, access to the resource would be priced by the market ensuring more efficient allocation and reducing overconsumption. From the standpoint of economic efficiency, the decision to give away the natural resource or to sell it is not important. Even if the government gives away the resource to someone who cannot use it efficiently, efficient users will make attractive offers to buy it from the initial recipients.

For the same reasons, the issue of who becomes the initial owner of the resource is also unimportant in terms of economic efficiency. However, it may be of critical importance in determining the political viability of privatization. If government-owned resources are sold rather than given away to those now using them, the present users may form a powerful group blocking privatization. On the other hand, sales bring in government revenues which could be used to pursue other objectives.

In cases where using a natural resource involves significant externalities, however, putting it in the hands of private owners will not solve the problem of market failure, since the prices private owners charge would reflect private costs and benefits rather than social costs and benefits. But government ownership is not the only way to deal with externalities. The actions of private owners can be regulated by laws such as those that make people liable for damages if they cause hillside erosion. Externalities can also be incorporated in private market decisions through taxes and subsidies, fines and fees, or other government action.

When natural resources remain in government hands, prices charged for access to these resources ought to reflect, to the fullest extent possible, the actual costs and externalities associated with using the resource. This policy can be implemented in any of three ways. First, when the appropriate price can be calculated, the government can set the selling price at that level. Second, when the market price is unknown, the government can auction rights to use the resource, allowing the auction to determine the market price. Third, the government can give away or sell at low prices the right to use the resource, and allow that right to be bought and sold. In this last case, the market for transferable rights will set prices and dictate the appropriate use.

Summary

- Markets for natural resources are sometimes characterized by imperfections, either when the resource is a public good or when the use of the resource involves externalities.

- Sometimes the market imperfection can be eliminated by assigning property rights. One way to define these property rights is by creating tradable permits to use the resource.

- When the government retains ownership of a resource, access to that resource should be priced to reflect social costs and benefits.

Discussion Questions

1. Why should the government own any forests? Why not sell them off?

2. Why should the government set the price for a resource it owns at the level where marginal social cost equals marginal social benefit?

3. Why shouldn't the government sell timber to firms at prices below the government's cost of providing the timber?

4. Why should recipients of federal water be able to sell their water rights?

5. What are the problems in measuring the value of nonmarket goods?